Best Seat
in the
House

Best Seat
in the
House

The Wit and
Parliamentary Chronicles of

FRANK
JOHNSON

Compiled and Edited by
Virginia Fraser

BOOKS

First published in Great Britain in 2009 by
JR Books, 10 Greenland Street, London NW1 0ND
www.jrbooks.com

Edited edition © Virginia Fraser

A catalogue record for this book is available from the British Library.

Photos: page 7 (all) – Joyce Kennedy; page 8, third from top – Tessa Keswick,
bottom – Pom Lampson; page 9, middle – Alan Davidson, bottom – Robert
Hardman; page 12, bottom – Getty Images; page 13, bottom – Tessa Keswick;
page 14, top – Corbis, bottom – Getty Images; page 15, top – Corbis, bottom –
Getty Images; page 15, top – Rex Features, middle – Getty Images, bottom –
Corbis; page 15 – Herbie Knott.

ISBN 978-1-906779-33-7

1 3 5 7 9 10 8 6 4 2

Printed by MPG Books, Bodmin, Cornwall

Contents

To Violet, Honor, Simon and Jack

In memory of Frank

Acknowledgements

With many thanks to the Telegraph Media Group, to William Lewis and Matthew D'Ancona, editors of the *Daily Telegraph* and the *Spectator* and The Times Newspapers Limited for facilitating access to their archives and allowing material to be reproduced.

Many thanks to those who provided a few lines setting the sketches in context: Jonathan Aitken, Kenneth Baker, Rachel Billington, David Blunkett, David Cameron, John Casey, Jung Chang, David Dimbleby, George Galloway, Grey Gowrie, William Hague, Roy Hattersley, Michael Howard, Boris Johnson, Gerald Kaufman, former Speaker Michael Martin, Charles Moore, John Nott, David Owen, Matthew Parris, Andrew Roberts, Dennis Skinner, Norman Tebbit, Margaret Thatcher and Alan Watkins.

A special thanks to Lady Thatcher, to William Rees-Mogg and to Simon Hoggart.

Introduction
by Virginia Fraser

It was Jeremy Robson, my publisher, who planted the seed of this book in my mind. After Frank, to whom I had the great good fortune to be married, died in 2006 Jeremy wrote me a graceful letter. He suggested that, having already published two collections of Frank's parliamentary sketches in the early 1980s, he would very much like to publish a third. Several friends encouraged me to consider this idea.

In France that summer, high up a mountain where we have a house, I reread Frank's two books and was entranced. Even the earliest sketches were effervescent, like quicksilver, with ideas and metaphors shooting into the sky. Acute and subversive, occasionally harsh but only very seldom too harsh, Frank had early on developed his own hallmarks: relentless waves of satire, the reversal of logic, and the puncturing of pomposity, all of which are invariably interwoven with a more serious thread. Drawing from his intellectual hinterland, he would both flatter and intrigue the reader by interlacing history and the arts into his pieces. He was never a slavish party line follower but always splendidly mocking of all parties. His 'conceits' as he called them, both contrary and irreverent, would target those at the top on principle. As I came to the end of the second book which brought us up to 1983, I felt strongly that the best sketches of the subsequent years should not be lost to posterity and that they would give great pleasure to many.

The thought occurred that, with a little imagination and much delight, one could follow the path of British political history over the last 35 years by reading Frank's sketches. But explanations would be needed and sketches would have to be set in context. I wondered

Frank Johnson by Nicholas Garland.

whether the politicians and others who were themselves the subject of the sketches might contribute a few lines of explanation and cast their own light on events. So I invited a number of them to do so. They responded with generosity and admirable good humour, for which I thank them all.

Frank's genius went hand-in-hand with the nature of Parliamentary sketch writing. The gallery of the House of Commons, where journalists from various newspapers gather, is 'the engine room' of political reporting. Until the Blair years, the Commons usually did not start its proceedings until after lunch. There would only be two or three hours in which to observe and write before the newspaper's deadline of 7.00pm: little time to check references and mull over your copy.

A voracious bibliophile, Frank would often be reading a book in the gallery of the House of Commons whilst listening to events unfold in the Chamber below him. He wouldn't plan or structure his thinking ahead of time but would wait for a phrase or an interjection by an MP to strike a chord as he pursued his own train of thought. Once something had caught his fancy he was off. His sketches were an instinctive response to what he witnessed. The writer A.N. Wilson described this to me so well: 'Something would have to feed into his stream of consciousness, not the other way round.'

Political history is often written from memory, edited after the events they describe with the benefit of hindsight. Frank's writing is the opposite. It captures a moment in time and has a freshness that makes it as interesting today as it ever was. His political antennae were finely tuned and he was often one of the first to recognise the dawn of a new movement within the political landscape such as Jenko–Thatcherism and New Labour.

'*La Comedie Humaine*' fascinated Frank throughout his life. Coming from a world of working-class respectability, he mingled freely at every level of society – the social, the intellectual and the élitist, instinctively absorbing every detail. I remember being fascinated that he could bring the same understanding to such a variety of subjects, be it in his sketches or in his descriptive writing. In one piece he might describe what it was like to be a small boy in the East End of London, being passed by his father overhead from person to person to the front of a football crowd; in another he might imagine being present in the boudoir of the Duchess of Buccleuch at the turn of the 19th century.

Late in life he embraced my family with this same empathy and with an inexhaustible *joie de vivre*: always delighted to advise my elder son Simon if he was crafting a speech or to help my younger son Jack with his application essays to the hotel school in Lausanne. In all family altercations, true to form, always challenging authority (how could I possibly not have predicted this?), Frank was on the side of the children.

Not all events over the 34 years of this book are reported as fully as others. During the 1990s Frank was editing and therefore not sketchwriting and during the early years of the new century he was sketchwriting, but often unwell. He wrote commentary pieces throughout his life and I have included many here particularly on the subject of opera and ballet which were a real passion. He cherished and nurtured his friendships and would be particularly delighted that many of his friends have contributed to this anthology. Above all I hope he would see this book, as I do, as a wonderful celebration of his life.

There are so many friends to thank: Jeremy Robson my publisher, for showing such faith from beginning to end; Simon Hoggart, David Ruffley and John Casey for being so generous with their time and helping me read thousands of pieces; Anthony Howard for checking the manuscript and Phoebe Dickerson for assisting me in pulling the whole thing together. Special thanks to William Rees-Mogg for his lovely tribute, to Simon Hoggart a second time for his revealing memoir, and to Richard and Caroline Ryder who looked over the work in progress and strengthened my resolve. Every friend I spoke to seemed to give me a good idea . . . special thanks to Joan Bingham, Michael Brown, Rupert Christiansen, Rebecca Fitzgerald, Orlando Fraser, Stephen Glover, my sister Talia Grose, Robert Hardman, David Heathcoat-Amory, Joyce and Michael Kennedy, Tessa Keswick, Peter Lilley, Charles Moore, Charlotte Mosley, John O'Sullivan, Julian Seymour, Stuart Reid, Andrew Roberts, Flora Soros, Alan Watkins, A.N. Wilson and Peregrine Worsthorne. And, of course, my thanks to the many contributors who have enlightened me and I hope the reader with their few lines of explanation under the sketches.

In addition to occasional descriptions from contributors, I have added, from time to time, a few lines of my own to explain the twists and turns of Frank's career or to remind the reader of relevant political developments. And of course all inaccuracies are my own.

A Tribute by
William Rees-Mogg

Frank Johnson had the most enviable of journalistic gifts. Everything he wrote was recognisably from his hand; every line was readable. His virtue as a writer of English prose was derived from his individualistic sense of humour and from the personality which flowed equally through his journalism and through his conversation. Indeed one of the pleasures of re-reading his past columns is that they remind me of lunching with Frank and Virginia, or visiting the Sistine Chapel with Frank some years before.

I suppose that one could call Frank a satirist. There must have been some leading politicians of the 1980s or 1990s who did not wholly appreciate his demolition of their contributions to debate. Yet Frank had little or none of the savage indignation which is supposed to be an essential weapon in the armoury of the satirist. His banter of the politicians was wholly without personal malice. He liked most of those who became the subjects of his ridicule. Indeed the best portraits in his sketches of Parliament are those of people of strong views whether or not he agreed with them. If the first words of a sketch are Norman Tebbit or Enoch Powell, one knows that they will be followed by a delightful report. Best of all are the pieces he wrote about Margaret Thatcher. He was splendid in his account of Margaret Thatcher campaigning in a chocolate factory.

Frank made jokes, both in his writings and in his conversation; some of his jokes did have a sting to them, but they were jokes derived from observations and from ideas. There was an underlying humour which ran through the whole piece, and that was derived from an idea and from Frank's own sense of humour. He referred to these ideas as 'conceits'. A Frank conceit would run through a passage of conversation just as much as it might through a column. If one should call Frank a humorist rather than a satirist, it is because he was too generous a sort for the satire of a Jonathan Swift. He should be called a humorist because he so delighted in the quirks and characterisation of human nature. He himself chose a quotation from Goethe as the motto for his first book, *Out of Order*, which he published in 1982: '*Der Ventaudige findst fast alles lächerlich, der Venrunftige fast nichts.*' 'The intelligent man finds almost everything ridiculous, the responsible man hardly anything.'

This is quite close to the epitaph written for himself by John Gay, who was loved by almost everybody in the backbiting Augustinian age:

'Life is a jest; and all things show it.

I thought so once, but now I know it.'

Gay, too, was a kind man, with a fondness for the absurdities of human life.

Frank had good fortune in the time that he was writing his parliamentary sketches for *The Times* and the *Daily Telegraph*, in the 1970s and early 1980s. It was a time when British politics had thrown up a group of exceptionally interesting politicians. Some of them were beached whales or quite rapidly became so, but there were figures in all three parties who were well worth writing about for their personalities, and a smaller number were also worth writing about for the interest of their ideas.

Frank's first parliamentary sketch was written for the *Daily Telegraph*, then still owned by the Berry family, in October 1972 – which either seems to one like yesterday or as an ancient part of British history, one with Gladstone and Disraeli if not with Nineveh and Tyre. The characters who make their first appearance included Harold Wilson, Ted Heath and Roy Jenkins who was indeed always one of Frank's favourite subjects: Mr. Jenkins struck Frank as funny, from the beginning, though his humour also had its respect. On this first encounter he wrote:

'This led on to Mr. Roy Jenkins, the Labour Member for Stechford. He offered the sort of wrist-flapping, torso-swivelling, adjective-emphasising performance that has been good enough to establish him, for many tastes, as a parliamentarian of the golden age . . . It was a speech studded with the sort of reflections on which have been based Mr. Jenkins's repute as a thinker. "You can never go back," he observed. "You always have to start from where you are." True, how very true.'

Many people who are self-taught have large gaps in what they know, and perhaps an exaggerated self-confidence in their opinions. Frank was largely self-taught, both in his body of knowledge and in his interests, which included an encyclopaedic knowledge of classical music and an early enjoyment of ballet. To read him, or to converse with him one would have had no idea that he was largely self-educated. He was, quite simply, a very well-educated man, who had read more widely than other people and had a wider range of interests. He had done an exceptionally good job of it.

He also had deep roots in a happy childhood in the East End of London and the blessing of an extraordinarily happy marriage to Virginia in his last years. Frank had a stock of happiness which he drew from his home life and gave to his friends and, indeed, to his readers.

Of all Frank's virtues as a sketchwriter, the most attractive is his compassion. It is the failed candidate or the fallen minister to whom his sympathy goes out. I would like to end by quoting his farewell to a fallen Prime Minister, Jim Callaghan, written not when Callaghan left office in 1979, but when he retained his Cardiff seat in 1983 – a disaster year for Labour:

'Mr Callaghan was both moved and moving. The rain kept on. A passing bus set up a tidal wave across the pavement. Canvassers, canvassed, Mr Callaghan, myself – a not unpleasant melancholy settled on us all.

'As we reached the end of the road, I asked him: "Why are you carrying on?" "We're not, we're going back in the van now," he replied. "No," I said. "I mean, carrying on in Parliament. You've been in since 1945. You've been everything. Why continue?"

'"I can give you a priggish answer, which is that I want to try to do something to help, to stop things I'm against. The unpriggish part of the answer is that I enjoy it. I'm fit. Why not?"'

Remembering Frank
by Simon Hoggart

We were all very envious of Frank when he was a sketchwriter because he was so brilliant. And worse, he made it look so easy. He sat in the Press Gallery and barely took a note, just jotting down occasional thoughts in his ungainly handwriting. These small spider scrawls would appear next day transformed into light, amusing, perfectly turned prose which also carried a crisp political message. (I loved his line about the late Tom Litterick, a left-wing Labour MP who was always calling for more public spending. Frank discovered that he had read economics at Dundee. 'Ah, the Dundee faculty of economics,' he wrote, 'home of the celebrated "tree-grown" theory of money.' The poignard went in so deftly that the victim was probably laughing until he realised what damage it had done.)

He loved to get a theme for a piece and to tease it, expand it and generally play with it. He would call the central idea a 'conceit', in the old sense of a witty and fantastical notion. Once, soon after he had joined *The Times*, he was delighted to learn that the then editor, Harold Evans, had told an editorial conference, 'Frank's gone up to Liverpool to do us one of his conceits.'

So insouciant could he appear that sometimes, when covering Parliament, he took a book into the Chamber. No point in wasting time listening to boring speeches or vacuous answers to questions. Generally it was a history book, often a battered volume published many years previously, which might fill a gap in his voluminous knowledge. So if everyone was chatting afterwards about some daft remark made by an MP, Frank was more likely to say what a disaster it would have been if Von Stuffenberg had succeeded in killing Hitler or some such thing.

Parliamentary sketchwriting is not uniquely British, but it has a longer tradition here than anywhere else. In America it would be impossible to sketch the debates in Congress, since there is almost no interaction between the speakers. Political humour there is clearly labelled and often very funny, but the notion of creating jokes out of the passing show would be a little too close to the bone, threatening to the idea of totally impartial – i.e. dull – reportage.

I suppose the first sketchwriter was Dr Johnson, though he laboured under the problem that reporters weren't allowed into debates in the House of Commons. This was because MPs then took the view that if the electorate were to discover what they really thought, they would be inhibited from saying it. No doubt some would prefer things if they had remained that way. Dickens wrote real sketches based on real observations, and they crackle with the back-biting, the conspiracies, envies, resentments and ambition that we still recognise today.

The great wartime *Guardian* sketchwriter was Harry Boardman, whose collected works were titled *The Glory of Parliament* – not a title you would be likely to find today. The late Bernard Levin was the first modern sketchwriter, writing for the *Spectator*. He had little time for most of the politicians he wrote about, and possessed a peculiarly savage wit. I still read out to audiences his description of trying to stay awake during a speech by Hugh Gaitskell, Leader of the Labour Party, and 52 years later it makes them laugh immoderately.

Frank was one of the greats in this long tradition, and like Levin he was delighted to weave his knowledge of a wider culture into his brief studies of politics. He was proud of the fact that, even with the most rudimentary education, he had become – well, 'learned' is the only word for it. And he had cracked the upper classes, being welcomed in privileged and aristocratic salons, having skipped straight past the bourgeois world where most of us live. Though it could occasionally be confusing. He had once been to a dinner where a fellow guest was the Prince of Wales. 'And do you know, he was wearing carpet slippers!' Frank said, not knowing that those slipper-type shoes are what the very poshest people always wear with black tie.

Frank had his enemies, lovingly created. In fact, he nurtured his foes in the same way other people cultivate their friends. Often they were on the same side of the political argument. I remember one particular pompous and self-regarding journalist. Spotting him wandering round a party conference, Frank said, 'I'm all for care in the community, but this is ridiculous.' Yet years later, when this man fell on difficult times, Frank quietly made sure he got work when he was editor of the *Spectator*.

He also loved running jokes, standing things on their head and seeing what resulted. For instance there was the conceit about those charity appeals: 'consider, for the cost of one new dress, you could buy mosquito nets for an entire African village . . .' He rewrote that as 'do you realise that for the price of just five artesian wells in India, you could buy a pony for a little girl in Esher . . .'

He was always eager to learn, no matter what the topic. Until he reached great happiness with his wife Virginia, he found women especially baffling, and I recall long conversations with him during which I tried to explain how they – and relations with them – worked. It was almost like instructing an apprentice how to repair a car. He and I both took the view that it was our stern duty to continue taking the mickey out of politicians no matter how serious the topic they were dealing with. When the Falklands War began, however, Frank immediately reported to the colours and wrote stirring patriotic prose – as beautifully crafted as ever.

He was never one of those sketchwriters who hold themselves aloof from the people they write about. (One of my predecessors in the trade, Norman Shrapnel, also wrote lovingly chamfered pieces, but did his level best to avoid meeting MPs. 'If I got to know them,' he explained, 'it might spoil the purity of my hatred.') Frank did not take that view – why, it was politicians who had the best gossip and often the best lines. His chosen friends were the dry, the funny, the loose-tongued and the entertaining – people such as Alan Clark, who always called him 'Franco', doubtless after the late Spanish dictator, and even Labour MPs such as Peter Snape. He helped run Snape's jokey and doomed campaign to become Labour Chief Whip.

Politics fascinated him, but he never let people's political opinions interfere with his estimation of them. He could despise a Tory and relish the company of a Socialist. For years he had a flat in the same house as his close friend Alan Watkins, the *Observer* columnist, and no Conservative himself. He loved plain English cooking, possibly to an exaggerated extent, and would be annoyed and just puzzled by over-fancy foreign food. Once a group of us lunched, as he loved to do, at Simpson's in the Strand, which is even more old-fashioned than Rules. To my surprise I thought the roast beef and Yorkshire was delicious and said how wonderful it would be to have seconds, like on Sunday at home. 'Oh, they'll bring you seconds,' said Frank, and they did: another slab of cow and opera hat-sized Yorkshire. No charge, of course; he was one of their most valued customers.

I suppose Frank's perfect working day would have involved reading at home in the morning, lunching at Simpson's with someone funny, clever and full of gossip, then on to the Commons – preferably for Prime Minister's Questions which were twice weekly in those days, and then half an hour of chat about what we'd all just seen at the regular sketchwriters' tea, and finally on to the Opera House. Being seldom rivalrous, we all often swapped ideas. If someone had his own conceit, the others would never dream of stealing it, but would happily chip in with adornments and curlicues.

At his memorial service in May 2007, all the elements of his life were present. Sir Willard White sang. David Cameron spoke. The place was packed with politicians, journalists and other friends. Then we all went to the Royal Opera House. He was taken from us far, far too early. But that was a fine way to be remembered.

PART ONE

Chapter 1

Frank's early years

These five pieces, drawn from various publications that form Chapter One, are ones in which Frank wrote about his childhood years in Stoke Newington. In several of them the descriptions of his early life hang on the coat-tails of events that he remembered, such as the Suez Crisis of 1956 and the Queen's Coronation of 1952. In the final piece, which was written as an introduction to a previous collection of his journalism, Frank described the first step of his career and the break given to him by Maurice Green (editor of the Daily Telegraph *1964–1974) appointing him sketchwriter.*

⚼ 25 June 1988 ⚼
Stoke Newington in the 1950s

What the sociologists and the romanticisers said about the old boroughs where native Londoners tended to be born and bred remained broadly true as late as the 1950s.

Your own few streets in Stepney, Hackney, pre-gentrified Islington, and pre-revolutionary Lambeth were as self-contained and insular as any of those 'tightly knit communities' about which we have heard so much during the miners' strike.

Everyone knew everyone else. People were always popping in and out of each other's front doors. The womenfolk wore aprons and those curious turbans made from brightly coloured scarves – an ensemble now seen only in photographs illustrating university textbooks on English social history 1900–1960. To many of us born into this world of warmth and sharing, there was one overriding question: how to get out of it?

If a neighbour was caught urinating in, say Clissold Park, Stoke Newington – other than in the park's public conveniences, that is – his punishment was not the £5 fine, but the report in such papers of record as the *Hackney Gazette,* which would use what was then the local newspapers' confusing euphemism for the offence – 'causing a nuisance'. No one knew that 'causing a nuisance' just meant urinating against a wall or a tree. I only discovered it myself when, years later, my disagreeable duty was to report the magistrates' court for the *Walthamstow Guardian.* So the imagination of the warm and sharing cockneys could wander at will. At those doors through which turbaned women were doing all the popping, the word would be passed: 'I read it in the *'ackney.* Course, what they didn't put down in the paper was that 'e bashed 'is missus. That's what I 'eard anyway.'

Fewer people living in those areas are now known to all, so many of them being non-native students, squatters, IRA fugitives and investment analysts. So the local *Gazettes* and *Guardians* are no longer such feared and pitiless forces for rough justice – with a consequent gain for the quality of mercy, if not for good behaviour in places such as Clissold Park.

Another instrument of social control in the 1950s was the corner shop – the equal of the typical pub and the National Health Service among over-esteemed British institutions. There were heard the phrases, however baffling their exact meaning, through which society conveyed its disapproval – such as *'she's* no better than she ought to be'. If customers opted for margarine rather than butter, or Weights cigarettes rather than Players, the world soon knew they were hard up that week. Today's fashionably maligned supermarket, with its anonymity, is a far more humane place.

Not that there was really much bad behaviour to disapprove of. Today, outbreaks of soccer hooliganism are always followed by outbreaks of articles explaining that we have always had soccer hooliganism. But at Tottenham and Arsenal in the 1950s, children really were passed down unharmed over the heads of the crowd so as to give them a better view at the front. The literary critic Raymond Mortimer, contributing to a book on London, could write in 1950:

'Foreign visitors 80 years ago used to remark upon the violence of the population; now it is our mildness which excites surprise.'

Unlike in the provinces, escape from the tightly knit community was only a shilling bus ride away. Once in the West End, you were in the wider world depicted on the films, in the *Daily Mirror*, or the BBC – the world of both culture and anarchy. For anarchy, you could sit in a Soho milk bar and speculate that the swarthy men reading Maltese newspapers on the corner were members of the gang led by Jack Spot, whose knife fight was one of the running tabloid stories of the period. For culture, a few shillings would get you into the Proms and the galleries of Covent Garden or – a mile or so from the West End – the Old Vic and Sadler's Wells. Anarchy may have been more popular among 1950s youth than culture. The point is that both were available, since culture had not entirely been polluted by people who were more interested in anarchy. That is why to grow up in 1950s London was to grow up in the last decade in which everything was more or less as it should be.

Spectator

⊰ 25 October 1986 ⊱
Suez remembered through a schoolboy's eyes

The Suez Crisis of 1956 was an armed invasion led by the then Prime Minister Anthony Eden in coalition with the French and the Israelis to regain the Suez Canal after it had been nationalised by the Egyptian President Gamal Nasser. The invasion, though initially militarily successful, resulted in political humiliation for Britain after the US withheld its support.

In the fateful autumn I was aged 13 and three-quarters, and was in form 2b of a secondary modern school in Shoreditch.

Like Dulles, it took us some time to realise that this Suez crisis would turn serious. I first heard about it during an informal dinner in front of the television at my home in Stoke Newington, while watching the television version of the *Goon Show*. The programme was interrupted for a news flash saying that the Israelis had attacked Egypt and were advancing towards the canal. News flashes were rare in those days. We assumed it to be one of the show's surrealist jokes. It was expected that Mr Spike Milligan or Sir Harry Secombe would soon come on in long white underwear and a fez – fezzes being prominent in mid-fifties humour. When the programme did not pursue the subject, it was assumed that someone could explain the joke at school the next morning. The school's standard of Goon scholarship was high. All of us did Goon voices, a nasal, semi-Irish sound. It was early in that Suez autumn that I used mine on Alfie Barber, the class brute. To his face, I boldly sang, 'High dreeem of Alfie wiv the light bro-hwn teeth'. This made for much popularity in form 2b, it being about time that Alfie were cut down to size. Alfie split my lip for it. It is my most painful memory of that difficult time.

Until very late, Suez for us was completely overshadowed by Hungary. In comparison, fighting Egyptians did not seem important. Britain was always engaged in such campaigns: in Malaya, Kenya, Cyprus. You could read about them every day in the *Mirror*. This being the age of National Service, we could hear about them from our older brothers and cousins. Fighting, involving Russians, in the streets of a European city such as Budapest was of a different order of things. Had we but known it, we shared with Spengler, and with Professor J.M. Roberts today, a sense of the unique importance of the West: a view of history now discouraged as 'Eurocentric' by ILEA [Inner London Education Authority], and doubtless banned in Shoreditch.

Then something odd started to happen in Suez: we seemed to be losing. Years later, I read about the uproar in Parliament. None of us noticed that at the time. In so far as we had any interest in politics, we were Labour, but it was assumed that Labour was as much in favour of defeating someone like Nasser as everyone else. In places similar to Egypt, these sort of wars usually ended with us winning. Now there was a suggestion that this Suez crisis would end with Nasser still on his radio.

For a while, we assumed that Sir Anthony was just playing for time before deploying his ultimate resources: our big brothers and cousins on National Service. Also, he would throw in the Gurkhas.

Then, inexplicably, there was a ceasefire without our having our canal back.

It cannot be said that we had all along had doubts about Sir Anthony's fitness for the premiership, doubts of the kind imputed to Churchill. This was mainly because the only thing we knew about Sir Anthony was that our mothers admired him, although he did look to us like the ambassador in a funny film whose trousers fall down at a posh party. One thing seemed certain. All this talk about the danger to the pound was an excuse. The Russians did not have many pounds and they had seemed to win in Hungary. No, Sir Anthony had been let down, probably by the Americans, who were always claiming to have won the war without us, and probably by these other men in dark suits and hats around him. We did not like the look of this Macmillan. Also, that Butler was said to be against capital punishment.

Years later, I read in Mr Richard Gould Adams's biography of Dulles that, when Selwyn Lloyd visited Dulles in hospital in 1957, Dulles asked, 'Why did you stop?' 'You wouldn't let us go on,' Lloyd replied. 'There was nothing we could have done, really,' Dulles revealed, thus confirming the view from Shoreditch of those of us who were there at the time.

Spectator

Apart from his passion for opera, Frank, like Billy Elliot, the hero of the film, had a secret life connected to ballet, though in his case it did not involve dancing. He would go whenever possible to a Saturday matinee performance of ballet at Covent Garden and tell his family he was going to watch Arsenal play.

⊰ 4 November 2000 ⊱
Frank's Billy Elliot life

One of the papers reported the other day that the makers of *Billy Elliot* had compiled a list of the many male critics, reviewing the film, who had written that it was they who were the original Billy. They, too, had braved the fury of their rough-hewn fathers and taken ballet lessons. Our film critics, in childhood, were, it seems, seldom out of their tights. None of them explained why they had given up and chosen to soar as film critics rather than as *danseurs nobles*. It looked as if their fathers prevailed.

I cannot equal those critics. I can, however, claim to have done something even more difficult, and needing still more bravery, than going to ballet lessons in adolescence. That is, going to ballet in adolescence; watching ballet, not dancing it. As Billy's father eventually accepts, being able to dance confers a certain status, even among the proletariat. The proletariat, steeped in soccer, rugby league and boxing, admires fitness and strength. Whatever else they may be, male ballet dancers are fit and strong. Raising Mlle Guillem aloft is no light matter. Billy would have been strong enough to hold his own against playground bullies.

But we ballet watchers, as opposed to ballet dancers, could not and still cannot suppress plebeian mockery by our strength and fitness. No one is frightened or impressed by someone who just sits. What we did, and do, then, takes real courage.

In my case, it happened thus. I was about Billy's age at the start of the film. I was already interested in opera. That was hard enough to explain to friends and large uncles. But the latter tended to admire Gigli, Mario Lanza and Harry Secombe. Some were with the Eighth Army when it reached Naples, and could therefore size up a tenor. Also, opera had great tunes. All the world likes a great tune. Counter-tenors were unknown to them. Opera, provided it was tenors and tunes, was all right. Also, so long as it was mainly about singers, opera had about it more than a suspicion of heterosexuality. It is different today, of course, when opera is mainly about producers. Opera production is not a profession in which heterosexuality is rife. I do not know why, but there it is.

But singing is another matter. Many of the anecdotes of the late critic Philip Hope-Wallace, at whose feet I would sit in El Vino in old Fleet Street, himself a homosexual, were about heterosexuality on the operatic stage, or, rather, just behind it. Thus he would, with wholly serious delivery, assure me of the great soprano Emmy Destinn: 'She did have a lover, the baritone Gilly – French Algerian, a very good baritone as a matter of fact. They often sang together at

Covent Garden. Often in *Aida*. He would be available to her in her dressing room during the interval. But he was not always in the cast. He had his own international career. When he wasn't in the performance, they would send across Bow Street for a policeman.'

Not that ballet had failed entirely to penetrate my household. Every now and then, as the commercial television company's gesture towards the elevated promises that had won it the franchise, ballet would top the bill at *Sunday Night at the London Palladium*. Today's young will never be able to appreciate what a ritual *Sunday Night at the London Palladium* was on British Sunday nights of the late 1950s and early 1960s when there were only two channels, and the alternative on the BBC was, say, Ibsen's *When We Dead Awaken*.

Neighbours and relatives would gather in whichever house along the stretch of street had a television. The womenfolk would sip Babycham, the men, bottled brown ale. Liquorice comfits and sherbet would be distributed to the children. The sherbet, in turn, would be distributed down one's sister's back. There would be adult calls to order. Then, *Sunday Night at the London Palladium*. The Tiller Girls in top hats and fishnet stockings. Tommy Trinder, a compère of exemplary vulgarity. But sometimes, as Tommy would say in the reverent hush he reserved for high culture, 'Dame Margot Fonteyn, partnered by Michael Somes, have consented to perform the PAH de DUR from *Swan Lake* by JAI-kovsky.'

The great partnership would take the boards. A beery uncle would inquire, 'Where's the bleedin' swan?' My father would explain, 'They 'ad it for dinner.' A mischievous child would ask, 'What's that he's got stuck down his trousers?' Another uncle would speculate, 'His lunch.' Someone would add the further observation, 'By the look of it, 'e ain't wearin' any trousers.'

So I knew that ballet could expose all connected to it to Hogarthian satire. Yet, being already an opera lover, I knew there was this other art form going on in the same buildings – Covent Garden and Sadler's Wells – and dealing with the same sort of themes. Why not investigate? I did. It was *Swan Lake*.

I have a theory about conversions to ballet. Ballet, unlike opera, does not tend to grow on people. They either like it immediately, or not ever. I liked it immediately; to the point of obsession. It was not just the surge and swell of Tchaikovsky's score. I was soon immersed in ballets of far lesser music. It was choreography. Choreography, when great, as in the case of *Swan Lake* Act Two, and the ballets of Ashton, Tudor and above all, Balanchine, seemed visual music. It did not have to represent something, or 'mean' anything, any more than a symphony did. It was enough just to be great choreography.

But how to conceal all this from the uncles? Mercifully, ballet, unlike opera, was given at matinees. But how to explain what I was now up to of a Saturday afternoon? On one such Saturday, early on, as I left home, a male neighbour inquired, 'Off to the football, then?' That was it! I would be at the football. But soon, on returning from *The Sleeping Beauty* or *Giselle*, the neighbour would observe, 'Lucky old Arsenal!'

'Yeah,' I would reply. 'They were rubbish. I nearly walked out at half time.'

'Whaddya mean? They were at Newcastle.'

'I mean Spurs.'

'Spurs! I was at Spurs. They played a blinder.'

I began to endure the stress of all who live lives of deception, be they balletomanes or adulterers. But summer was worse. Where was I officially going on summer Saturday afternoons? A neighbour, possibly the same one, had the answer, 'Off to the Oval, then?'

But I knew somewhat less about cricket than I did about football. Time spent on *Wisden* would have been time lost on Beaumont's *Complete Book of Ballets*, the *Wisden* of the dance. I sensed the dangers when the neighbour asked me who had taken most wickets that day for Surrey, and I had replied Trueman or possibly Bradman. It could all go horribly wrong. There was just a shortage of cricketers in my head.

'You must have seen that six that hit the pavilion. Who got it?'

'Er, Markova. I mean, W.G. Grace.'

So it was best to admit everything. People took it badly. I do not believe in Billy's father. It was I, and not some soft film critic, who was the real Billy Elliot.

Spectator

⊰ 2 June 2003 ⊱

**The Queen's Coronation (2 June 1953). Relatives and
neighbours heaved into our front room to watch it on
television, the only one in the street.**

The weeks preceding the Coronation were important. You could collect cut-outs of the impending procession, almost in its entirety, from successive Kellogg's cornflakes boxes.

We lived in London on the Stoke Newington side of the border between Hackney and Stoke Newington – then two separate boroughs, now one – the frontier of the East End and North London. My father's main employer, as I discovered years later, always paid him the average national wage. We were a mother, a father, a daughter and a son. We were, then, the average British people.

It is often said that the Coronation coincided with the coming of television. In fact, it was not until a year or so later that sets came within the average working man's pocket, there being few working women to help meet the cost. But we were among the first in our street to afford one because my pastrycook father augmented that average national wage in the evenings by making cakes for weddings and bar mitzvahs.

He would secure the ingredients from his employer without the latter's knowledge. In our world, such requisitions from the ruling class were not considered improper. The family wealth, then, was built on tax avoidance and the surreptitious expropriation of raw materials.

On the day, much of the street, as well as relatives from deep within Hackney, heaved into the front room of our narrow terrace house: 68 Belgrade Road, the name having been changed from Wiesbaden Road in 1914 when Germany became our enemy and Yugoslavia our ally. As representative of the nation's future, I was allowed to turn on the set.

Nothing appeared. Tall uncles who had fought in Normandy, and vast aunts who had fought Hitler on the home front, laughed. Aunt Lill said that the only thing that worked in our house was a bar mitzvah cake.

'It's just warming up,' said my father – now worried. The set was a Bush, he emphasised: the best. It was so long ago that even the televisions were British. Thank God, a picture appeared: the same as was to appear, with minor variations of personnel, for the next several hours: troops from England, Ireland, Scotland, Wales and the newly invented Commonwealth marching around a rain-lashed London in the broad direction of Westminster Abbey.

The uncles greeted all of those who were not obviously white with cries of: 'There's the Gurkhas. Terrified of 'em, the Japs were.' The aunts drank cherry brandy, the uncles brown ale from bottles, and there was 'Tizer the Appetizer' for us children.

I cannot remember the Queen's coach, but it must have been in there somewhere, though an uncle said it must have taken a wrong turning and got stuck in Mare Street, Hackney. Eventually, we were inside the Abbey. To the horror of myself and my generation, some sort of High Anglican service seemed imminent. 'Be a laugh if the skypilot dropped the crown, eh?' thought my father, referring to Archbishop Fisher.

We, the young, had these services inflicted on us every Sunday morning in the Butterfield church at the bottom of the road, built when High Anglicanism sought with some success to win the London working class from, among other diversions, drink and revolution. Our parents never attended. They said we had to because it was good for us, and would stop us stealing – which was a bit much, given the source of that television.

My best friend, Johnnie, and I fled the screen to my bedroom, where we re-enacted the Coronation procession with broomsticks for rifles. Later, we went into the deserted streets to steal copies of the 'naturalist magazine' *Health and Efficiency*, left in racks outside temporarily closed newsagents in those trusting, socially cohesive days.

We returned to the screen only when marching resumed. After the balcony scene outside the Palace, we went out to the trestle tables beneath bunting in the street. There were fishpaste sandwiches, R. White's lemonade and wobbly jelly on paper plates, and all the adults assured one another that every country in the world envied us because of our monarchy.

Daily Telegraph

⊰ 1982 ⊱

From the *Sun* to the *Daily Telegraph*

For some time before 1972, I had a silent, nagging and increasingly hopeless ambition to hold the post of parliamentary sketchwriter. Politicians would be justified in deriving a certain satisfaction from that admission. Backbenchers are much mocked for the way in which they live in endless hope of being called by the Prime Minister and granted even the most tedious junior office. Such mockery is a staple of the Irreverent School of political journalism. But the irreverent also strive after their little satisfactions. Journalism has much in common with politics. Journalists and politicians are as one in their search for recognition, status, praise.

The clown who addresses the audience directly in the Prologue of *I Pagliacci* sums up the 'irreverent' journalist's predicament. It went particularly well in the terrible English translation I recall from the cheap seats at Sadler's Wells as a boy. 'And so, sweet people, when you look upon us, clad in our motley and tinsel . . . we are but men like you of gladness and sorrow, with the same broad heaven above us . . .' (I quote from fallible memory). On and on some hoarse baritone would bellow. I was under the impression at the time that here was profundity. How true, how true, I would reflect. It seemed so much more persuasive than poetry of the better sort. Later life did indeed reveal that the clown had described the condition of all performers – including a type of journalist. It was profound after all.

In 1972, Mr Andrew Alexander left the *Telegraph* sketchwriting job to do the same work on the *Daily Mail*, though more lucratively. He suggested I apply for the *Telegraph* job. By that time, I had moved from a provincial paper to become one of no fewer than three lobby correspondents whom Mr Rupert Murdoch's *Sun* saw fit to employ at Westminster, even though politics was not the reason for the vast circulation the paper remorselessly achieved from the moment of its launch in 1969. I was unsure whether to act on Mr Alexander's suggestion. I doubted whether the *Telegraph* would offer the job to someone from the *Sun*.

It is perhaps forgotten how appalled people were by the early

Murdoch *Sun* before its excesses became a national institution. I shared a house with my parents at the time. When the paper was delivered, I used to hurry downstairs and, if there was a particularly blatant bosom on the newly notorious page 3, would remove the page. This was in order to avoid the censure of my mother, a London matriarch who embodied traditional morality. 'Your paper's a bit short-weight today,' she would subsequently complain. 'It says here page 2 on one side and page 5 on the opposite.'

'I know, I know,' I would reassure her. 'It's all on account of those print unions. Some nights they refuse to print whole pages.' That did not really surprise her. The unions were holding the nation to ransom, she would explain. For I had found that with my mother, it was safe to blame most things on the unions.

There was another problem about applying for the *Telegraph* job. It was an outer branch of the higher journalism, involving metaphors, conceits, quotations, mandarin irony – that sort of thing. I had never written anything like that. Indeed, I had written scarcely anything other than 'Premier Ted Heath lashed Labour Leader Harold Wilson in a new Commons storm last night', which is the other main language of the profession.

How to persuade the *Telegraph* that – despite one's mode of employment – one was a man of immense culture? (Saying 'one' when you mean 'I' would do for a start, I decided.)

There was next an interview with the editor of the *Telegraph*, Mr Maurice Green, formerly of *The Times*. He was a courtly, shy, unmoralising man whom little had ever been known to amaze, nearing the end of his editorship. 'You may wonder what I'm doing for the *Sun*,' I mumbled during one of several silences in the conversations. No, not at all, he replied. We all had to work somewhere. Why should I think it would cause him any wonder? Well, because the *Sun* was sort of . . . trivial. Also, it was pro-Labour (for at that time it was), and I was some kind of a Tory. He replied that in journalism where one worked was largely a matter of chance. He had nothing against trivia. As for politics, the *Sun*'s advice on the subject had so far done considerably less harm to the British economy than the *Guardian*'s, in his view. I was beginning to admire this man.

Concerning the work I had submitted, he thought the trial sketches 'rather overdone, perhaps' but the *Sun* pieces were 'damn good'.

He gave me the job. It took someone of Green's social imperturbability to do so. I suspect I would have fared less well at the hands of one of those youngish, exciting grammar-school meritocrats who had for some years been taking over the country.

Chapter 2
1972–1977

These early sketches, in Chapters 2, 3 and 4, were written for the Daily Telegraph *over a period of five years.*

⇥ 30 November 1972 ⇤
All is calm as the Lords turn to pornography

Lord Longford (1905–2001) and Mary Whitehouse (1910–2001) were both tireless campaigners against sexual liberalism over many decades. In 1972 Lord Longford set off for Copenhagen to research the subject of pornography and the Danish Government's attitude towards it. Here he is reporting back to the House of Lords. His daughter, the novelist Rachel Billington, adds a further word of explanation below Frank's piece.

With Mrs Whitehouse on sentry duty in the public gallery, it was to be hoped that all entendres in the Lords yesterday would remain undoubled.

Given the debate's subject – the Earl of Longford's pornography report – much self-denial was therefore expected of their lordships as well as of anyone attempting to describe the proceedings.

In the end, the House did not disgrace itself.

Phrases capable of imaginative interpretation by the more baroque minds among us averaged out at only around one a speech. About par for the course, I would say.

Admittedly, the Bishop of Leicester, Dr Williams, introducing the debate, did call for the Longford legal proposals to be given 'a fair crack of the whip'.

But I rather suspect that this was a naughty, episcopal joke – the sort of thing that has them in stitches at the Athenaeum – designed to set Press Gallery pens racing, which ploy was entirely successful in the case of this reporter.

For the Bishop swiftly added: 'If that is not an unfortunate metaphor.'

Elsewhere, it is true that there was a tendency for some peers to defer – with a roguish chuckle – to one or other of their colleagues' 'greater experience' of the subject under debate, while adding that they, of course, meant nothing untoward.

And there were undoubtedly a number of entendres too double to be retold here – or so I was informed.

But generally, participants and spectators – of the debate that is – remained so calm that it was as if we had endured, prior to the start, a number of cold baths in the approved public school manner.

From Dr Williams, we had confirmation that Lord Longford's honour remained unsullied through recent ordeals.

'I particularly admired and approved his action in going to Denmark and in entering the places of questionable repute which he felt it his duty to enter,' the Bishop told the House. 'And I admired his good sense in leaving them at the precise moment when he did.'

Dr Williams's main case was that Lord Longford's critics had dismissed too early the report's belief that outrage to the public sense of decency could be a new criterion for successful prosecution.

The Bishop's case may, ultimately, have been unconvincing. But what was totally convincing – and should have compelled admiration – was his profound loathing for the pornographers' trade and obvious foreboding about the health of a society in which it flourished.

The Government's spokesman Baroness Young and Lord Shackleton for the Opposition, clearly shared that loathing. But they did not share the Bishop's view about the legal criteria for prosecution.

At the start of her speech, Lady Young heaped huge praise on the usefulness of the Longford report – a sure sign that she was going to disappoint the report's supporters by the end.

Without saying so, she made it plain that the law would not be changed in the way they wanted.

And Lord Shackleton was even more resolutely opposed to the change.

The standard of debate fell sharply with the intervention from the Liberal benches of an apparition – complete with suede shoes and naturally disdaining a dog-collar – of the 1970s' switched-on cleric incarnate, the Rev. Lord Beaumont.

He did not know why everyone was getting so worked up, really. Few had ever been harmed by a spot of porn now and again. He implied that the contemporary capitalist ethic might be to blame for encouraging pornography anyway.

Daily Telegraph

My father, Frank Longford, took his report on pornography seriously, but I fear, after his personal research into Danish sex clubs, few others did. Malcolm Muggeridge advised against the Copenhagen jaunt, and Gyles Brandreth and others have made gentle comedy out of it ever since.

However Cyril Connolly gave his assessment in The Sunday Times: '. . . *respect-worthy, reasonable, well-documented, cool, unbiased and with no sense of an inquisition'. So I was wrong to suggest no one ever took it seriously. That was the notable thing about my father: he never feared sticking his head above the parapet if he believed in the cause.*

Rachel Billington

≼ 28 June 1973 ≽
A glimpse of Foreign Secretary, Alec Douglas-Home

The aristocratic Alec Douglas-Home (1903–1995), having renounced his peerage, had briefly been Prime Minister in 1963–64. He became Foreign Secretary in 1970 and is seen here leading a debate about suspending Portugal and Greece from NATO.

Most of the world's ills were being made worse, if not actually caused, by a septuagenarian Berwickshire landowner.

This appeared to be the gravamen of the case put forward by a succession of Labour speakers during the first half of a two-day foreign affairs' debate in the Commons yesterday.

Repression in Greece, Portuguese colonialism in Africa, French nuclear testing in the Pacific and many a sundry woe – all were being fostered by a certain Sir Alec Douglas-Home, British Foreign Secretary.

And while that statesman was dealing with these matters, would he kindly sort out the drought in India?

Poor Sir Alec, still among the wisest, but no longer among the nimblest of men, had enough trouble sorting out his notes.

Once they had been assembled in correct order however, he delivered a speech that remained true to those sound principles of diplomacy that were good enough for Castlereigh and Curzon, if not for Mr Frank Allaun (Lab. Salford East).

It was true, as well, to that almost equally venerable tradition whereby Sir Alec's sibilant tongue betrays a tendency occasionally to say the opposite of what its owner intended.

Thus 'Asia' momentarily saw service as 'Europe' and the 'impotence' of the recent Nixon–Brezhnev declaration of principles was emphasised, only to be hastily corrected to 'importance' – though some of us felt that Sir Alec was right the first time.

As ever, the Foreign Secretary had to contend with an Opposition which believed – or in the case of its leaders, affected to believe – that the prime aim of British foreign policy should be to bring Fabian democracy to Greece, Portugal and Mozambique.

'There are some who argue,' said the Foreign Secretary, 'in the context of NATO that, because of the internal policies of Greece and Portugal and Portugal's policies in Africa, that these two countries should be expelled or suspended from NATO.

'This seems to me to mark a fundamental miscalculation of what foreign policy and security are all about.

'Foreign policy and defence is too serious a matter to be conducted on the basis of emotional reactions to aspects of other Government's policies over which we have no control.'

Many on the Labour side rolled around in their seats, purporting to be repelled by such naked siding with – indeed, encouragement of – outright Fascism.

Mr Kaufman (Lab. Ardwick) would have had us believe that he was outraged, a sure sign that an unexceptionable sentiment had been spoken.

Mr Maclennan (Lab. Caithness and Sutherland) intervened to assure Sir Alec that the last Government had been far harsher on the Greek regime than the Tories.

We searched our memories but could not recall the occasion of Col. Papadopoulos being summoned to Downing Street to receive the rough edge of a Yorkshire tongue.

Perhaps it was around the time the late Labour administration debated whether to sell arms to South Africa? Or was it when it decided to retain the British nuclear weapon?

It turned out, however, that Mr Maclennan was referring to something or other that the Labour delegation had got up to in the Council of Europe.

Sir Alec produced, in reply, a quotation about the pointlessness of British sanctions against Greece from a speech by Mr George Thomson, when a Labour Cabinet Minister.

Some of the Labour benches refused to accept Mr Thomson as a fit representative of their party. Mr Kaufman tossed his head with an air of 'Oh! Him.' Mr Wilson, it seemed, had harboured a minister blatantly sympathetic to the colonels.

Alas for Sir Alec! He had hoped to use the debate to focus attention on what our attitude should now be towards a Slavonic tyranny that was not actually a member of the same alliance as ourselves. But détente-crazed Labour politicians had no time for that old stuff.

Daily Telegraph

⋇ 15 November 1974 ⋇
Margaret Thatcher, Opposition front bench Spokesman
on the Environment, and her dimples of iron

On sitting down after her speech yesterday, Mrs Thatcher became the first Tory frontbencher in this Parliament to win from Tory backbenchers a cheer prompted by enthusiasm rather than by hope of distant knighthoods or peerages.

In her first appearance as her party's finance and public expenditure spokesman, Mrs Thatcher proved, as was once said of a deceptively easy-going operatic prima donna, that she has dimples of iron.

Her principal target was the Chancellor. But before she launched into Mr Healey, a glancing blow was sustained by Mr Lever, the Dr Schacht of the present Wilson regime. Mr Lever's answer to any problem was to borrow, she claimed.

'There are four ways of acquiring money – make it, earn it, marry it, borrow it. The Right Honourable Gentleman (Mr Lever) seems to know about all four.'

Moving on from Mr Lever's personal finances to those of the nation she said: 'Yesterday, it was suggested that there should be a penalty on companies which went beyond the social contract.

'It seems very odd that employers who were not parties to the social contract pay a penalty if the contract fails, but those who were parties to the contract seem to take no part in the penalty.'

She also drew attention to the economy of detail shown by Mr Healey in his Budget speech over the precise magnitude of the price rises and other privations, inherent in the Budget strategy.

'The first was petrol, followed by nationalised industry price increases, then deductions arising from public expenditure cuts, and then, in April, increases in taxation and rates,' she said. 'It is going to be sacrifice by instalments.'

Finally, she made admirable play with the corny patter in Mr Healey's Budget speech about accumulation of material goods not bringing happiness.

She produced a newspaper cutting in which Mr Healey was quoted as saying that he never saved, and that whenever he got any money, he would 'go out and buy something for the house'.

Mr Healey jumped up to demand the source of the quotation. 'The *Sunday Telegraph*,' said Mrs Thatcher. The Chancellor and his supporters seemed unwilling to regard that publication as a scholarly guide to the personal habits of the major politicians in the Workers' Party.

For Mr Healey denied ever having said it. Alas, his evidence for not making the remark rested solely on the grounds that it was 'preposterous'. He did not behave in that way towards money, we gathered.

Mrs Thatcher said how pleased she was to receive this assurance that, far from being a spendthrift, Mr Healey apparently took the excellent investment advice of his colleague Mr Lever.

'Certainly, I know he's spent money on buying houses in good Tory areas,' she added.

The male chauvinist thought crossed the mind that she might be about to scratch his eyes out. But soon she was learnedly discussing the Treasury's net borrowing requirement.

Reluctant though I am to risk the lady's wrath by questioning her undoubted femininity, let it be said that the Tories need more men like her.

Daily Telegraph

⊰ 27 November 1974 ⊱
It is 'time we finished with this folly' – John Prescott on the Channel Tunnel

Anthony Crosland (1918–1977), as Minister of the Environment under Harold Wilson, defended the viability of the Channel Tunnel. John Prescott, who later became Secretary of State for Transport and the Environment had his own view.

Like one of those gallant but not very subtle British officers in Colditz, Mr Crosland was caught yesterday trying to tunnel his way out of any commitment to the increasingly expensive-looking Channel Tunnel.

True, Mr Crosland did not admit that he and the Government were attempting an escape. But, as he read out a statement on the future of the project, the evidence of surreptitious spadework began to pile up around him.

One such tell-tale heap of earth was his announcement that 'The Government have now completed their examination of a revised cost estimate by British Rail. This amounts to £373 million at May 1974 prices.

'This excludes the additional environmental works which have been canvassed in Surrey and Kent; the greater part of the cost of compensation under the 1973 Land Compensation Act; and the cost of enabling the link to carry freight which was not previously envisaged.

'It is out of the question that the Government should approve or finance an investment of this magnitude. We must find some less expensive means of enabling the through traffic, which forms so essential an aspect of the tunnel project to gain access to London and the British Rail network.'

He had, therefore, formally proposed to the Government's partners in the project – the French Government and the two Channel Tunnel companies – that it be delayed 'to enable alternative lower-cost rail links to be thoroughly examined before we decide to build the tunnel or not'.

The Environment Secretary said that the French Government expected present studies to confirm 'the economic and financial viability of the project'.

Still burrowing (it being almost as difficult for me to extricate myself from this subterranean metaphor as it is for Mr Crosland to extricate the taxpayer from this tunnel), the minister added that the French Government's optimistic opinion 'may or may not be so'.

Did the Tory front bench punish Mr Crosland for his desperate adventure? After all, it was not all that long ago that Mr Heath assured us that Maplin, Concorde and the Channel Tunnel would be hugely beneficial to the national future.

Yesterday, however, Mr Channon, Shadow Environment Spokesman, had no harsh words for Mr Crosland's decision.

He largely confined himself to asking what had caused the 'astonishing increase in cost', and to insisting that any cheaper version be 'environmentally desirable'.

Mr Crosland un-astonishingly replied that cost had risen because of inflation, environmental factors and problems caused by the fact that no one had any experience of building railways in this country since the turn of the century.

Mr Prescott (Lab. Hull East) said it was 'time we finished with this folly', but Mr Crosland was not yet ready to dig that deeply and urged that the time for a final decision would be the spring.

And Mr Snape (Lab. West Bromwich) felt that, amid all this concern over the cost of the tunnel, the Government should look again at Concorde, which he called 'the flying albatross'.

Mr Crosland replied that he was not the minister responsible for Concorde. To vary the metaphor at last, Mr Crosland – having gone some way towards digging himself and the taxpayer out of a potentially costly hole – could not be expected to fly an even more expensive aircraft on a suicide mission.

Daily Telegraph

⊰ 19 February 1976 ⊱
James Callaghan as Dixon of Dock Green

Frank portrayed Foreign Secretary James Callaghan (1912–2005) as the plodding policeman Dixon of Dock Green, the thoroughly decent hero of the BBC soap opera. Here Callaghan is conducting a debate on the activities of the Soviet Union in Angola. He went on to lead his party as Prime Minister from 1976–1979.

When he was Home Secretary in 1967–70, it was the cartoonists' custom to depict Mr Callaghan as your friendly neighbourhood policeman – the repository of much homely wisdom, but firm with it.

As Foreign Secretary, he brings to world events – no matter how vast or fearful they may be – the same avuncular banality.

At Question Time yesterday, the Talleyrand of Dock Green was faced with the impending triumph of the Soviet Union and its Cuban mercenaries in Angola, and the potentially cataclysmic effects which this may have on Rhodesia and South Africa: a fit subject for the broad sweep approach, one would have thought, if you are going to say anything about it at all.

But his tone was essentially one of: 'Now, now, you MPLA blokes, move along there please.'

Certainly, there was nothing he could do, for good or for ill, to influence these events. Why then, did he pronounce upon them at any length?

After confirming the British Government's decision to recognise the MPLA as the Angolan Government, he issued another one of his requests for Cuban troops to be good lads and leave the premises forthwith, since it was well past hours, he had a job to do, and it would be better for all of us if they did what they were told, since they knew it made sense, didn't they now?

Because of his party's grotesque assumption that the South Africans were just as (if not more) naughty, he had to couple this with an appeal for South African troops to get out as well, even though most of them were by now at home, captured or dead.

But, to give him credit, it was the Cubans whom he regarded as the villains who were really making life unpleasant down at that particular manor. 'The presence of Cuban troops represents a potential danger to the neighbouring countries of southern Africa,' said Mr Callaghan, as he proceeded on his rounds and noted a disturbance emanating from a former Portuguese colony.

'Although they may have been invited into Angola by the MPLA, they have not been invited into any of the neighbouring countries.' For the Cubans and the South Africans to withdraw would be 'far the best thing', he added.

The Tories questioned Mr Callaghan about the fate of Rhodesia in all this. Mr Amery (Con. Brighton Pavilion), to the irritation of Labour backbenchers, said that, if there were an invasion of Rhodesia from Mozambique, 'we should not be a party to continuing sanctions'. Mr Callaghan did not agree.

Mr Maudling, Shadow Foreign Secretary, wanted to know what assurances Britain had received from the MPLA before giving it recognition, that Rhodesia's territorial integrity would be respected. The gist of Mr Callaghan's reply was: None.

There is, of course, nothing that the Foreign Secretary can do about Rhodesia either. And that, for a Labour politician, is an ideal setting in which to moralise.

'Time is running out' for Mr Smith, he said. The Rhodesian Prime Minister's 'last chance was to get together with the black Rhodesian leader Mr Nkomo and work out a transition to black rule.'

After all, suggested Mr Callaghan, this kind of carry-on doesn't make my job any easier y'know.

Daily Telegraph

⊰ 26 April 1976 ⊱
Henry Kissinger pronounces on Africa

Anthony Crosland, Foreign Secretary from 1976–1977 was asked about Dr Kissinger's speech and the reaction to it of Rhodesian Prime Minister Ian Smith.

Drawing on his lifelong lack of interest in foreign affairs, Mr Crosland made a successful début as Foreign Secretary at Question Time. The fact that it was successful is no argument for extending the principle of the gifted amateur to, for instance, brain surgery. But Mr Crosland's appointment is a reminder to Britain's expensive and frequently patronising Diplomatic Service of their true place in the scheme of things. For he is reportedly only at the FO for a few months in order to fill in time before succeeding to the Treasury. The Foreign Office, then, is nowadays just a superior sort of dentist's waiting room – whose inmate leafs through briefs about, say, Ethiopian Cabinet reshuffles instead of copies of *Punch*.

But no disrespect is here intended to Mr Crosland, who is one of the cleverest men in the Commons, as he would himself concede. And yesterday he donned world statesman's drag and comported himself in the manner associated with the 'Great Department of State' that harboured Canning, Sir Edward Grey, Burgess and Maclean.

Moreover, when it comes to being patronising, most people on the FO payroll will find Mr Crosland a hard man to beat. He was asked yesterday about his meeting with Dr Kissinger. Now almost certainly he believes Dr Kissinger to be a chubby, rather boring little fellow, perfectly amiable in a superficial sort of way, but not up to much intellectually. Furthermore, he should grapple – as Mr Crosland himself had done for years – with something really difficult, such as the British rating system, instead of going in for all that easy, 'broad sweep' stuff about Metternich – who was no doubt an equally tedious character – and the 'Decline of the West'.

The evidence suggests that Mr Crosland would not be far wrong. But he thought it prudent to tell the House that the doctor's speech this week on Africa was a 'major contribution to African policy'.

He was also asked about Mr Ian Smith. Now he, of course, in the Crosland lexicon, would be a very vulgar and tiresome figure indeed – worse even than all those hysterical and tiresome black men from all those outlandish countries about which people like Mrs Judith Hart become sentimental in a perfectly ludicrous fashion. If he had his way, he would have no part in any of it.

However, he explained that: 'The essential thing is for Mr Smith and the white community to grasp the full significance of the Kissinger speech and realise that they are dealing with an opinion now held by the whole world community.'

Furthermore, 'in terms of national interest and the global balance of power, I would suggest that if the UK Government and Dr Kissinger had not taken the line they have taken, we would have undermined every moderate black leader in the entire continent of Africa.'

Note such 'broad sweep' touches as 'world community' and 'global balance of power'. Mr Crosland had mastered the patter without any trouble at all, proving that being Foreign Secretary was nowadays a form of upmarket, unskilled labour. He did spoil it at one stage by showing a certain amount of knowledge of the cod war, but that could be explained by the fact that he is MP for Grimsby.

Mr Tugendhat, an Opposition foreign affairs spokesman, asked him what he thought about Mr Jimmy Carter's reported sporting of an 'England-get-out-of-Ireland' button. To Mr Crosland, Mr Carter would be a really rather absurd person whose advance towards the Presidency only went to show what preposterous and boring people the Americans could be when they set their minds to it. But the Foreign Secretary stuck to deploring the illegal American arms shipments to Ulster.

As for Rhodesia, we must not lose sight of the conditions for a settlement recently laid down by the British Prime Minister – 'Otherwise we should simply set off again on that long, stony road we have tried to inch up in the last twelve years.'

A telling phrase, if I may say so, Foreign Secretary. God bless you, in these troubled times, sir.

Daily Telegraph

⊰ 8 December 1976 ⊱
Norman Tebbit, Swain and fisticuffs in the House

Without once having to read from notes, Mr Tom Swain – a Derbyshire miners' MP – whose syntax is normally more muddled – yesterday exclaimed to a Tory, 'If you say that outside, I'll punch your bloody head in.'

It was the best and most articulate speech Mr Swain had made in his 17 years in the House.

A moment later he illustrated his observation with a diagram: He seized the Conservative by the tie, but by that time other Members had understood the broad sweep of Mr Swain's argument and interposed themselves – at some personal risk – between the two men.

This example of punk politics took place during Question Time – a peak viewing hour – while many impressionable politicians and sensitive journalists were watching. I myself subsequently jammed numerous switchboards in protest.

Throughout it all, the Speaker said nothing. One had always known that it was wrong for Mr Bill Grundy to be passed over when last the Chair fell vacant.

It happened as questions to the Education Department were drawing to an end, and Prime Minister's questions were about to begin.

Which immediately raises the interesting side issue: What is the hitherto concealed link between Mr Swain and education? But no matter. Mr Swain was in his place.

Opposite him sat Mr Tebbit (Con. Chingford) – tall, thin, dark-jowled, ideally equipped for his role as Labour's current Tory back bench stage villain, but who would also be excellent as the wicked Sir Jasper in one of those Victorian melodramas now being fashionably revived.

Mr Tebbit was recently described by Mr Michael Foot as 'the most studiously offensive man in the House'. A signal honour. Let us hope Mr Tebbit proves worthy of that sacred trust.

Certainly he did his duty yesterday. Mr Swain was complaining to the Speaker about not being called by the Chair to put questions to the Education Ministers.

Mr Tebbit muttered something studiously offensive. It was then that Mr Swain spoke eloquently about the likely fate of Mr Tebbit's head.

Mr Swain turned to the Chair, complained to the referee that 'the Honourable Member accused me of being drunk', and sat down.

Out of earshot of the rest of us, Mr Swain and Mr Tebbit continued to exchange ideas across the floor of the House. It seemed unlikely that they were discussing the economic situation.

Suddenly they rose and walked to the Bar – the Bar of the Chamber that is. Mr Tebbit was smiling. Mr Swain seemed to grab Mr Tebbit's tie, and pulled back a huge miner's fist of the kind idealised – highly implausibly – by D.H. Lawrence.

A Tory backbencher continued to drone through a question to the Government front bench.

But Mr Tebbit had stopped smiling. After all, Mr Swain – a large, beetle-browed person, shaped like a bulky wardrobe – is no joke. Well, he is a joke. But you know what I mean. In such a mood as yesterday, Mr Swain, once a bolt had been shoved through his head, would make an effective Hollywood Frankenstein.

Rescue action was clearly required. Only MPs could supply it. That was only proper. They are always urging sacrifice.

The press, one must report, displayed exemplary cowardice. Throughout, it was left to several Members standing by the Bar to usher Mr Swain away.

The two returned to their seats – Mr Tebbit with his head still mercifully intact; Mr Swain with his as intact as it is ever likely to be.

Daily Telegraph

In this early column, Frank highlights one of those incidents you will not find reported in Hansard when Tom Swain and I had a tetchy disagreement which I thought might be better resolved outside the Chamber.

Knowingly or not, Frank's not infrequent references to me rescued me from the obscurity of the backbenches to modest fame as 'the Chingford Strangler', 'the Chingford Skinhead' and, courtesy of Michael Foot, 'the semi-house-trained polecat'. In this incident I detected that Tom was a little the worse – or the better – for drink, and advised him to calm down. He didn't, and to avoid a scene in the Chamber I suggested we sorted things out outside – which he interpreted as a challenge to a fight.

Norman Tebbit

⊰ 16 February 1977 ⊱
The lavender honours list and the 'Beast of Bolsover'

Following Prime Minister Harold Wilson's shock resignation announcement in March 1976, rumours circulated that his much-criticised resignation honours list had been drafted on lavender notepaper by his Political Secretary, Marcia Falkender – a suggestion she has always fiercely rebutted. The list included the business tycoon, Jimmy Goldsmith. It was at about this time that the redoubtable Dennis Skinner (Labour MP for Bolsover from 1970) was nicknamed the 'Beast of Bolsover', a phrase that was widely attributed to Frank.

Mr Callaghan was questioned for the first time yesterday about a matter connected with the affair involving Haines [Wilson's Press Secretary], Falkender, Wilson and airborne whisky – changing at Crewe, and stopping at lavender notepaper, and Goldsmith.

The subject was alluded to by the left-winger, Mr Skinner (Lab. Bolsover), who, as a full-time proletarian, is unlikely to hold with all those decadent goings on under what was supposed to have been a 'People's Government'.

It was only proper that Mr Skinner should be the first man to raise the subject in the House. For Mr Skinner's function as 'A Difficult Sort of Character' is now as much a part of the British Constitution as Black Rod, and a good deal more useful.

The fact that Mr Skinner is also a shameless publicity seeker is neither here nor there. So too, it could be argued, is Black Rod – going around in those absurd black gaiters, and carrying that silly wand.

Anyway, Mr Skinner had a question on the order paper asking the Prime Minister to list his official engagements for the day.

This is a procedural device enabling a Member to raise virtually any matter once the Prime Minister has read out the engagements.

Mr Skinner acidly asked whether he would be meeting 'his political advisers'.

'Political adviser' is the euphemistic title often used to describe the various Pagliacci-like strolling players who made up Mr Harold Wilson's inner circle – Mr Haines, Lady Falkender, and other unintentional exponents of the custard pie, the water-squirting carnation, and the whisky-soaked Press Officer.

Mr Callaghan had his own political advisers. But alas, they seem to be a serious lot who are unlikely to contribute as much to the gaiety of the nation as their now-immortal predecessors.

'If he does meet his political advisers, will the Prime Minister engage in a discussion about the honours list?' Mr Skinner asked.

'Would the Prime Minister take out a sheet of clean . . .'

The Tories, in virtual unison: 'Lavender notepaper!'

Mr Skinner decided to treat that flippant intervention with what a less literate MP once described as a 'complete ignoral'.

'. . . would the Prime Minister take out a large clean white – not lavender – paper and write on it . . .'

The entire Tory Party: 'Skinner!'

Mr Skinner laughed. But now he had an air of: Er, where was I?

Ah yes, 'Would the Prime Minister write on this paper "the honours list is undemocratic and I intend to abolish it"?'

It had taken some time to reach the fundamental essence, indeed the quintessential kernel – not to mention the point – of Mr Skinner's question. But now, all was well. We were there.

Mr Callaghan said he took note of Mr Skinner's denial that he would wish to appear in an honours list.

'I am not sure whether it is mock modesty,' he added, 'or whether he got somebody over there to shout his name in order to put into my head something that would never otherwise have been there.'

But as we all know, Mr Callaghan is an old Tory at heart. And he strongly defended the honours list as an institution.

'I have no intention of abolishing it,' he said. It was a 'suitable vehicle' for rewarding people who had done work 'frequently voluntarily'.

He made it clear that he was referring to such people as 'those who worked voluntarily with handicapped children', rather than with handicapped Prime Ministers.

Daily Telegraph

⊰ 8 November 1977 ⊱
Ritual murder and homosexuality in Lancaster

Mrs Kellett-Bowman, the Conservative Member for Lancaster, demanded of the Speaker that an emergency debate be held about public money being given to an Indian institution called the 'Arnand Marg'. This turned out to be not one of those tandoori restaurants with a potentially lethal cuisine but merely (as she told the House) 'an Indian terrorist group which practises homosexuality and ritual murder'. Mrs Kellett-Bowman was indignant. Understandably. Ritual murder is one thing, but homosexuality is always to be deplored.

Mrs Kellett-Bowman, who represents a marginal constituency and could therefore lose her seat if she offended any significant minority taste, courageously came out against both. But it was a sign of these permissive times that the ritual murder seemed to be causing her most concern. For, when certain Labour backbenchers laughed as she described the twin activities of the Anand Marg, she sharply told them: 'I am surprised that Members of the Government side should find ritual murder amusing.'

She swept on. It emerged that these gay necrophiliacs, or whatever is their precise hobby, had a branch on Merseyside. They had received a £60,000 grant from the Government's Manpower Services Commission. But, as Mrs Kellett-Bowman explained, Professor Ridley, the chairman of the Merseyside Job-Creation Committee, had said it was all right because the ritually murderous gays from the subcontinent had been given the cash so that they could rejuvenate a Victorian theatre in Liverpool. (Are you able to follow all this? I confess that I cannot, For instance, why did Professor Ridley think that the most obviously suitable people to rejuvenate a Victorian theatre in Liverpool were these deviants of a homosexual, and indeed homicidal, tendency? Perhaps it is all part of the timeless, unfathomable mystery that is teeming, changeless Merseyside.) We never did get to the bottom of it all.

Soon it was time for the Speaker, Mr George Thomas, to read out the application for an emergency debate. He said that, under Standing Order Number Nine, Mrs Kellett-Bowman was asking for precedence over other business to be given to a debate about a grant to a group 'which practises ritual murder'. He left out the homosexuality, the squeamish man!

'And homosexuality!' Mr Norman Tebbit, the Conservative MP for Chingford, smilingly obliged.

Mr Speaker is a Welshman and a Methodist. Presumably, although ritual murder is well-known in the valleys, folk know nothing of that other matter. He ignored Mr Tebbit and refused an emergency debate.

Daily Telegraph

⊰ **13 December 1977** ⊱
The Labour Party finances Poland to buy British ships

From the Government Dispatch Box, the always dependably outrageous Mr Gerald Kaufman last night wound up a debate forced by the Tories on the Polish ships deal with a brilliant speech which won him a deserved cheer from his party.

He was particularly impressive on this occasion because, like all the most heroic actions, his speech was a defence of an impossible position.

The Poles have shown no inclination to buy British ships under normal circumstances, but this difficulty is to be overcome by our more or less giving Poland the money with which to do the buying.

It was this last point which has enraged the Tories. From the Opposition front bench yesterday, Mr John Nott (St Ives), the Shadow Secretary for Industry, and his deputy, Mr Norman Lamont (Kingston) effectively exposed the horrendous financing of the deal.

Mr Nott thought that the arrangement would probably cost the British taxpayer £38 million and the resultant British-subsidised Polish merchant ships would take away business from British interests.

'We all know that for the love of one Labour marginal seat the Prime Minister would ski down Mount Everest in the nude with a carnation up his nose,' Mr Nott observed, drawing on his wide reading of current affairs.

'Would it not have been better to spend the money on the Royal Navy? The Royal Navy is at least on our side.'

The laconic Mr Nott is one of the Opposition front bench's best debaters – which praise is not meant to be as faint as it sounds – and his speech was delighting his backbenchers. It was also outraging Labour backbenchers. Everyone, then, seemed satisfied.

As the debate wore on, Labour Members from shipbuilding areas twitched with irritation. It was now reported that the Indians were going to get a similar deal, one Tory complained.

'So what?' a Labour voice inquired. 'It's the unemployment that's important,' another Labour man cried.

A collective mania for such ruinous commercial arrangements seemed to be sweeping the Labour benches. One could quite believe that these MPs were angry at the lack of similar shipping deals with Czechoslovakia, Switzerland and Tibet – regarding such a lack as sheer water-ism: discrimination against landlocked countries.

The Minister of State for Industry, Mr Kaufman (Lab. Ardwick), defended the deal to such tremendous effect that generations of Polish schoolchildren will be brought up to revere the name of Gerald of Ardwiczki, the Father of the Polish merchant navy.

First, he produces a letter from a Merseyside Tory member, Miss Lynda Chalker (Wallasey), asking for the propellers to be built in her constituency.

She got up and gave a complicated explanation about how this did not mean she approved of the ships' order as a whole.

Then Mr Kaufman impaled a north-east Tory backbencher with a quotation – from the backbencher in his local paper – seemingly favouring the order.

He too got up and gave a rather involved explanation which resulted in Mr Kaufman calling on the shipyard workers of the Tyne to note that this Tory 'wants them on the dole'.

Mr Kaufman accused Mr Nott of wanting unemployment in the

shipbuilding areas. Mr Nott rose and noted that unemployment in his constituency of St. Ives was worse than in the shipbuilding areas, and what was the Government going to do about that?

Mr Kaufman replied that if Mr Nott was calling for more Government expenditure he had better sort it out with his Tory front bench colleagues who were against more public expenditure.

Next Mr Kaufman mocked the Tories for apparently being against these sorts of deals with communist countries. He noted (to a large Labour cheer) that over the recent visit to Yugoslavia, Mrs Thatcher had praised a certain project (which involved British credits) as an admirable example of 'Anglo-Yugoslav cooperation'.

Then he took up an earlier complaint from Mr Nicholas Ridley (Con. Cirencester) that the Government had not released enough details of the Polish shipping order's financing.

He said that Mr Ridley, when a Minister for Industry in the Tory Government, had been asked to supply similar details, but had refused in a Parliamentary reply which had noted that 'this is a purely commercial matter'.

Finally, Mr Kaufman pointed out that work was being carried out at Warsaw Airport by a British firm called Cementation. It involved British Government credits.

'Like the *Daily Express* (an opponent of the Polish ships deal), this company is a subsidiary of Trafalgar Investments,' Mr Kaufman said.

And he triumphantly added: 'I am sorry I cannot give further details of this deal because, in the immortal words of the Honourable Member for Cirencester, this is purely a commercial matter.'

Daily Telegraph

Frank's sketch about the debate on the Polish shipbuilding deal is my all-time favourite, and not just because he wrote in such laudatory (if tongue-in-cheek) terms about my own contribution.

This agreement between the UK and Polish Governments, which we regarded as so important that I went to Warsaw to clinch it, was precisely as Frank depicted it, namely that we paid the Poles to sign up for ships for their use to be built in British shipyards.

We did so because those shipyards were in danger of closure, and we were desperate to protect jobs for the workforces. The Conservatives had a very strong case, and it was my role to put them on the defensive, with every ruse at my command.

This sketch is notable not only for its wit and acumen, but for the fact that Frank stayed until the end of the debate to listen to the speeches. No sketchwriter today could have written its equivalent because deadlines are such that no sketchwriter would stay so late. Also, whatever the time of day of the debate, none of today's sketchwriters would bother to report in such detail. O tempora! O mores!

Gerald Kaufman MP

Chapter 3

1978–1979
The Winter
of Discontent

The 'Winter of Discontent', a phrase of propaganda genius, was one of widespread strikes by the unions demanding higher pay. The Callaghan Government struggled to cope, a particularly difficult task given that they were supposedly representing the unions in Parliament!

⊰ 1978 ⊱

**The Chamber is graced with a visit from
the young Prince Charles**

Prince Charles paid a visit to the House to see how Parliament works – or, as the case may be, doesn't. There had been much advance interest in how the Labour left-wingers would react to his presence. The last time a royal personage with his first name became particularly interested in Parliament, their predecessors on the extremist wing of British politics cut off his head. But one had the fullest confidence in Mr Dennis Skinner.

The Prince strolled into the Peers' Gallery accompanied by the amiable, smiling figure of Lord Peart of Workington, Lord Privy Seal and Leader of the House of Lords, who in real life is dear old Mr Fred Peart. Mr Peart's duty was to sit next to Prince Charles and explain what was going on. This would have made the Prince notably confused. Every now and then, he would lean forward and whisper in the Windsor ear. 'See that fellow sitting in the big chair in the middle, Your Royal Highness, the one with the full-bottomed wig and the black tights,' Fred was no doubt saying, pointing towards the Speaker. 'That's the Prime Minister.'

At the time of the Prince's arrival, the Minister answering the questions at the Dispatch Box was that other Fred-figure: Mr Mulley, the Secretary of State for Defence. This was appropriate. Mr Mulley and the Prince have something in common. They have both fallen asleep on or near the Prince's mother's lap.

The sight of a member of the Royal House seemed to revive, in the Secretary for Defence, memories of that single heroic action for which he is famous, and for which his name will live forever in the annals of the British Armed forces – so long as men still tell of these things. He began to sound distinctly drowsy.

And the Labour Left's reaction to the royal visit? They turned out to be a cowardly lot. For they treated both us and his Royal Highness to a disgraceful show of good conduct. One cannot see the point of having a Left if they are going to behave like this.

And Mr Skinner? The visit of such a person as Prince Charles would no doubt have been particularly provocative to him. But Mr Skinner, with centuries of tradition and breeding behind him in these matters, knew exactly how to behave. He left earlier than usual.

Daily Telegraph

⊰ 1978–1979 ⊱
The gravediggers' strike. Dennis Skinner's outbursts come from the heart.

This is the strike in the north-west of England by workers responsible for gravedigging and crematorium operating: the dying industries. Messy work of this kind, among ministers, is normally palmed off on Mr Denis Howell, the Minister of State for the Environment. In his time he has looked after Sport, Drought and Snow. But this time he seems to have dug in against being landed with Death.

So the statement was made by the Secretary of State who is the head of Mr Howell's department, Mr Peter Shore. It was a tricky one both for him and for any Member who might want to put a question to him. It is agreed on all sides that this dispute is fabulously horrible. But supposing some Tory suddenly told Mr Shore that it was a grave situation? Supposing some left-winger accused the Tories of inflaming the crematorium problem? It did not bear thinking about. In particular, we in this column, conscious of the way in which we tend to set the tone in these matters, would have to proceed warily.

In the event, we all acquitted ourselves rather well. Not a single MP doubled his entendre. Everyone was appropriately mortified by this strike.

Actually, Mr Michael Heseltine, the Shadow Secretary for the Environment, rather overdid it. His tone became more and more theatrically sombre as he pressed Mr Shore to make another statement within a day. One harboured the suspicion that if he was *that* upset he would surely be on the train to Lime Street, with the intention of wielding a shovel himself.

Mr Shore, on the other hand, seemed genuinely aghast. 'The matter goes much wider than one of public health,' he said. 'It affects the feelings of those confronted by death in the family and in the community.'

Mr Heseltine rose again, and tuning in his sepulchral tones, he once again played undertakers – although, since he was standing beneath that elaborately sculptured blond hair-do, and was encased in several yards of expensive suiting, he would have been one of those prosperous American members of the funeral profession to be found in Evelyn Waugh's *The Loved One*. He vaguely demanded action. Mr Shore asked him 'to wait until a little later' to see what the response was to various talks among the local authorities and unions concerned.

The left-wing Liverpool Member, Mr Eric Heffer, who had long seen himself as the First Gravedigger of many a Labour Government incomes policy, said he was 'deeply concerned at the distress being caused to bereaved families. But the man must have a decent living wage,' he added, with the nearest we came to an unfortunate phrase.

All the piety proved rather too much for Mr Dennis Skinner. He told Mr Shore that both sides of the House were 'with only a few

exceptions indulging in a bout of utter hypocrisy'. Mr Skinner probably regards death as a bourgeois custom. It holds no terrors for him. The House and the Government could 'get rid of these dead bodies', he said, by paying 'a decent wage'. And he added: 'There is no one, but no one, in this House who would do the job these people are doing for a take-home pay of £40.'

This was an honest and impressive outburst. It was very different from the false emotion – surely the definition of sentimentality – which was deployed by other Members. But honest and impressive, too, was Mr Shore's reply. He rounded on Mr Skinner with real feeling, something one does not often see displayed in the House. He said he hoped that Mr Skinner 'will at a later stage today consider what his sense of priorities and values are. Death is not hypocrisy, nor is human grief, nor is a common sense of humanity. There ought to be some sense of common fellowship and decency between members of the same community.' (Huge Tory cheers: Labour silence.)

Mr Skinner sat back in his seat with a look of considerable disapproval. Two of his left-wing cronies appeared to commiserate with him. He stared at Mr Shore. These middle-class Labour ministers, he seemed to say, would be the death of him.

Daily Telegraph

⊰ April 1978 ⊱
Ordure, thrown from the Gallery, rains down
upon the Scottish Devolution Bill

Manure was propelled in the direction of MPs yesterday. Your correspondent was in the Press Gallery bar at the time, engaged upon in-depth research. He therefore cannot, for once, be held responsible. By the time he arrived in the Chamber, MPs were filing out with impressive calm – women and children first. Various attendants were busy with brushes and brooms.

Relatively few MPs or journalists were present for the incident. This was because the House was debating the Scottish Devolution Bill.

The news that excreta was raining down upon the Scotland Bill sent one hurrying into the Chamber for an eyewitness account from, among others, the parliamentary sketchwriter of Another Conservative Newspaper, who has a perverse and expert interest in the subject (the Scotland Bill, that is). This informant was shaken – although possibly with glee. From his, and other, accounts it seems that a man and woman in the Public Gallery yielded to a temptation which a lot of people must feel from time to time, and launched the rude substance in what appeared to be several half-open plastic bags.

Mr Tam Dalyell, the Labour Member for West Lothian, was in mid-point of order. This of course rapidly became a point of odour.

The Speaker shouted 'Order!' but, according to some reports, it might have been 'Ordure!' (The reader will be burdened with no further puns.)

The fall-out covered a wide area and was non-ideological in its choice of victims – it ranged from the Tribune benches to the right-winger Mr Ian Gow (the Conservative Member for Eastbourne). Our condolences to relatives, particularly wives.

But it was the Tribune benches, just under the Public Gallery, which got the worst of it – this causing a lot of people in all parties to reflect that life may not always be unfair. And the worst affected area was Mr Dennis Skinner, the Labour Member for Bolsover, but he has always claimed that politics under capitalism were a dirty business. There was a direct hit on the new sports jacket which Mr Skinner has worn for the first time in the Chamber this week. Understandably, he jumped up and rushed to the door. MPs looked aghast, almost as much as they would have had the stuff missed Mr Skinner.

Visitors in the Public Gallery gazed down impassively – the Americans, Japanese and Arabs among them being presumably under the impression that it was all a regular part of the unchanging ritual of the oldest Parliament

Mr Dalyell, a remorseless critic of Scottish devolution, was forced to stop speaking – something which only dung from heaven could have achieved.

The couple in the gallery shouted slogans at least as odorous as their missile. They were removed.

Small deposits of the substance settled throughout the Chamber. Even the very Dispatch Boxes were defiled. Mr John Smith, the Minister of State in charge of devolution, looked down to find that his briefs were soiled, so to speak. The first instinct of the Speaker, Mr George Thomas, must have been to consult Erskine May, the parliamentary rulebook, to discover the precedents. But under what heading to look? Pollution? Agriculture? No, George was on his own. So he established the historic precedent that when proceedings begin to leave a nasty smell, the House has to be suspended for 20 minutes.

Daily Telegraph

Chapter 4

March–May 1979
The dawn of the
Thatcher years

⊰ 28 March 1979 ⊱

Callaghan loses a vote of no confidence by one vote

*On the 28 March 1979, Prime Minister James Callaghan lost a
parliamentary vote of no confidence by one vote and called an election
for 3 May 1979. The Conservatives under Margaret Thatcher
triumphed.*

All evening we waited for the answer to the question: Would we
get a drink? For the Commons catering staff had chosen this,
of all nights, to go on strike.

Even those of us whose history is rather hazy had no doubt that
this was the most dramatic debate since Simon de Montfort did for
Ramsay Macdonald over Norway. Yet it was taking place in an eerie
void, without tea, without coffee, without the famous House of
Commons rock cakes made from genuine rocks, and without booze.

The political columnist of the *Guardian*, who has a sense of
history, informed one that, as well as being the first time for over 50
years that a Government had lost a confidence vote, it could also be
the first ever time that a Government had lost a confidence vote with
everyone sober.

He spoke too soon. As the night wore on, passers-by were
confronted with that most frightening spectacle: a sober mob of
journalists. It roamed the streets of Westminster in search of a pub
that had not been taken over by the equally desperate mob of MPs.

Police with dogs were on hand to keep the two groups apart.

Back in the Chamber, the debate had opened amid the traditional packed House and constant hubbub.

As ever on these occasions, one's eye was constantly drawn to the Peers' Gallery and its picturesque collection of defunct politicians resembling the Twentieth-century History section of Madame Tussaud's. Some of the likenesses were rather unconvincing. There was a shrivelled owl, purporting to be Lord George Brown. It did not look a bit like him. There was also a large, round character – resembling one of those jolly porcelain figures surrounded by children which one sees in the windows of Chinese restaurants – purporting to be Lord Thorneycroft.

A sighting was reported, on a distant Labour bench, of Mr Frank Maguire, the Independent Irish Republican, who has hardly set foot in the place since being elected in 1974, but none of us really knew what he looked like. It could have been someone in from the street. Next, word went round that it was impossible to get into any of the loos because Liberals were locking themselves in as their explanation of why they did not want to vote. So anything could happen. The excitement was tremendous.

For about half an hour, however, it was dispelled. Mrs Thatcher spoke. Within minutes of rising to open the debate and move the motion of no confidence, it was clear that she was in pedestrian form. Labour Members sensed it and fell silent. The bounders decided to give her a fair hearing. Remorselessly, she heaved statistics at us to demonstrate Governmental failure in every field of human endeavour. Her backbenchers began to fidget and even to talk among themselves. The much-loved Mr Freddie Burden, the Conservative Member for Gillingham, appeared to nod off.

Suddenly, Mrs Thatcher brought a heavily statistical passage to an end by raising her voice. Her backbenchers took this as their cue to stop muttering to one another and to cheer. Unfortunately, the unaccustomed noise caused dear Freddie to wake up with a jolt. Labour Members gave him a huge cheer.

Mrs Thatcher sat down after only half an hour amid Labour cries of, 'That all?' and 'More! More!' But, although she had not done herself much good, she had not done herself much harm either. No one was much interested in the speeches, only in the vote.

The Prime Minister's was nonetheless a great success, its close bringing Labour backbenchers to their feet cheering and waving their order papers. This was because the speech was a roguish mixture of denunciations of Mrs Thatcher's heartless capitalism, of clever playing upon the divisions in the Shadow Cabinet, and of talk about microprocessors. (He was either for them or against them.) It ended with an impressively shameless announcement of higher pensions soon for the old folk. Many Tories helped by heckling him. They included Mr Burden at one stage. 'I'm glad the Honourable Gentleman has woken up,' Mr Callaghan told him.

A look of utter relief crossed the face of a tired and pale Mrs Thatcher at 10.18pm. A tall Conservative Whip was standing over her and whispering something. She drew in her breath. Mr William Whitelaw, seated next to her, put his arms around her shoulder. She had won.

A few seconds later the Conservative and Government Whips lined up in front of the Speaker's chair and a Tory among them barked – as is the prerogative of the winners of a division – the news that the Conservative motion of no confidence in the Government had been carried by one vote. A huge cheer went up from the Tory benches, which became a forest of waving order papers . . . The final scenes of the debate and vote were the most exciting anyone could remember. Mr Michael Foot, the Leader of the House, whooped and bawled his way through a magnificent, outlandish winding-up. He was in full Footage. If Mrs Thatcher is half as much a threat to socialism as he made out, the country is saved.

After denouncing her every policy, he found himself still with 10 minutes to go. So, in a marvellously gaga passage, he started raving about how it was always Labour who had to save the country – for example, in 1940. Developing the theme, he bellowed, 'It was a Labour motion in this House which brought Churchill to power.'

The Tories became rather angry at this failure to mention that Churchill was a member of their party at the time. But Mr Foot stormed on. 'Yes, we saved the country then, and we'll save it again.'

The fact that Labour was already in charge of the country seemed lost on the Labour benches, which were receiving Mr Foot's speech with delirium. He sat down to a vast ovation.

After the result, Mr Callaghan rose and the House fell silent. Smilingly, he announced a general election. Amid Tory jeers, some Labour Members, including Mr Heffer of Walton, Mr Cryer of Keighley and Mr Price of Lewisham West, stayed behind and sang 'The Red Flag' which must have been worth a few votes to the Tories in the marginals.

Daily Telegraph

⊰ April 1979 ⊱
Mrs Thatcher is filmed electioneering in a chocolate factory!

Mrs Thatcher's image maker was Gordon Reece, who realised that in a TV age it was powerful visual images which mattered. This was really the first full TV election in Britain.

Mrs Thatcher continued to travel around the country telling everyone she met that a Conservative Government would be all right. On a more serious note, she also ran amok in a Birmingham chocolate factory. For those of us who have been on the trail with her this was indisputably the big event so far.

Finding herself by chance in the extremely marginal constituency of Selly Oak – Labour majority 326 – she decided to call in on the voters on the Cadbury assembly line who bring you your walnut fudge in soft caramel, hazel crispy cluster, and bitter lemon crunch, and who are therefore responsible probably for more coronaries than anyone in Britain apart from the pro-jogging lobby. It was a discreet visit – just the Leader of the Opposition and about a hundred television and press photographers and reporters.

Before we were disgorged into the factory, we all had to put on white coats and hats to make us hygienic. We then advanced on the unsuspecting folk on the conveyor belts. The famous factory is as superbly organised as legend has it, but is rather noisy. Apparently the manufacture of chocolates is a process which makes a noise like

Niagara Falls. Into this existing uproar erupted Mrs Thatcher, pursued by a hundred white coats. The whole effect resembled perhaps a lunatic asylum in which the doctors had themselves gone berserk; or possibly a convention of mad surgeons.

The entire surrealist canvas was the most picturesque which your correspondent has witnessed in a decade or so of observing politicians trying to become Prime Minister. Mrs Thatcher would descend on a chocolate woman (that is to say, a woman making chocolate). They would have a conversation. Because of the din, neither could hear the other. This is the ideal arrangement for conversations between party leaders and voters at election time since it cuts out a lot of unnecessary detail.

Meanwhile, Mr Denis Thatcher, the husband, would lurk on the fringe of the affray conversing with employees who did not quite get to talk to his wife. He has developed an impressive line in Duke of Edinburgh factory visit chat. It goes something like: 'This is the assortments section, I gather . . . Interesting . . . Do you export much? . . . Really? Africa as well . . . But surely it would melt?'

Back at the base, the Leader of the Opposition would inevitably be urged to try chocolate packing herself. The problem of course, would have been to stop her. Maniacally, she would raid the hazel crispy clusters and shove them in passing boxes. At this, those of the deranged doctors who had cameras would ecstatically close in with their tripods, lights and in the case of the TV men, those strange objects which look like small bazookas and are to do with the sound. Some of them would clamber on chairs and machines to get a better angle. Thus clustered together at many different levels, they became not just mad surgeons, but mad Martian surgeons as a result of their extra, deformed electronic eyes and cables coming out of their heads. In the midst of the tiers of lenses and faces, the visage of the occasional Japanese photographer or correspondent would peer out, framed perhaps by huge piles of Bourneville selection. This was an extra loony touch.

What a scene! The genius at Conservative Central Office who thought it up must get a knighthood.

In the middle of it all, the little chocolate woman who was the object of Mrs Thatcher's rapt attention would rather tend to get forgotten. Eventually we would all move further on down the conveyor belt or up to the next floor, the entire progress taking place before the disbelieving gaze of the Cadbury's employees on the conveyor belts. The squeals were understandable. It was exciting for me. It must have been mind blowing for the folk who have to sit all day transferring the plain-coated nougat into the boxes of 'Contrast'. From department to department there was no abating of noise. Squeals! Roaring machinery! And Denis still doing his stuff: 'Fascinating . . . but how do you get the walnut exactly in the middle of the fudge?'

It was occasionally hazardous for those of us caught up in the heavy, swaying throng. Machines bubbled and clattered within inches. The Leader of the Conservative Party, borne irresistibly on by the deranged mob, was herself at times fortunate not to be converted into a large mass of delicious hazel crispy cluster.

Daily Telegraph

⊰ 3 May 1979 ⊱
'Parris is well worth a mass'

'If we're not careful, we'll have a dead calf on our hands.' Thus, Mr Denis Thatcher, delivering an aside out of radio and television earshot on the first day of the Tory campaign. It was the climax of the now-famous scene in which the Conservative Leader clasped a fragile, newly born calf to her bosom as determinedly as if she were Cleopatra with the asp.

Denis never looked back after that masterly opening mutter. From Norfolk until the end in the south London marginals yesterday afternoon, he fought a campaign conspicuous for its dignity, candour, laconic humour, and avoidance of nationally divisive issues or, in fact, of any issues.

For these reasons my vote for 'Man of the Match' goes to Denis Thatcher. The only thing which can stop him reaching Number 10 tomorrow, is his wife. But of her more later.

Before we get on to that, a suggested runner-up for Man of the

Match is Mr Matthew Parris. He is the Conservative candidate in the safe Conservative seat of Derbyshire West. But he was also a member of Mrs Thatcher's office, in which capacity he had to reply to correspondence on behalf of his leader.

He turned out to be English literature's frankest letter-writer since Byron. He seems to have lived out the sort of fantasy life coveted by most normal MPs of all parties. Faced with endless communications from menacing senior citizens and allegedly stricken council tenants, they long to write back: get lost, you don't know when you're well-off, you old moaner.

Well, though, he had to wrap it up and Matthew more or less did just that. A Mrs Collingwood complained to Conservative Central Office about the possibility of the Tories putting the council house rents up. Mr Parris wrote back saying, in essence, that she ought to be grateful for a council house in the first place.

The letter found its way into the *Daily Mirror* and thence into half-a-million Labour leaflets bound for the council estates. One's hopes rose that there were other Parris letters in the possession of the underprivileged all over Britain, ready to reach print any minute and enliven the campaign.

Sure enough, one turned up in a few newspapers last week without, unfortunately, getting the show it deserved. The correspondent was grumbling on behalf of his relatives who were council tenants. Mr Parris told him that if he (Matthew) were paying in housing costs 'only twice what your relatives will be paying after the rise in council rents, I should be well content. Thank you for writing.'

Matthew, then, is probably the only candidate standing today who says what he thinks. The fact that the letters went out on behalf of Mrs Thatcher rather than himself may detract a bit from his heroism. Nonetheless, to quote the newly converted Henry IV, 'Parris is well worth a mass'.

Indeed, he may be in need of a mass. A lot of Tories are said to be in a mood to murder him. But even if he survives, we can, alas, be reasonably sure that, despite his imminent arrival in the Commons, nothing much more will be heard of Mr Matthew Parris.

Daily Telegraph

It may surprise you to know that in context this was the most forgiving of all the commentaries published. The others were just abuse – Auberon Waugh said he had never met me but assumed I had an unsatisfactory moustache, and Paul Foot described me as probably the nastiest new MP in the House. But there was an undertone of kindness in Frank's piece, and it did not hurt me during so wretched a time that his pay-off line – that I would never be heard of again – was almost comforting. I just wanted to disappear from the face of the Earth.

Matthew Parris

Chapter 5

April 1981–March 1982

Frank moved from the Daily Telegraph *to* Now! Magazine, *the new publication founded by the business tycoon James Goldsmith in 1979, and he wrote for it for 18 months until it folded. He then joined* The Times *as sketchwriter under Harold Evans' editorship.*

⊰ April 30 1981 ⊱
Richard Wagner and Mr Roy Hattersley

Unsuccessfully, as it will now emerge, I had resolved from the outset that there were two subjects which had received sufficient airing on this page and would not be mentioned further: Wagner and Mr Roy Hattersley.

Concerning the one: nobody in his right mind would deny his capacity for the sublime, his surges of lyricism, his sheer weight and scale, but there is also his torrential prolixity, his essentially outdated nineteenth-century ideological attitude towards his art, his foggy symbolism and an epic tedium which modern audiences should surely not be expected to endure. These are some of the drawbacks of Mr Hattersley.

Wagner, for all the intimidating left-luggage that comes in his train, is a less fascinating figure. But, entombed as one was in a performance of *Lohengrin* at the Royal Opera House, one was forced into some embittered reflections about him. After an incandescently wonderful prelude has put us into an ethereal mood (for I do not deny that, when Richard really wanted to, the boy could write), we are suddenly washed up on the banks of some dank river somewhere in the Low Countries of Rhineland. For getting on for forty minutes or so, various disagreeable Teutons stump about bawling '*Heil*

Koenig Heinrich', and similar observations, to a dullard of a bass who seems to be in charge. My relatives fought in the war to put a stop to that kind of thing.

Eventually there is a mysterious visitor carried in by a swan. He is the tenor (the mysterious visitor, that is, not the swan: the swan does not sing, being one of the few characters in any of Dick's operas who is mercifully silent all evening). In this production, the tenor was an East German. He was driving this swan without a crash helmet, itself an offence under English law, and without a rear-view mirror. He explains himself by saying that he has come from a far-off land to champion the beautiful Elsa in combat with the wicked Friedrich, not to be confused with the boring Heinrich, provided Elsa does not ask him his name. Any British copper, routinely hauling an East German tenor off an illegally-ridden swan and faced with such a tale, would robustly respond along the lines of: 'Oh, yeah, and I'm the Ayatollah.' Not so these German rozzers, who astoundingly allow the lad into their country for his big fight with Friedrich. Whereupon, the tenor addresses the beast as '*mein lieber Schwan*', which potentially suggests tastes which, though unfortunately common in rural areas, would also be illegal in this country, but which do not seem to put off the beautiful Elsa over in the Low Countries.

To be fair to Dickie, all scenes involving the swan are radiantly beautiful. But the rest of the work consists of music endlessly stopping and starting. The Wagnerians defend *Lohengrin* by saying that it was an early show and that their boy only hit peak form later in his career when setting up a really big gig like *Gotterdammerung*. This is undoubtedly true. But the biggies also contain many an hour of *Lohengrin*-type windbaggery. *Parsifal* contains a character, the wounded Amfortas, who does nothing else but moan all evening on a stretcher. 'Amfortas is the wisest man in the theatre this evening,' the *Manchester Guardian* critic Samuel Langford once whispered to Neville Cardus during a notably slow performance of the work, 'he's brought his bed with him.'

Debussy, a composer disgracefully maligned by Mr Levin, was one of the earliest to see through the massively-hyped German. 'The two Sunday concerts were in competition,' he wrote when he was the superb critic of *La Revue Blanche* in 1901. 'Each played us Wagner. The result? No score on either side.'

None the less, it will be some years yet before the dilettanti, cowed by the mighty reputation, stop allowing themselves to be herded into the opera house for all those hours of monologues and papier-mâché dragons, mention of which brings us to Mr Hattersley. Those racists who beat and kicked him at a public meeting which he addressed recently were 'the product of society in the same way that the people in Brixton were: in the same way, we have alienated them and made them feel rejected'. In effect he is arguing that they were disturbed, not responsible for their own actions, and not simply evil. Here, encased in Mr Hattersley's sickly and obviously bogus compassion towards his assailants, was the behaviourist fallacy: the claim that someone's behaviour is primarily caused by 'society'.

But to want to sock Mr Hattersley is not evidence of mental disorder. No one would be incarcerated in a special hospital on such a rap. For the desire is widespread in his party and in the country as a whole. It is just that most of us, on the whole, do not give in to it.

Such is the dominance of the sociological explanation of riots and criminality, we seem to be losing sight of the fine old British concept of the yobbo: the low type who simply wants to throw Molotov cocktails, pillage telephone boxes, or assault Mr Hattersley because it is fun. Such conduct should be condemned, not verbosely explained.

Still, as a rule, we will no longer be anti-Hattersley in this space. As this latest, shameless playing to the radical gallery shows, he is a divertingly professional politician who knows precisely when to go left and when to go right in the practice of his profession, which is to become leader of the Labour Party. Society is not to blame for that, either.

⊰ 8 May 1981 ⊱
The Conservative Philosophy Group meet in
Jonathan Aitken's house

Hugh Trevor-Roper (1912–1998, historian and academic) and
Enoch Powell (1912–1998, politician and scholar famous for his
'Rivers of Blood' speech about immigration) had their say. Jonathan

*Aitken and the mischievous and legendary Cambridge don John
Casey add their memories of the evening below Frank's article.*

A few months ago the Prime Minister was in conversation with
the Master of Peterhouse.

The subject of the conversation was Christianity and freedom, or
some related topic. Lord Dacre did not agree that Christianity was
dependent on freedom. If the Russians overran Western Europe, it
did not necessarily follow that things would go badly for Christianity.
Look at Poland. Christianity was pretty strong there. Remember the
Roman Empire. That was overrun. Christianity did not do too badly
subsequently in those parts.

Now, you have to be especially careful when attributing practically
any opinion to a mighty academic, as the letters column of the *Times
Literary Supplement* proves. I am perhaps vulgarising what may have
been a more elegantly subtle piece of reasoning by Lord Dacre,
although his argument sounds wholly persuasive to me. But Mrs
Thatcher was not persuaded: 'You are being deliberately provocative', she told him.

Mr Enoch Powell was present. He did not agree with the Prime
Minister that we could defend Christian values: 'Values cannot be
defended,' he said. Mrs Thatcher: 'What do you mean?' Mr Powell
slipped into overdrive. Militarily, values could be neither defended
nor destroyed.

They existed in a transcendent Platonic realm beyond space and
time. Territory was what could be defended. For territory was not in
space or time but here on earth. All this remorseless logic was issuing
forth in that haunting voice with its Black Country accent which
makes Mr Powell sound like an admixture of St Thomas Aquinas
and an Aston Villa trainer. As he pressed on, Mrs Thatcher shot him
a look of 'wise guy, eh?' Then, index finger to cheek, she began to
study his work like a grammar school teacher confronting a brilliant,
but perverse essay by a boy who had a great future ahead but little
common sense and who needed to be taken down a peg or two for
his own good. 'Create, Enoch dear, don't destroy,' she said.

In this, the week of the second anniversary of her election victory, it should be emphasised that Mrs Thatcher is if anything even more interested in what may seem to many to be idle speculations but which can loosely be described as right-wing ideas and ideology. She still loves to chatter about them to clever people whom she regards as being broadly on her side, just as she did in Opposition. But temperamentally, she is something of a Stalinist. Freedom, Christianity, Western values, the theological justification for nuclear weapons . . . they all swirl around together under that coiffure. And she would prefer that those who support her on one should accept the right-wing line on all the others.

Possibly this is because she seems to have come rather late in life to all these profound matters. For the first decade or so of her parliamentary career she was influenced by such figures as Mr Macmillan, Rab Butler and the late Reginald Maudling – clever men, but men distrustful of all that abstract theorising. It was the Tory loss of office in 1974, coinciding as it did with the emergence, for good or ill, of some sort of Conservative intelligentsia, which seems to have galvanised her. Consequently all the ideas seem to have got hastily and happily jumbled up together.

At the gathering to which I have referred she seemed content to stay on into the night – going on fascinatedly about the nature of authority or whatever. As people started to debate the perhaps still more pressing issue of which trattoria or tandoori to make for, it would have surprised no one had the Prime Minister suddenly chirruped, like Miss Brown at that party in *Vile Bodies*: 'Why don't you come to *my* house?' (Miss Brown was living at home with her father who, if you remember, was Prime Minister at the time.) Fortunately, Mrs Thatcher did not do so. The spectacle of various professors, Conservative thinkers and sundry poseurs piling out of taxis would have caused some concern to the Downing Street police.

None of this is to suggest that she actually does much about all this ideology. Possibly it is a form of escapism or relaxation. She knows that, come the morning, she will encounter some starchy permanent secretary or wet minister telling her that such and such an ideological course of action would be counterproductive or upset the Arabs. She has not been a particularly 'ideological' Prime

Minister. She constantly changes her policies in a wettish direction. The ideology is literally 'all in the mind'.

This makes her a more, rather than less, serious person. She ponders the inert, moderate mass that is 'government', 'Whitehall' and 'expert opinion' in the only manner consistent with seriousness – with disappointment and irritation at how little can be changed. This week, after two years, she still sounds like a Leader of the Opposition. Her first response to any outrage is to say that the Government should do something about it, only to realise 'I am the Government'.

Well, perhaps she is not really. It could be that she is a right-wing counter-revolutionary trapped in an essentially social democratic state. As did Chairman Mao, on the opposite wing of politics, she presides over a government apparatus against which she is spiritually in revolt.

The Times

Frank was one of the earliest and most perceptive observers of Margaret Thatcher's mind. He was given a ringside seat in this endeavour by his membership of the Conservative Philosophy Group, a quasi-intellectual discussion group which met in my house from the mid-1970s to the late 1980s. Margaret attended quite frequently, particularly in her years as Leader of the Opposition. She enjoyed sparring over political ideas and theories with the CPG's regular coterie of Oxbridge dons, Conservative columnists and brighter backbenchers. Part of her enjoyment was that our Chatham House ground rules preserved confidentiality.

Frank found the temptation to circumvent these rules too hard to bear. One indiscreet column in The Times *headlined 'The Whirling Thoughts of Mrs Thatcher' earned him a warning after he divulged some entertaining exchanges at a CPG supper between Hugh Trevor Roper, Enoch Powell and the Prime Minister on the esoteric subject of whether or not a value could be defended.*

Frank's next breach of the CPG's omerta code was more ingenious. In prime position as the main political column of the New Statesman *there appeared a verbatim account of a meeting of the group, including direct quotes from Thatcher. If memory serves, the headline was 'Everything from Harrods'. The column's message was that the CPG organised evenings in which the food, the curtains, and above all the ideas seemed to have come straight off the shelves of the Knightsbridge department store. The line I most clearly recall was 'even the host, Jonathan Aitken, looked as though he'd been gift wrapped at Harrods'.*

The most surprising aspect of this article was its purported authorship. According to the by-line it had been written by the then political columnist of the New Statesman, *James Fenton. Needless to say he was not a CPG member, nor had he been present at the evening so amusingly reported under his name.*

It was the humour that gave Frank's game away. It did not take a sleuth from Scotland Yard to spot that the spoof, the jokes, and the style of writing were unmistakably his. There was some huffing and puffing from one or two indignant CPG members. But after extracting a promise that Fenton alias Johnson would not repeat his dastardly deed we laughed it off and Frank continued to come to our suppers as a much enjoyed guest.

Jonathan Aitken

The occasion was piquant, because the Dean of Peterhouse was addressing the Conservative Philosophy Group in the presence of his mortal enemy, the Master of Peterhouse. The speaker was advancing Christian arguments for our possessing nuclear weapons, which delighted Mrs Thatcher, who said that it might be necessary to use them 'to defend our values'. This led to the notable exchanges described between the Prime Minister and Lord Dacre and Mr Powell. Frustrated by Mr Powell's Platonic arguments, she descended to the personal when he had to depart early in order to vote in a Commons division. 'You shouldn't have left us, Enoch dear – then you would have had a pair this evening!'

John Casey

⇥ 11 May 1981 ⇤
Women's Rights Festival: Is it bourgeois to feel possessive about one's biological child?

A few days ago, a deputation of women, including Miss Jill Craigie, the wife of Mr Michael Foot, handed in a letter at Number 10 summoning the Prime Minister to a day-long 'women's rights' festival in London to stand trial for 'putting her class above her sex' and other crimes.

Come last Saturday, and I hurried to the secondary school north of King's Cross where the festival was being held; too late, unfortunately, for the morning seminar, advertised in the programme as: 'Why the Tories want us to be heterosexual'. So, one is unable to bring you the answer to that age-old question. Perhaps it is something to do with the public schools.

But I was in time to snap up from a stall the last copy of *Sisters in Song: a collection of new songs from the women's liberation movement.* 'Ben and I were young together, said our lifestyles would be of our choosing' one began. And there was a tragic ending when their lifestyles went all wrong. On p.30 you could sing along to 'Class Struggle Widow' and on p.34, to the tune of 'There's a Hole in the Bucket', you could be moved by the hauntingly entitled: 'There's a Hole in the Condom'.

There was no sign of Mrs Thatcher. Perhaps she had skipped bail? But there was plenty to do while we waited. Here were seminars and workshops and pamphlets about: sexism in school; El Salvador; nuclear weapons; rape; abortion; National Health Service cuts; rent strikes; South Africa; every conceivable form of racism and exploitation; more rape; a spot more abortion; women's health hazards at work; nursery closures; the need for women not to be browbeaten by capitalism into using deodorants. On the dozens of bookstalls, what the organisers regarded as all respectable political points of view were represented; Trotskyism, anarchism, Maoism, Sinn Fein, plus ordinary communism for any passing moderates.

A booklet reporting the proceedings of a day school on 'Children and Socialism', organised by a ladies' socialist organisation demurely named 'Big Flame' contained an invaluable report of the findings of the school's Possessiveness and Jealousy Workshop. 'To start the ball rolling, A. from Leeds discussed the problem of living with kids with whom he had no biological connection. In his case he wanted Ben (presumably not the same Ben who was having trouble with his lifestyle in the song) to have an ongoing relationship with him specifically . . . However, he felt possessive about Jesse, his kid, 15 months . . . a lot of this he felt had to do with feeling "indispensable" with your own kid. He wondered whether it was part of our bourgeois conditioning . . .'

Swarming all over the building were thousands of pairs of jeans containing women of all shapes and of none. But there were *some* men and women wandering around hand in hand. One fell idly to speculating about courtship rituals among the radical classes. 'I think you're wonderful,' he presumably says to her. 'There's not a sniff of deodorant on you. In fact, you stink like a polecat. Will you share my lifestyle?'

Come late afternoon, and there was still no sign of Mrs Thatcher. She was still on the run. She'll never get away with it. Loudspeakers called us to the final rally in the playground. Orators talked of such matters as rape and abortion.

The radicals always seem to have an extraordinary relish for the latter. It would never be surprising to hear them suddenly argue that, not only should there be abortion on demand, but non-pregnancy should be no bar to abortion either. They just can't get enough of abortion.

A ferocious Irish woman called on us to support the IRA prisoners in the H-block. An astounding and somewhat confused resolution was passed about [Jack] the Ripper who, because of his assaults on women, was a figure only slightly less hated all afternoon than Mrs Thatcher.

Coverage of the Ripper case, said the resolution, ignored 'women, who experience danger and fear from men every day of our lives' – the suggestion being, presumably, that we chaps – as a general rule – wander around with a pinhead hammer and a screwdriver just on the off chance.

Next, a minute's silence for the late Robert Sands. More speeches, doubtless about abortion. Suddenly a cry from the crowd: 'What about the prostitutes?' To which a voice from the microphone promisingly replies: 'They will be later.'

What was all this about prostitutes? Where did they fit in to the general ideology? I went in search of a prostitute, so to speak. Soon I found a woman who offered me a leaflet from the English Collective of Prostitutes. What to say to her? 'How much?' did not seem quite proper. One wanted to inquire: 'Are you yourself a fallen woman?' but that did not seem right either. The pamphlet was much the best written of the afternoon and put forward an overwhelming case for changes in the law.

Here was the central problem. The feminist cause is a great one. As Mr Paul Foot's fine new book on Shelley shows, it has been championed by some of the greatest souls. How to stop it being swamped by idiocy and worse? Easily the day's best speech came from Mrs Ditta from Rochdale who successfully fought the Home Office Minister, Mr Raison, to allow her three children admission to this country from the subcontinent. In her Gracie Fields accent, she was very good at his expense: 'Why doesn't he have a blood test? After all, his children might be Mrs Thatcher's.'

But there seems to be some iron law of radicalism which ensures that good causes like this one – and the prostitutes' – get subsumed in darker struggles such as that of the IRA.

The Times

⊰ 5 June 1981 ⊱

In January 1981 Roy Jenkins, Shirley Williams, David Owen and Bill Rodgers, known as the 'Gang of Four', founded the Social Democratic Party (SDP). After losing the election of 1979 the Labour Party had taken a sharp turn to the left under Michael Foot and the Gang of Four split away, citing major differences over Europe and defence policies. In 1988 the SDP and the Liberal Party merged and became the Liberal Democrats.

**William Hague, aged 20, addresses Shirley Williams
at the Oxford Union**

Entering the crowded Union to debate the motion, 'This house would support the Social Democrats', Mrs Shirley Williams looked like polling strongly in Oxford last night. Unfortunately for her, the looming by-election was in Warrington. That geographical-cum-social detail apart, it was a heartening evening for Mrs Williams, irrespective of the eventual fate of the motion.

While the other debaters walked in through polite applause, she received a goodly cheer. And even her opponents in the debate fought shy of questioning that fabled niceness. As the undergraduate from Balliol who proposed the motion put it, she was 'notorious perhaps for being the nicest and most well-liked person in politics'.

The first undergraduate speaker against the motion said that to question Mrs Williams was rather like mugging your granny. She was the only politician in the land who could be the most popular politician in the country and still lose a 10,000 majority, he added to widespread hisses.

On Mrs Williams's side, a girl from New College, with a red dress, a red rose in her hair, but suitably pink policies in her head, fought back against that sort of thing by saying, 'Oxford fell in love with Shirley Williams 20 years ago. I hope it will do so again and join her in her fight for liberty, equality and fraternity.'

All this was too much for Mr William Hague, of Magdalen, the treasurer: the same Mr Hague who, at the age of about 16, galvanised a Tory Party conference a few years ago, receiving vast publicity in the process. He has overcome that initial disadvantage to be, in mid-career at the age of 20, the Tory star of the Union.

He hoped the Social Democrats would not 'degenerate into some sort of heterosexual wing of the Liberal Party', but was not sure. He praised a party for its ability to win support from 'such diverse sources as a Conservative MP and the Communist former leader of the National Union of Students, without either saying there had been any change in their views'. Such a party deserved to be taken seriously. Sir Hugh Fraser MP, a former president, praised him for 'a brilliant speech which makes him the next Prime Minister but 14'.

Mrs Williams eventually rose amid huge applause and engulfed us all by being torrentially articulate about everything; the new Nationality Act, which she was against; overseas aid, which she was for; and much else which it was not clear she was either for or against. The house listened spellbound. She said nothing new. Indeed, she, in reality, said nothing much at all, but impressed us with the conviction – the passion – with which she said it, or did not say it, as the case may be!

She took issue with the Shadow Home Secretary, Mr Merlyn Rees, another of her opponents in the debate, for claiming 'that we are essentially a party of the small Hampstead circle'. That was not the impression she had gained in Scotland and the north. No one intervened to ask why, in that case, she was not contesting Warrington.

Somehow we forgave her, for her niceness batters one into submission in the end. Her peroration hushed the house: 'Stalin betrayed Communism. Hindenburg betrayed Christian Democracy in Germany. Both parties in Britain are betraying the principles into which they were born . . . social democracy is the last hope and I believe that history is not going to give us much longer.' She sat down to tumultuous applause. Moderation had infected our young. Where was the nation coming to?

The Times

The background to this packed debate in the Oxford Union was the formation of the Social Democratic Party three months earlier. The new party was leading in the opinion polls in Warrington and on the brink of a huge by-election swing there, with Roy Jenkins as its candidate.

Yet as Shirley Williams swept in that evening we young Tories and our Labour friends were determined to derail the bandwagon, in Oxford at least. We fought long into the night to defeat the SDP, but Oxford, in the phrase coined by Kevin Brennan, now a Labour MP, turned out to be unwilling to 'mug its granny'.

William Hague MP

⊰ 19 June 1981 ⊱
The Trade Union Conference – Michael Foot
meets the workers in Bournemouth

Simply to look at, he was like any other old-age pensioner from the traditional public service class enjoying Bournemouth this week: white-haired, courtly, still with his wits about him, though occasionally a little forgetful, and perhaps rather out of place while the resort was taken over for the annual delegate conference of the Iron and Steel Trades Confederation. Yet this was no ordinary Leader of the Labour Party. This was Mr Michael Foot.

In these days of rapid change, he tends to be forgotten. But he still takes a lively interest in what is going on. For example, they tell him that the country now has a woman Prime Minister. Bless my soul! And from what he has heard, he didn't like the sound of her. 'I repeat, the economic policy of this Government is a CATASTROPHE,' he bawled at the steelmen.

Mr Healey and Mr Benn have got all the publicity this early summer as they have toured the union conferences at the seaside resorts, fighting each other to the death, or to the Deputy Leadership of the Labour Party, whichever is the sooner. But Mr Foot goes too. While Mr Healey and Mr Benn are saying terrible things about each other at the fringe meetings, Mr Foot travels quietly down the train, makes a speech to the conference itself, and receives a presentation consisting of some product connected with the workers concerned (at Bournemouth, it was some fine steel goblets; at the hospital workers it is probably something contagious).

What thoughts are passing through that noble old head as all this is going on? What does he make of this modern world of ours? Let it be emphasised at the outset that no adverse criticism is intended of Mr Foot by drawing attention to his age.

Since the 1960s – the truly low, dishonest decade – we have had enough of brilliant young politicians. It was always astonishing that youth should ever have been associated with ability, idealism or even vigour. Still more astonishing was the fact that Kennedy's age on assuming the presidency, 43, was widely considered to be of itself a point in his favour – it being much overlooked that Hitler also assumed power at the same age.

It is difficult to know what the Leader of the Opposition makes of it all. But one suspects that he is rather melancholy. After a lifetime of romantic left-wingery – in journalism, in biography, on a thousand television panels and editions of *Any Questions?*, in set-piece orations in the Commons – he suddenly, against all augury, became Leader of the Labour Party.

Sometimes, in the late 1950s, a popular newspaper did a jokey piece about the things least likely to happen. One of them was Mr Michael Foot becoming Leader of the Labour Party. I happen to know the man who wrote it. For, until he was propelled by fortune into his present position, Mr Foot had attained a quite different, though equally formal and traditional position in our national life. He was Her Majesty's Leader of the Left.

It was a position just as dignified as Black Rod or the Lord Warden of the Cinque Ports. But as a result of an unforeseen concatenation of circumstances, Her Majesty's Leader of the Left finds himself Her Majesty's Leader of the Opposition. Moreover, on achieving this further dignity, Mr Foot has made a mortifying discovery: there are lots of people to the left of him.

Indeed, we now have a completely different kind of left. He is now in the centre of his party, perhaps on the right. For, while Mr Foot was ranting happily away all those years under the impression that he was the left, a different, less respectable, less comfortable left was coming into being.

To a traditionalist such as Mr Foot, accustomed all his life to a left which shared his bourgeois taste for parliamentary oratory and for belles-lettres, it must be a baffling, faintly menacing, universe. Watching him at Bournemouth this week, it seemed that he resolved the difficulty by ignoring it.

He was helped by the fact that the steelworkers were an old-fashioned lot who were on his side – solidly built characters loyal to Old Labour, who seemed to embody a vanished industrial Britain. Folk tough enough to chew steel as well as make it.

And that was only the wives!

Mr Foot must have been further helped by the fact that, from its outward appearance, the resort remains an idyllic place which might have stayed still at some happy point in the mid-50s or even earlier. It is very much the town of a certain Mr Heath (no relation) whose very name should inspire waves of nostalgia. Neville George Cleverly Heath! A classic mid-40s story; a handsome fellow who, in the town's genteel hotels, would charm impressionable women until such time as he would dismember them. He was hanged. Since then there has been no further unpleasantness in Bournemouth and Mr Foot did not disturb that situation this week.

He gave the delegates some familiar, much-loved Footage. He

scorns a text or notes or even any particular theme. He spins it out as he goes along, repeating the last idea, or a related idea, in various forms while he thinks of the next one.

'The Common Market, the EEC, the European Community, or call it what you will.' That sort of thing. It is the *Roget's Thesaurus* school of oratory. For some minutes, Mr Foot – or Mr Boot or Mr Sock or call him what you will – simply kept the steelmen happy by running down the list of members of the Government. The mere phrase, 'Sir Keith Joseph' was enough to get them amiably falling about.

'Then there's Denis Howell, the Minister of Energy,' he added. 'The only reason he's got an energy policy is because he's been told one by Joe Gormley.' He was thinking of Mr David Howell. Denis Howell is a member of Mr Foot's front bench – having been in the last Labour Government. But Mr Foot is a man for the broad sweep rather than petty detail. His speech was a great success.

Mr Foot got his goblets and set out for London, leaving the conference to abstruse speculation about the precise nature of their industry's ownership and similar matters.

Back at Waterloo, one hovered in the background, as Mr Foot made his way past a group of his fellow senior citizens. They noted him warmly. He adopted a genially seigneurial manner: 'Where you off to? . . . splendid . . . hope it keeps fine . . . jolly good . . . carry on.'

But the Bournemouth Idyll was already gone. He was back in London and reality.

The Times

⊰ 6 July 1981 ⊱
Roy Jenkins: A grand, stupendously distinguished and largely incomprehensible magnifico

When nominations close today we shall know whether Mr Anthony Keane, a Manchester barrister with a grievance concerning the Social Democratic Party's alleged breach of the copyright of the title, makes good his reported threat to change his name by deed poll to 'Roy Jenkins' and stand as a Social Democrat in this by-election.

If he does so, interesting aesthetic and philosophical issues will intrude into the campaign. How will it affect the real Roy Jenkins? Furthermore, can the real Roy Jenkins – the grand, stupendously distinguished and largely incomprehensible magnifico from another world who has been introducing himself with a courtly bow of his smooth shiny head to incredulous passers-by in this town all week – in any sense be regarded as real? Will both be make-believe? Here is a theme worthy of the great Pirandello. Nearly all of his plays, it may be remembered, are about whether we are who we are pretending to be. What is truth? What is fable? And, for all one knows, who is Ruth? Where the hell is Mabel? To return to the Warrington by-election.

The surprising news, perhaps, after this first week of campaigning is that the people rather like Mr Jenkins. That does not mean a majority will vote him in. The one opinion poll so far strongly suggests that they will not. Rather, it means that he is seen as a figure above and outside politics, like the Queen.

How else can folk explain the extraordinary Jenkins carry on? That incomparable voice, beside which Sir John Gielgud sounds like rough trade! That distinction of manner! People may not know precisely for what he is distinguished, but it must be for something. 'Roy Jenkins, a miner's son . . .' began one of the campaign leaflets. True, certainly; but only in the way that it is true to describe Mrs Jacqueline Onassis as the widow of a Greek merchant seaman. It simply does not do justice to Mr Jenkins' position in café society.

Nor was it really necessary for the leaflet to brandish Mr Jenkins' sole proletarian credential. Those who wrote it must have assumed the Warringtonians to be inverted snobs. This seems not to be so. They like an aristocrat. They see characters like Mr Jenkins engaged in idle, brittle chatter with groups of bejewelled bosoms, in the salon scenes of series like *Edward the Seventh*. He's the one to whom some heaving duchess exclaims: 'You're so clever, Lord Melbourne.'

Sadly, for Mr Jenkins, he is engaged in Warrington in politics. And politics is something which the people associate with less graceful figures such as the Labour candidate. He goes under the blunt, utilitarian-sounding name of 'Doug' Hoyle. He is short, grey-black-haired, has a small moustache and is somehow both round and compact, so that he resembles, as Alice Roosevelt Longworth said of the hapless Governor Dewey, 'the man on the top of the wedding cake'. One suspects that, to the people of Warrington, Mr Jenkins is some sort of ideal vision. Mr Hoyle is your husband, or yourself, and you vote for reality.

Mr Jenkins has turned out to be much more famous among the people than many of us thought. It is because of the European Community. This has nothing to do with, say, his activities in the cause of European monetary union. It is to do with his activities in the cause of European money. He is thought to possess an enormous amount of it which, relatively speaking, is correct. But the local attitude to this is not what might be expected. 'What did you think of him?' I asked Mr Alexander Done, of Dickenson Street, after he had been approached by Mr Jenkins in the shopping centre. 'A gentleman, an educated man,' he replied.

Why educated? 'Well, the Common Market.'

Was Mr Done in favour of the Common Market? 'No, detest it.'

What was this about Mr Jenkins and the Market, then? 'Well, he got paid a lot of money by it, didn't he?'

Did Mr Done disapprove of that, then? 'No, everyone's got to get what they can, haven't they?'

Mr Done was not untypical.

It all goes to confirm a theory of the crusty Tory backbencher, the late Charles Curran, who used to say that the British working class did not object to vast wealth, provided it was of a random or windfall nature. What they couldn't stand were people who had worked for it. Mr Jenkins' fabled riches seem to be regarded as being in the same category as those of pools winners or of the Aga Khan or of Lady Docker in the 1950s.

Here is a theme on which the SDP must build if they are to have any chance of winning here. They must convince the voters that Mr Jenkins is not too good to be true at all, but is a bit of a card – with even a touch of the rascal about him. Look at all that swag he got paid in Europe.

I have long seen him in that way myself, believing that over the years he has been rather spoilt by the quality press. He has been depicted as the courageous liberal, a man more honest than other politicians.

There is rarely much courage required to be liberal, outside places like the Soviet Union, South Africa or Haiti. That is not to say it is wrong to be liberal, just that it is not courageous. In the Labour Party, Mr Jenkins was often a consummate politician. At the Dispatch Box, he was invariably superb, but to be superb at the Dispatch Box requires a considerable measure of low-minded demagoguery designed to impress selected people. This is true of Mr Enoch Powell, seeking to impress the masses on immigration, but also of Mr Jenkins, seeking to impress polite society, on race relations.

The Times

⋈ 16 July 1981 ⋈
**Harold Wilson, now a little forgetful, resumes his place
in history at the Warrington by-election**

No one was quite clear who had invited Sir Harold, for he and the present Labour candidate – indeed, he and the present Labour Party – are not of the same persuasion. It was thought that perhaps he more or less invited himself. Old bruisers sometimes feel the urge to haul themselves back up between the ropes for a final lunge. Perhaps Sir Harold felt the old tongue itch at the prospect of one more press conference, one last evasive answer, just as it was in the old days.

So we found him at Mr Hoyle's daily campaign press conference. All campaign long, there had been a duel between ourselves and Mr Hoyle to get the candidate to admit he was for Mr Benn as Deputy Leader. The rest of Warrington had remained oblivious to this epic struggle, but nonetheless it was a point of honour among us to resolve it on this last day. 'Did Mr Hoyle agree with Sir Harold's recent remark that Mr Benn had immatured with age?' one asked, and sat back triumphantly. That had got him. He was in trouble now. Harold was right beside him. How would he get out of it, eh?

Mr Hoyle shot me a look of simple hatred. He cleared his throat for a long time, so that it sounded like a gargle. Or a death rattle? No!

Suddenly, he recovered. Tony Benn? Not standing in the by-election. Warrington interested in policies, not personalities. What mattered was Leader, not Deputy Leader, and Doug Hoyle was for Michael Foot. Mr Hoyle had won again. Your correspondent subsided, beaten, demoralised. Sir Harold stirred. 'Tony Benn?' he muttered. 'Now, Tony Benn was a good minister . . .' Mr Hoyle nodded gratefully. '. . . a good Postmaster-General. He introduced lots of pretty stamps.'

Mr Hoyle stopped nodding gratefully, for he had remembered that Sir Harold was a master of irony. '. . . everyone in this town should remember that Tony Benn introduced the Queen's Award for Industry.' Mr Hoyle started nodding again. '. . . he wanted to call it the Parliamentary Award for Industry, but it had to be the Queen's Award because she's the fount of honour, I told him stuffily . . . as far as Mr Benn is concerned, he has no following in the parliamentary party.'

Mr Hoyle, about to be one of Mr Benn's followers in the parliamentary party, had stopped nodding some time before, and was generally more relaxed when Sir Harold devoted his attentions to Mr Roy Jenkins.

'Roy Jenkins? . . . Tended to knock off at 7 o'clock . . . a socialite rather than a Socialist . . . The SDP. It's not a party, it's a clique or a click, as they say up 'ere. As for Dr Owen and Mr Rogers, I never thought of them as Cabinet calibre . . . perfectly good junior ministers. Jim took a different view. I had retired by then – voluntarily – which is a very unusual thing in politics.'

Past glories now intruded into the shabby little committee room into which we were all crammed. There was one night when the whole government machine was working late, Sir Harold continued. Time of the seamen's strike in '66. He had sent out for fish and chips all round 'for which I got knocked in the press for doing some kind of a gimmick. Mind you, if I hadn't intervened that night, we could have had a six-month strike.' In comparison with such tales of encounters on the high seas long ago, the puny Warrington by-election seems to be far away.

Sir Harold was asked about his opposition to the next Party Leader being chosen by an electoral college. It was a constitutional issue, he said. The Queen may need a Prime Minister immediately after an election. It could be a time of crisis. Sterling. That sort of thing. She shouldn't have to wait for Labour choosing its leader.

But he was not the right man to ask, because he did not know much about such matters. What could explain this unprecedented flash of modesty. Soon we learned. It was because 'I've very little experience of the party not being in power.'

With that wicked thrust at Labour leaders subsequent to him, who had lost an election or looked as if they could lose one in the future, Sir Harold, winner of four out of five general elections, brought the discussion to a close and resumed his place in history

The Times

⊰ 28 July 1981 ⊱
Michael Heseltine gets lost in Merseyside

In 1981, after terrible rioting in Toxteth, Michael Heseltine,
Secretary of State for the Environment (1979–83), was appointed
by Margaret Thatcher to look into the problems of Merseyside.

For over seven days and nights now, Mr Michael Heseltine has been running amok over Merseyside. At his temporary office in the Royal Liver Building, they said he was to be found at the community centre at Skelmersdale. At Skelmersdale, they said he had been there but had just left for Runcorn. At Runcorn I asked a policeman where Mr Heseltine was. 'Who was he?' this constable gratifyingly replied. Some years on the political trail have taught me that one of the great strengths of British democracy is that there are always pockets of ignorance about even the most self-publicising of our rulers.

One explained to the policeman that Mr Heseltine was the new minister for places like Merseyside and that sort of thing. You could not miss him. He was about seven foot tall with what looked like a blond wig but was, so far as we knew, real hair. This man was believed to be in the area. 'The public have been warned not to approach him, but to call the police instead,' I said, adding a tentative 'Ha, ha, ha'.

The constable looked bleak. Never try to be funny with police-men, one's auntie used to say. The policeman radioed headquarters: 'I've got a fella 'ere who says he's a reporter and he's looking for Mr Heseltine, who's the Minister of Merseyside. He's about seven foot tall and he's got blond hair that looks like a wig . . . no, not the reporter, the minister.'

Someone at headquarters told the policeman to turn down his radio, presumably so that I could not hear what was being said. After a conversation, the constable explained: 'No, we don't know where he is.' It seemed clear that the forces of law and order knew of his whereabouts, but assumed, as authority always does, that ministers do not want to be bothered by their subjects.

Parting from the constable, I explained that Mr Heseltine had been sent up after the riots. 'I blame the parents,' said the policeman. 'Oh, I don't think old Heseltine's parents are to blame for the way he turned out,' I replied. The policeman stared. It was time to be off.

'Perhaps Mr Heseltine doesn't want any publicity,' said another constable later. Mr Heseltine not wanting any publicity! As soon argue that Dracula did not want any blood. Nonetheless, it was time to retire to the hotel and bed. But there, the following morning, in the lobby, encased in seven foot of Savile Row suiting and four foot of Jermyn Street shirting, awash in half a gallon of aftershave, was Mr Heseltine. He was roaring off to a couple of job training centres. It was not, of course, entirely true that he was avoiding publicity, but there was some truth in it.

Becoming an 'emergency' or 'crisis' or 'special' minister is a perilous adventure for a politician. Everybody says it is a gimmick and, in any case, too little too late. Afterwards, when nothing much happens which would not have happened in any case, he gets blamed. Also, people are apt to laugh at him and ask questions like: 'Who needs a riot when you've got Michael Heseltine?' Look at Lord Hailsham on the north-east, Mr Denis Howell on the drought.

The assignment does have its good side. He gets in the papers and on television a lot. But the publicity is difficult to control. He gets pictured going importantly in and out of meetings, staring at slums with a look of concern, and he gives interviews in which he can say statesmanlike things such as that there are no easy solutions, and that he is at present here to listen.

But it is difficult to control what is said at all these meetings if there are difficult people there.

Terence Moore, of Caryl Gardens – which are no gardens but an unrelenting block of flats – was waiting for him with a few inmates, being rather cynical. 'Tarzan, they call him,' Mr Moore explained. 'So they should tell him to plant some trees around this place.' Terence's brother, Albert, said his wife had read out from that morning's *Mirror* where it said Mr Heseltine had spent £10,000 over the weekend on his daughter's birthday party – 10,000 quid, Albert emphasised. It would have been better spent getting the fungus off these walls.

The suit containing the crisis minister turned up. Terence waylaid him. 'Why wasn't Mr Heseltine meeting the people here in the houses they had to live in?' Mr Heseltine replied that he had gone into some houses yesterday. 'He's got three houses himself,' I whispered to Terence's brother, Albert, hoping to make the full and frank exchanges still more constructive. 'You've got three houses yourself,' said Albert, 'I saw it in the papers.' But Mr Heseltine was still engaged with Terence.

'My job is to see as many things as possible. I think I've got a picture of the housing problem.'

Terence interrupted: 'It's a corrugated jungle.' Mr Heseltine had not seen these particular houses. 'I looked up carefully as I drove in, Mr Heseltine replied, adding reassuringly: 'I've seen dreadful housing conditions.' But today he was dealing with jobs. He couldn't deal with houses when he was dealing with jobs. Only in this way could he 'try to get a better impact for you'. Mr Heseltine made for his car: 'I'm awfully sorry,' he said.

The minister was being perfectly reasonable. And observing him on his rounds there is no doubt that he is moved and appalled by much of what he sees. We hurried off to an employment exchange, or a job centre, in the Old Swan district.

Lured by the television cameras, a small crowd had gathered. A Mrs Durant, of Alston Street, approached me to ask whether this

Mr Heseltine was worried about employment. If so, her husband had a scrapyard, but they were making him close it down because they wanted the land for trees. 'They don't need trees around there,' she said, 'they just break them down to hit each other with.' (Terence's complaint, if you remember, was the precise opposite. He wanted more trees. The public, you see, cannot agree on these matters.) I urged her to raise the problem with Mr Heseltine, who would be here in a moment.

'Do you think I should?' she said. Certainly. He would be very interested. The suit entered, suffused in television lighting and was escorted forward by the manager. Fortunately, Mrs Durant managed to nip in. 'Mr Heseltine,' she said, 'You're here about jobs. Well, my husband's got a scrapyard but they want it for trees and . . .'

Mr Heseltine thanked her and said he couldn't deal with that now and turned her in the direction of 'one of my officials'. A luckless official was right behind. Mrs Durant got going again. He produced a pen and a notebook. 'I'll follow it up with the city,' he could be heard saying, 'I can't promise anything. Scrapyards *are* unpopular . . .'

The Times

⊰ 20 October 1981 ⊱

Edward Heath campaigns in the Croydon North West by-election

Mr Edward Heath campaigned for the Conservatives yesterday in the Croydon North West by-election, and said nothing.

For Mrs Thatcher, it could have been a lot worse. He might have said something. But it would be an error to assume that his visit was un-newsworthy. On the issues, Mr Heath silent is as interesting as Mr Heath talkative, as well as easier to understand. His seminal silences yesterday on the subject of Mrs Thatcher were the most definitive public statement so far of his position on the matter.

Mr Heath appeared in support of Mr Butterfill who sounds like a crunchy item of confectionary advertised disgustingly on TV, but is in fact the Conservative candidate. They had lunch in a pub and then advanced through the saloon bar for a Meet the People Tour.

Some lunchtime drinkers called out. Mr Heath pressed on towards the street. As always, he preferred an Avoid the People tour. Mr Heath is not at his best with people. A TV crew asked him to turn back and engage the citizen in conversation. He agreed.

'What are your policies?' said the voice of the people at the bar. 'Yes,' Mr Heath replied slowly – or rather, 'years'. The average citizen repeated his question. 'He's the candidate. It's him you're voting for,' said Mr Heath, placing a hand menacingly on Mr Butterfill's shoulder. 'I thought we were voting for the Government,' said the typical voter. 'You vote for them as well,' Mr Heath replied. He made the 'them' sound like the title of a horror film – them as in *The Thing!* ('vote for *Them*,' says Ted). But it was the most wholehearted endorsement Mrs Thatcher was to get all afternoon . . .

We left the pub and advanced on the rest of the electorate. Mr Heath and Mr Butterfill wandered up and down the High Street for a while in the middle of a tight pack of cameramen. A couple of times they all piled into a small grocery shop. Other times, they would waylay passing housewives. Considering the difficult situation in which he found himself, Mr Heath was good-natured, showed none of his fabled quick temper, and even seemed at times to enjoy the proceedings. And there was no doubt that for him it *was* a difficult situation. He believes this Government to be disastrous, but the remorseless rituals of the Conservative Party, with its emphasis on unity, compel him to put in at least a token appearance at this by-election.

Nonetheless he managed to convey an impression of distance from it all – as if, in his cashmere coat, arms at his side like a Burton's dummy, he was simply being borne along, possibly against his will, by the tide of cameras and microphones. A passer-by would recognise him and shake his hand.

The talking would then be done by Mr Butterfill, whom Mr Heath would introduce as 'the candidate'; this was just as well. So distant did Mr Heath seem, so impatient is he with verbal nuances at the best of times, that any attempt at the exact name would have been bound to come out as Mr Butterscotch, Mr Buttermilk or Mr Buttermountain, a fellow European.

Eventually, we found ourselves in a Betjemanesque suburban idyll called Briar Avenue. We all charged up and down a couple of gnome-infested front gardens shaking hands with convinced Tories. A woman said she was voting Conservative because of Mr Ken Livingstone, the hated left-wing leader of the GLC [Greater London Council] whose name parents use in these parts to frighten disobedient children. 'I must say, Livingstone's a great help,' Mr Heath observed as he moved on. 'Where did they find him?'

Another woman hurried out of Number 33 with an autograph book for Mr Heath to sign. She had an SDP–Liberal poster in her window.

'I'd vote Conservative if they got rid of Mrs Thatcher,' she said. Mr Heath had no alternative but to reply that he was not interested in personalities but in issues, and that in any case, while he had his differences with the Prime Minister over certain matters, there was no question of, as the woman put it, 'getting rid of her'.

After an hour and a half it was time for Mr Heath to go. He turned and waved to the photographers. One pressed forward in the hope of getting an exclusive silence. Instead, he observed that Mr Butterfill was a good candidate: 'very good on the doorstep'. Was Mr Heath predicting a Tory win on Thursday? 'I don't make predictions,' he said as he lowered himself into his car which made off away from the clamour of the hustings.

The Times

⊰ **22 October 1981** ⊱
**The SDP wins and 'at the name of Goodman,
every pen shall cower'**

A Mr William Pitt, of the SDP–Liberal Alliance won the Croydon by-election. Arnold Goodman (1913–1995 heavyweight London lawyer and adviser to politicians) bludgeoned two constituents with a letter.

It is time for a summing up of the Croydon North-West by-election, as well as a cautious prediction of the result. In which case, the reader is referred elsewhere. For something interesting has happened at last.

Not Lord Goodman himself could find a smear worthy of his name in this unhealthily polite contest, one had mused in the comatose depths of the constituency the other day. But one should not take the Lord's name in vain. For one thing, to do so tends to cost thousands. Yesterday, in its closing hours, there came an unscheduled guest appearance from the face that launched a thousand writs, the man who put the junk in injunction: the greatest solicitor since Cicero, Lord Goodman.

Two housewives had allegedly made certain remarks to two Liberal canvassers about Mr William Pitt, the SDP–Liberal Alliance candidate, in his capacity as chairman of a local residents' association. Whereupon, astoundingly, both women received through their letter boxes a terrifying letter from Messrs Goodman Derrick and Co. – a letter of the kind that Lord Goodman has unleashed to bludgeon mighty newspapers and giant corporations down the ages.

The document's existence was discovered by the Labour Party, which yesterday reproduced it in 5,000 leaflets warning voters, immortally, that if you tell Mr Pitt to get lost you might receive a letter from Lord Goodman. The pamphlet ends triumphantly: 'Stan Boden, your local Labour candidate, doesn't need a top peoples' lawyer. His door (47, Eversly Road) will always be open – whether you want to deliver bouquets or brickbats.' The pamphlet omits to mention that Lord Goodman, as a public figure, was largely invented by the Labour Party. But no matter.

At this stage, we must proceed warily. For at the name of Goodman every pen shall cower. It must be emphasised that everyone mentioned from now on is a person of unblemished reputation, total integrity and personal freshness, except if Messrs Goodman Derrick and Co. say they are not. Furthermore, there is not a jot or tittle of evidence for any suggestion to the contrary – or jit or tottle, tittle or bottle. There is not a scintilla, whatever that may mean, of any other evidence. It is all a farrago of untruths, and indeed, a fandango if required. (Lord Goodman's prose style is infectious on these occasions.)

The letter demonstrates once again that Lord Goodman has no peer as an exponent of the legal-pomposo school of English. 'Dear Madam' it begins. (A little impersonal, that, but it is probable that, just as with a Bellini or a Veronese, not all of the letter comes from the hand of the master himself, but from lesser members of the School of Goodman. That opening may have been the work of Derrick.)

'We act on behalf of Mr William Pitt' the document continues. (All his life, the history-conscious Lord Goodman has regretted that he has never been able to write that sentence. Another ambition achieved.) 'It has been drawn to our attention that on the 17th October you made certain allegations . . .'

Some of the phrases are rather dead, admittedly. More work by Derrick, one suspects. At this point a colleague has reminded me that Derrick is dead. That would explain it. Nonetheless, experts would agree that the work is still priceless. For, one after another, the familiar phrases roll out. 'Our client strongly refutes these allegations . . . without prejudice to our client's rights . . . in respect of allegations already made, we are instructed to inform you . . . proceedings . . . forthwith . . .' It is all there. A masterpiece, albeit a minor one. The work ends with a tremendous, overwhelming, life-enhancing: '. . . including, if necessary injunction proceedings to prevent you from repeating these allegations.'

Asked to comment yesterday, one of the recipients, Mrs Joyce Adams, understandably observed: 'When it arrived I couldn't believe it.' But she added: 'I'm not frightened,' which is more than can be said of the present writer. Nonetheless, one will hazard the protest that things have come to a sad pass when you cannot slander a by-election candidate to a couple of his canvassers without there thudding through your letter box a missive from the most numbing notary in the history of the British legal system.

The Times

⊰ 10 November 1981 ⊱

*After the Party conferences, Frank returned to the gallery of
the Commons.*

The baiting of Norman Tebbit

*Norman Tebbit, Secretary of State for Employment (1981–1983), made
the famous remark about his father when unemployed. 'He got on his bike
and looked for work.' It was endlessly misconstrued, as though he was
suggesting to the unemployed that they should do the same . . . perhaps he
was! Tebbit was teased about this for months with MPs calling out 'On
your bike!' every time he rose to make a statement in the House.*

Mr Norman Tebbit, the Secretary for Employment, rose in the
Commons yesterday to the by-now traditional cry – this time
uttered by the gravel-toned Scots left-winger Mr Canavan – of 'On
your beak . . . on your beak.' Mr Tebbit must by now be regretting
that remark about his father's bike.

The minister's beak pecked away at his opponents for 35 minutes.
Later, Mr Callaghan, the former Prime Minister, speaking from the
back benches, referred to Mr Tebbit as 'the most unlikeable man in
the House'. Mr Tebbit was visibly moved. Let us hope he proves
worthy of such a sacred trust.

'I turn to the matter that is perhaps the dominant question of
the day,' Mr Tebbit had begun. 'Myself,' he should have added.
Throughout the rest of the debate, speaker after speaker returned to
him personally.

Mr Eric Varley, the Shadow Secretary for Employment, referred
to Mr Tebbit as a street corner thug, and as a bovver boy whose
symbol of office was the knuckleduster. During a passage in which
he was trying to be less personal, he likened Mr Tebbit to Dracula.
Mr Varley had seized on a certain facial resemblance.

How did this boy Tebbit from an ordinary London working-class
home turn out as the only Cabinet Minster regarded by his opponents as evil? Just lucky, one supposes.

Yesterday, much of his speech was taken up with the usual inoffensive statistics, comparing our unemployment with that of Germany, France and elsewhere. But that was not what the punters on the Labour side had come to hear from him. Soon, he was referring to 'the old Labour Party' adding with a glance at Mr Michael Foot: 'Or perhaps by the look of them lately, the senile Labour Party.'

Then, in a passage especially parcelled for Crosby, he asked what SDP policy was on trade union law reform, reminisced about Mrs Shirley Williams's time on the Grunwick picket line, and added: 'Would she change it (the new law he intended to introduce) so that she could get back on the picket line?'

Spirits rose on the Labour benches. Happily, they simulated outrage. With so many Tories losing their Right nerve and, therefore, making themselves less easy to denounce as hard-hearted, Mr Tebbit is a raft in a sea of wets.

The Tories were subdued throughout the speech. A few extremists muttered under their breath: 'Year, year, year.'

Later, Sir Ian Gilmour, dismissed from the Cabinet at the same time as Mr Tebbit's accession to it, rose to make his first Commons speech for his new constituency, The Wilderness. He wanted to know when the recovery would come. Perhaps the Treasury knew. 'But judging by the interesting speech of the Secretary of State this afternoon, they have not told him.'

The irony of the 'interesting' was not lost on Mr Tebbit. From the direction of the Government front bench there was a creaking as if a vault were being opened. Mr Tebbit brought his legs to the ground. Dracula was rising.

Cautiously, Sir Ian stood back and allowed the dark-suited, pale, cadaverous figure to put a question: 'I assume that the Right Honourable Gentleman, like me, is a very practical man and has a great deal of experience of what goes on in the economy . . .'

That was Mr Tebbit's way of saying that Sir Ian, unlike the former airline pilot Tebbit, was a dreamy baronet, who could not screw on a light bulb. The minister demanded to know how Britain, after the reflation advocated by Sir Ian, could sell such goods as cars when other countries made them cheaper.

Sir Ian replied that if Mr Tebbit thought three million unemployed was the right way to run the economy, he could not agree.

Sir Ian resumed by telling us about some statistics which he had arranged to be given to something called 'the Treasury model'. One was not sure of the identity of this Treasury model, but she sounded a reckless and expensive girl who had led Sir Ian into trouble.

Sir Ian promised more jobs, but one was unable to say how much they would cost.

As a wet speech, Sir Ian was upstaged by that of Mr Julian Critchley, Tory member for Aldershot who, in the course of denouncing virtually the entire Government policy and the rhetoric with which it is presented, mocked the Prime Minister, the Treasury team and of course Mr Tebbit: 'What is life, Mr Speaker, but a series of errors?' he asked. Year, year, year.

The Times

In November 1981, I was the relatively new Secretary of State for Employment in the midst of a recession. I had to deal with unemployment peaking at over three million and reforming trades union laws which had given Britain the worst industrial relations of any leading industrialised society. I had no option but to attack my opponents, both on the benches opposite and those like Ian Gilmour on the benches behind me, who shared responsibility for the crisis in which Britain found itself. Such vigorous plain speaking, whether in the elegant style of Enoch Powell or my own north London grammar school (and former fighter pilot) style, was regarded with horror by my opponents and many Conservatives alike.

Norman Tebbit

⊰ 17 December 1981 ⊱
Roy Hattersley (Deputy Leader of Labour Party 1983–1992): Shameless rascal and politician for the connoisseur

Mr Roy Hattersley, the Shadow Home Secretary, yesterday made an eloquent, concerned and compassionate speech advocating a reduced rate television licence fee for old-age pensioners. What a shameless rascal he is.

But he is loveable with it. We know that, when he is visibly moved (as happens often) about the plight of elderly people or of the disabled or of racially disadvantaged groups in our so-called equal society, he does not really mean it. That somehow makes it less offensive.

There is a certain type of person the admiration for whom is almost entirely confined to others practising the same profession. There are lawyers' lawyers; journalists' journalists; conductors' conductors. Generally, they are not the same as the ones who are admired by outsiders. Mr André Previn, for example is admired by us outsiders, but not by his fellow conductors. Perhaps it has something to do with the fact that he is a little ridiculous. That is always popular.

Well, Mr Hattersley is a politician's politician; one for the connoisseur; not the sort of figure popular with the masses. It would not be safe to use him in wallpaper advertisements or party political broadcasts. No Previn, he. Instead, a performer to whom his fellow professionals flock whenever he consents, as yesterday, to give a virtuoso display.

Actually, they took some time to do the flocking. For a long time, the Labour benches were rather deserted. This is always the way after an Opposition demands an urgent debate on some Government announcement.

A few days ago, Mr Whitelaw, the Home Secretary, announced the increase in the television licence fee. Seemingly hundreds of Labour members rose, lamented the effect on old people's incomes, and insisted that nothing less than a full debate would suffice. Came the debate yesterday, and the Chamber was practically deserted. The art, you see, is to saddle the Government with the tiresome debate. The assumption is that the old-age pensioners, or whichever is the subject, should have noted the original uproar, and perhaps the debate itself – but not the empty Chamber.

Mr Hattersley rose with about a dozen Labour members strewn across the large expanse of the benches behind him, including several older folk for whom the Chamber is a place to stay in the warm and not be moved on by authority. Not that this deterred Mr Hattersley.

Effortlessly, he moved into his act – speaking now sombrely, now passionately, as if a full House hung on his words. In a masterly opening passage, he lamented the necessity for exempting old-age pensioners from any payments for anything. 'In an ideal world, pensioners would have what we've all got,' he said. This was of course shamelessness on an heroic scale. Mr Hattersley has not the slightest intention of allowing pensioners to have what he's got.

But by now he was well into his stride. Of the wretched pensioners, he claimed: 'Television is their single, sustained pleasure.' What impertinence! Does he assume they are capable of no other pleasure? He will be old himself one day. Then he will change his tune.

Meanwhile, Mr Hattersley swirled compassionately on. Eventually, Mr Michael McNair-Wilson, a Tory backbencher, intervened to ask why Mr Hattersley, when in the Labour Government, had not supported his much cheaper bill to provide free television for a still more deserving group: the deaf. Mr Hattersley was stopped in his tracks. He admitted he did not support that scheme. No doubt he toyed with the idea of reminding us about his compassionate policy of free radios for the deaf. In the end he settled for saying that his present reduced rate proposals could have a 'wider application'.

But we professionals can forgive Mr Hattersley. He is a master politician. Incidentally, he writes (in *Punch*) one of the few good columns anyone has ever written about the press, though, on the principle that they should have what he's got, he will presumably be giving that work eventually to some deserving pensioner.

The Times

I was, of course, delighted by these words. Frank Johnson's sketch was not the most complimentary article that had ever been written about me. It was not even entirely accurate. But neither compliments nor accuracy was Frank's style. His style was style – acerbic, elegant, fearless style. The art of sketchwriting has descended into vulgar abuse or dull description. At their best, sketches were both offensive and gratifying to their subject. Frank Johnson was able to combine both ingredients.

Roy Hattersley

⊰ 31 March 1982 ⊱

On this day Frank was named columnist of the year in the Newspaper Press Awards for the 'daily delight of his reports from Parliament'.

**Glasgow's unlikely hero, Roy Jenkins,
wins the Hillhead by-election**

Roy Jenkins won Glasgow Hillhead for the SDP, but his triumph was eclipsed by the Falklands War.

Mr Roy Jenkins yesterday took the seat he won last Thursday. And by exchanging warm greetings over the course of the afternoon with a baronet (Sir Ian Gilmour), a Tory backbench knight (Sir Hugh Fraser) and the owner of part of Cumberland (Mr William Whitelaw), he demonstrated to us all that he was back among the simple folk from whence he had come.

Among them there was much quiet rejoicing. It is nigh on six years since he went away. His travels had taken him to Brussels, Warrington, Hillhead and Morgan Grenfell. But he had never forgotten his roots. Through all that exotic voyaging he had remained as insufferable as he was on the day he left the Commons in 1976.

Insufferable, that is, to people who do not buy his act; such people include the entire Labour Party, the rougher half of the Conservative Party, and half the Gang of Four. This prejudice is not shared by this column. In common with most of the British people, we love a lord.

When Mr Jenkins strolled through those doors yesterday, positioned himself at the Bar of the House, put his hands behind his back, swayed on the balls of his feet, and pointed his nose in the direction of the rafters, we knew it was the miraculous return of the golden age.

Before being invited by the Speaker to take his seat, Mr Jenkins had to stand for more than half an hour, through exchanges involving Mr Rossi, Minister for Social Security, on the subject of the death grant, the sum paid by the state to the relatives of the recently deceased to help to defray funeral expenses.

Mr Jenkins continued to rock serenely to and fro. Sir Hugh Fraser came up to him and clasped him warmly about the shoulders. Mr Jenkins inclined his head in greeting, and whispered something in Sir Hugh's ear. The knight laughed, patted Mr Jenkins on the shoulder and moved on.

Various Labour Members continued to rave about the Tory intention of 'discriminating' between people who receive the death grant (presumably they objected to the fact that you had to die in order to qualify).

Sir Ian Gilmour came by and paid his respects. Mr Jenkins beamed at him.

Sir Anthony Royle, another backbench Tory knight, exchanged a nod and a smile. The lower orders on both sides of the House kept their distance. Mr Whitehead, a Labour man with a beard, shook Mr Jenkins' hand. But he is a former television producer and, like nearly everyone in television, probably has a mistaken impression of where he stands in the social order. Mr Enoch Powell streaked past, ignoring Mr Jenkins. Mr Jenkins ignored him back.

Eventually, at the Speaker's call, Mr Jenkins advanced down the Chamber to take the oath flanked by the two Scottish SDP Members who were his sponsors: Mr Robert Maclennan, and the man whose name resembles that of some African dictator, Dr Dickson Mabon.

The combined SDP and Liberal resources on the backbenches managed to muster a rather good cheer. 'Another merchant banker', cried Mr Dennis Skinner from the Labour Left. This was understood to be a reference to the hobby, which Mr Jenkins took up to while away the time on leaving the Commons, of collecting currency.

On taking the oath, Mr Jenkins passed behind the Speaker's Chair to be greeted by Mr Whitelaw. Meanwhile, as a foretaste of all those terrible Scottish Question Times yet to come, both Labour and Tory Members pursued him with such cries as 'och aye' and 'whisky, not claret'.

It was a reminder that, as some mother says in a Noel Coward play on hearing that her son is taking up boxing, Roy is so dreadfully *un* that sort of thing.

The Times

Chapter 6

April–June 1982
Eleven weeks
The Falklands War

In the spring of 1982 both President Reagan and the Pope were due to visit. Although there was a royal pregnancy and the World Cup to look forward to, all these events were overshadowed by the invasion of the capital of the Falkland Islands, Port Stanley by Argentina in the early hours of 2 April.

⊰ 5 April 1982 ⊱
To war

Peter Carrington resigned as Foreign Secretary (1979–1982), having taken full responsibility for failing to foresee the war, and Francis Pym succeeded him. John Nott, at this fateful time, was Secretary of State for Defence.

Outside: the sunshine, breeze and pale blue sky of a London spring; inside, for three hours on Saturday, the House was swept by storms not seen in this place since (ominous and, pray God, inapt comparison) Suez.

A huge queue had formed for the Public Gallery. The motive above all was no doubt curiosity. But there was also an air among the queuers of quiet, well-ordered concern. Argentina's equivalent at times of national crisis is the vast Buenos Aires rabble on behalf of whose depraved passions 1,800 Falkland Islanders have been set upon.

The civilised world will agree that we come best out of the

comparison. Inside the Chamber, men whom we had long seen as Tory Party hacks or place seekers became people of independent mind and righteous anger.

It was clear that their feelings were genuine. Indeed, perhaps it was the previous timidity which was the pose: the sad, necessary requirement for getting into the House in the first place. On the routine exchanges about the economy which had made up the stuff of a British political career these 25 years, there could have been little point in expending true feeling. But here was a subject to engage the emotions.

For three hours, all time-serving was suspended. How long it will last, we cannot say. But the Government had not bargained for such a mood as the debate got under way. Mr Pym and Mr Whitelaw sat huddled together on the front bench, heads down, occasionally whispering to one another: nature's party men, two former Chief Whips, professionals with half their lives behind them of string-pulling, elbow squeezing, thwarting backbenchers who were 'unhelpful'.

When they came into the Chamber on Saturday, they may have thought the emergency debate to be a routine party unity job; the same sort of thing as a tricky law and order one. Must stop any witch-hunt against Peter Carrington; must make sure enough backbench speeches helping poor John Nott.

But it was not to be as easy as that. Indignation swept and roared around the Government. Mrs Thatcher sat transfixed. She understood the feelings involved all right. For a start, she undoubtedly shared them. Yet she was, at the opening phase of the crisis, still at the mercy of the experts who draft the briefs.

When she said: 'Yesterday morning at 8:23am, we sent a telegram,' she adopted a heroic tone as if what was sent at 8.23am was a gunboat.

When Mr Enoch Powell reminded us that Mrs Thatcher had once gloried in the name of the Iron Lady, and when he added: 'In the next week or two the House, the nation and the Prime Minister herself will learn of what metal she is made,' she looked across at him, nodded slowly, and appeared to mouth something in agreement.

Mr Foot made the only speech since he became Leader that recaptured his old glory. Of course Mrs Thatcher was right when she said that, had the Government moved ships immediately, Mr Foot and his party would have raged at her for sabre rattling. But the Tory backbenchers did not want to hear that, for they were in no mood this day for the party game.

Throughout the debate, there was a closing of ranks against what so many see as Britain's traditional enemy: its foreign office. 'Someone has blundered,' said Mr Cormack, a Tory.

When Mr Whitney, a diplomat turned Tory backbencher, counselled understanding of the Argentinian position, he made the most courageous speech of his political career, which was just as well because that career was manifestly finished by it.

With his crinkly black hair and shiny moustache, Sir Bernard Braine looks, if he will forgive the expression, like an Argentine. But he displayed a healthy hatred of them. 'The thought that our people are in the hands of these criminals makes an Englishman's blood boil,' he boiled.

Of Mr Nott we will say little, except that he is a self-confident, nimble debater who has never had much trouble at the Dispatch Box before, which only went to show how wretched was his brief.

Let us hope for the sake of the Falkland Islanders and our fleet sailing towards them, that the Government fares better in the debates that lie ahead.

The Times

⊰ 7 April 1982 ⊱
Mrs Thatcher stands alone

In between yesterday's Prime Ministerial Question Time and the previous one last Thursday, the world has fatefully changed for Mrs Margaret Thatcher, and the fact showed.

She had about her an almost visible aura of being alone. If things go well in the South Atlantic she will have a House full of friends, followers who were with her from the beginning. If it is fierce, or worse, the corridors will be abuzz with realists who knew from the start that this adventure was madness. But yesterday, we were in that strange interlude between triumph and tragedy. Prudent men were hedging their bets.

Last Thursday she had been a Prime Minister whose fortunes were faintly, but perceptibly, turning for the better. At Hillhead, her candidate had been by no means humiliated. The opinion polls were beginning to move her way. She had no trouble at the Dispatch Box that day.

For an average Prime Minister's Question Time, the House is well-attended, but not full. Yesterday, it was full. The Peers' Gallery, a good guide to how much interest the Commons is arousing at any given moment, was crowded. Among their Lordships, the aged, the embittered, the patriots, the sympathetic, the worried, the simply curious, or the half crazed, all gazed down on the beleaguered commoner from Grantham.

She slipped into her place on the front bench while Social Service Ministers meandered towards the end of their questions,. There were some exchanges about the death grant. That is this month's cause among the compassionate classes. The grant is still too low apparently. Either that, or people should not have to die in order to qualify. Or it should also be paid on behalf of the living so as to make it a life grant. Who knows what the precise complaint is? Or cares?

Mr John Silkin, the Shadow Secretary for Defence, lowered himself into his seat on the Opposition front bench opposite her, and began silently to ooze stratagems. Mr Eric Heffer squeezed in beside him. Into the small space remaining at the top of the bench, the Labour Chief Whip Mr Cocks, almost as ample a figure as the other two, determinedly forced himself.

The frail form of Mr Michael Foot seemed to emerge from under Mr Silkin's armpit. The Prime Minister rose. In the second of silence before she embarked on her first answer, the Scots left-winger Mr Canavan shouted: 'Resign!' The cry was taken up by the Labour benches, pierced by the high cackle of another left-winger, Mr Winnick. When the noise subsided, Mrs Thatcher launched into an answer to two Tories about British Leyland. Labour remained silent. The second question on the order paper was about

President Reagan's visit to Britain and would afford greater opportunities.

The question about the visit came from Mr Cryer, an ally of Mr Benn's, a hater of Mrs Thatcher. She was trying to 'cover up her failing position' he said. He added that 'even President Reagan' had called for a peaceful solution to this crisis. Someone else should receive Mr Reagan. She should resign. Mrs Thatcher welcomed Mr Reagan as 'president of our senior NATO ally and the most powerful defender of liberty in the West and liberty in the world'. A Tory backbencher showed his neighbour the London evening paper, with news of Mr Reagan's desire to mediate between his 'two allies'. We are being equated with Argentina, it seems. Ominous.

Mr Foot made his first move. Were these reports true that we knew well in advance of Argentina's intentions? Mrs Thatcher in effect denied it. Several times Mr Foot persisted. Mrs Thatcher struggled through further denials, amid Labour glee. But her backbenchers looked on. They believed that we did indeed know, that she had not been told, and that the rules of politics forbade saying so.

The Opposition knew this too, particularly the cleverest or most cynical. Still, it was a good issue for them at this early stage. So there was an air of make-believe about these opening exchanges of the crisis, perhaps for the last time. Mrs Thatcher gathered up her papers quickly and left the Chamber on her own.

The Times

⊰ 25 May 1982 ⊱
HMS *Ardent* and HMS *Antelope* are sunk

Seven weeks and three days ago, Mr John Nott, the Secretary of State for Defence, had stood at this same Dispatch Box, a sorry figure. The Falklands had been lost the previous day: so, it seemed, had his career.

War is not only about the serious matter of real lives, but also about the minor matter of political lives. Yet minor matters can still be the stuff of drama, and it was a dramatic reversal of personal fortune when Mr Nott entered the chamber yesterday to make the first Commons statement since British forces returned to the Falkland Islands.

He was greeted with a cheer from the Tory backbenchers, not a prolonged or ecstatic cheer but a decent cheer nonetheless. Doubtless some of those cheering were exactly the same ones cursing him seven weeks and three days before. But then, he had about him the bedraggled air of fiasco; yesterday he was associated with success.

Strictly speaking, he probably had little responsibility for either. It may eventually become apparent that his greatest contribution to success was to have supported the Prime Minister against the negotiation party within her Government and beyond. But the Chamber of the Commons is not a place for subtleties or layers of meaning. Yesterday Mr Nott was a winner and that was good enough.

He began by saying that seven weeks before, his Right Honourable Friend the Prime Minister had stated that it was 'the Government's objective to see that the Islanders were freed from occupation'. He added: 'On the night of Thursday 20 May Her Majesty's forces re-established a secure base on the Falkland Islands and the Union Flag is today flying over the settlement of San Carlos in East Falkland where it will remain.'

Mr Nott surely lived a lifetime of hope and anguish in those seven weeks. There was the original facing of the Commons on that Saturday, 2 April. There was the time of the loss of HMS *Sheffield*, when the anti-war faction on the Labour benches flocked into the Chamber during some Scottish local government debate to bay for a Government statement, and Mr Nott had to hurry to the House to confirm the bitter news.

There were the last few days, when the forces for which he was responsible, 8,000 miles from home and exposed to onslaught from the air, began the operation in Falkland Sound, with Opposition politicians able to quote from their small print if it all ended in tragedy.

Through these weeks Mr Nott has gone about these occasions with dignity, avoiding both the bellicose and the feeble. Yesterday, he was manifestly relieved to be announcing a success. But he also had a warning. Our forces still faced 'formidable problems in difficult terrain with a hostile climate'. As he read on, it was clear that victory was being won at a steady cost in lives, as all victories so often are. He confirmed the toll on HMS *Ardent*: 22 dead, 17 injured. And HMS *Antelope*: one dead, seven hurt. But one thing was certain, he concluded: 'It will not be long' before victory. Several Labour backbenchers seized on the losses to urge a ceasefire and negotiation. They were figures such as the left-winger, Mr Frank Allaun, for whom this was a consistent attitude since they had opposed the use of the force from the start.

Such a recommendation would have sounded especially shameless coming from the Opposition front bench, which was why we did not hear it. Perhaps. If the capture of Port Stanley costs many lives and proves protracted, we will hear it soon enough.

But yesterday, the Shadow Secretary of Defence, Mr John Silkin, replying to Mr Nott, was carefully nonpartisan. 'The Opposition is very glad that a number of our fellow citizens in the Falkland Islands have now been liberated,' he said.

This was not the time for questions, he added. He was beginning to sound too good to be true. But he does have a divided party behind him, so he was swift to add that neither was it the time to ask questions about 'why the islands were invaded in the first place', thus promising his party at least some fun if it is faced with the total victory of Thatcherite arms.

The Times

Frank understands that throughout the Falklands Campaign I had responsibility for the success or failure of our forces but no power to command the outcome; power lay entirely in the hands of the military who, as it turned out, performed superbly. I had expressed privately to Margaret Thatcher – before the Fleet sailed – my doubts about the logistic viability of sending an opposed Task Force to the other end of the world. But once the Fleet sailed, there was no other option, in spite of the huge risks involved, but to support the venture in every possible way. It was made easier by the courage and leadership shown by Margaret Thatcher.

John Nott

⊰ 26 May 1982 ⊱
Michael Foot considers all Peruvian negotiators,
including Paddington Bear

Faced with the (to him) appalling prospect of the Argentines being removed from the Falkland Islands without the assistance of the United Nations or the President of Peru, Mr Michael Foot flew a heroic last mission against Mrs Thatcher at Prime Minister's Question Time yesterday.

'Can she clarify the attitude of the Government on the state of, or possibilities of, negotiations now?' he asked, braving a Tory back-bench surface-to-air missile: a cry from the direction of Sir William Clark of, 'Come off it, Foot.'

It was sheer suicide. How long can Mr Foot go on flying these missions? That was the question defence analysts were asking themselves last night. Mr Foot has kept it up now for seven weeks. First, he bombarded the Prime Minister with demands that Mrs Thatcher put her faith in the negotiating skills of the United Nations Secretary General. He is a Peruvian.

When Mrs Thatcher withstood that onslaught, Mr Foot roared down on her with a new negotiator, the President of Peru. He too, one assumed, was Peruvian. What was this mystical bond, we asked ourselves, between Mr Foot and Peru? One assumed it must have been because Ebbw Vale was a traditionally pro-Peruvian part of south Wales.

Yesterday, Mr Foot did not name his new negotiator. But it was clear that the Leader of the Opposition was prepared to negotiate to the last Peruvian. With the UN Secretary General and the Peruvian President seen off by Mrs Thatcher, the only other powerful Peruvian is Paddington Bear. (Readers with young children – or readers who are young children – will recall that Paddington was born in Peru.) He was presumably the mediator whom Mr Foot had in mind when he yesterday told Mrs Thatcher: 'Does she not agree that it is essential, in the interest of saving lives, British or others, that the possibilities of negotiation should be kept open along with the military action?'

The precise opposite was of course the case. The possibilities of negotiation would *prolong* the military action. But Mr Foot is the Leader of the Labour Party, while a Tory Government is engaged on an apparently victorious military operation. He is not expected to make sense. Mrs Thatcher declined Mr Foot's implied suggestion that we call in Senor Paddington. She pointed out that United Nations Resolution 502, the one which called on the Argentines to withdraw seven weeks ago, had not yet been implemented. 'If it were and Argentine troops withdrew, peace would follow,' she told Mr Foot.

Mr Foot had resumed his seat to refuel. Bravely, within seconds, he set out again. He told her: 'That is not the question.' Of course it wasn't. It was the answer. He was the one supposed to be asking the questions. The war has rather confused Mr Foot.

Nonetheless, to humour Mr Foot, we were all prepared to agree that that was not the question. It turned out to be: did Mrs Thatcher fully agree 'with what was said by the Foreign Secretary at the end of the debate on Thursday when he said we remain ready to negotiate'?

Of course Mrs Thatcher does not 'fully agree' with her Foreign Secretary. Otherwise it is extremely unlikely that we would be pressing ahead with the war. Everyone knew that, including Mr Foot. But Mrs Thatcher could hardly be expected to phrase it that way. So she avoided the question, and repeated what she had said about resolution 502.

Gamely, Mr Foot struggled to his feet yet again, displaying magnificent fighting spirit – that is to say, from his point of view, negotiating spirit. 'She cannot leave the matter there,' he protested. Did she agree with the Foreign Secretary, he repeated. She replied that she did not think the Foreign Secretary disagreed with her 'for one moment', a remark which caused widespread hilarity.

Mr Foot called off his attacks for the day. But where was Mr Healey? Why did not Mr Silkin put to sea? The Labour bankbench masses will undoubtedly turn on their leaders when this war is over. In turn, the junta will accuse each other of cowardice. The regime could totter. Mr Benn is waiting and watching. There could be terrible times ahead – we must hope.

The Times

⇥ 9 June 1982 ⇤
President Reagan (1981–1989) addresses Westminster

Below Frank's piece John Nott recalls sitting in on a private meeting of Reagan and Thatcher.

Mr Reagan's address yesterday was the sort of thing that, before the presidency restrained him, he presumably gave for years to small town rotary clubs: naïve, simplistic, determined to depict the Soviet Union as the supreme evil, insensitive to the multipolar nature of the modern world. For all those reasons, I liked it.

The speech was a sophisticate's nightmare. But then, so is everything about Mr Reagan. This is his great virtue. He knows that there is something fundamentally wrong about the Soviet Union and something fundamentally right about his own country and ours. Most people start out on their adult lives with this understanding, and most people retain it, but a number of people have it bludgeoned out of them by years of watching and making rotten television documentaries, or reading and writing rotten journalism.

One had feared that, because he was among Europeans, Mr Reagan might have felt that he had to make his tone more acceptable to polite society. He had been as much mocked in our enlightened prints as in those of his own country for his reliance over the years on such sources as the *Reader's Digest* for his information.

Now, no dispassionate soul, presented with the relevant material, would deny that *Reader's Digest* has been a more reliable source of understanding about the world than, say, *Le Monde*. But it just does not have the same social cachet.

At one stage in his speech yesterday, Mr Reagan launched into a passage about Soviet agriculture. 'A country which employs one-fifth of its population on agriculture is unable to feed its own people. Were it not for the tiny private sector tolerance in Soviet agriculture, the country might be on the brink of famine. These private plots occupy a bare 3 per cent of the arable land but account for nearly one-quarter of Soviet farm output and nearly one-third of meat products and vegetables.'

There was a *Reader's Digest* ring to that passage, but there was also a ring of truth. More sophisticated speakers or journals would blame that Soviet agriculture problem on the dislocation caused by the Second World War or by the Tsars. But Mr Reagan and the rest of the unfashionable classes suspect that it is because there is a bit of a flaw in Marx's ideas about agriculture.

Mr Reagan was equally interesting on the subject of El Salvador. 'For months and months the world news media covered the fighting in El Salvador. Day after day we were treated to stories and films slanted towards the brave freedom fighters battling oppressive government forces on behalf of the silent, suffering people of that tortured country . . . Then one day those silent, suffering people were offered a chance to vote to choose what kind of government they wanted . . . an unprecedented 1.4 million of them braved ambush and gunfire, trudging miles to vote . . . The real freedom fighters of El Salvador turned out to be the people of that country . . .'

Now, no doubt that account of Mr Reagan's was a partial account of recent history in El Salvador. No doubt, proportionately, the poll was indeed low – though not much lower than the ones that elected Mr Kenneth Livingstone. But Mr Reagan's version of El Salvador was at least as well-documented as the one on *News at Ten*, and I suspect more informative.

Mr Reagan had a respectful audience. This was largely because of the absence of many Labour MPs. But Mr Foot wandered in. Because of the heat, he was without the donkey jackets he wears on grand occasions. He wore a rather smart suit, giving himself another black mark with the Bennites.

Mr Reagan entered, preceded by a blast of trumpets, some Yeoman wardens, more men with moustaches, the Lord Chancellor, and a Britisher who would not go down well in Middle America on account of the fact that though wearing black tights, he was a man. He was the Speaker. The President turned out to be a genial man, a walking tribute to the avoidance of jogging, health foods, and psychoanalysis. It was a privilege to have him among us.

The Times

Reagan's visit to London towards the end of the Falklands War and his speech to Parliament reminded me of his more private visit to No. 10. He sat opposite to Margaret Thatcher at the Cabinet Table and Francis Pym and I attended at her request.

Margaret Thatcher put her head down and, without pausing for breath, reeled off a long list of detailed issues for discussion. It would have been impossible to question her or interrupt her flow. I watched Reagan who sat there, clearly bemused, and smiling sweetly as he doodled on a notepad. After what seemed an interminable time, she lifted her head from her brief and said:

'Thank you. Ron, what would you like to say?'

'Oh thank you, Margaret, it was very interesting but I have nothing to add.'

As he left the Cabinet room, I saw that he had left the presidential doodle on the table, but as I went to retrieve this interesting archive, his Chief of Staff, Meese, hurried back from the door and gathered up the doodle. Thus was I denied this piece of history.

John Nott

⊰ 16 June 1982 ⊱
Victory for Margaret Thatcher. Foot and Benn find fault.

Suddenly made real in the Chamber for Mrs Margaret Thatcher yesterday were her own dreams of these last 11 weeks, and the nightmares of both sides of the House, and in the world of the high-minded beyond, who loathe her.

For as she slipped on to the front bench for Prime Minister's Question Time while a junior social services minister meandered through some statistics, her triumph was total: the most complete a British Prime Minister had achieved in a generation. Overnight the news had got better and better. Not only had the Argentines accepted a ceasefire; that much she had told the House the night before. Now, they had surrendered – moreover, thousands more of them than we even thought were there. Amid the derision and disbelief of Britain's sophisticated classes, she had vowed to the world all those weeks ago that she would free those islands. And now she had. As she sat there, much of the House must have pondered in relief, exultation or dismay: the old girl had actually done it.

Meanwhile, she leafed through her notes, perhaps trying to give the impression that she regarded this as just another working day, from time to time smiling sweetly about her. But she knew that, life and politics being what they are, she will never again have a day such as this.

Naturally, she rose to a great Tory cheer. If things go well in the South Atlantic, I remember writing in this space shortly after the fleet set sail, 'she will have a House full of friends who were with her right from the start'. If it ended in farce or worse, 'the corridors will be abuzz with realists who knew that this adventure was madness'. I thought I would keep the cutting to hand whatever the outcome. Yesterday, they were with her from the start.

Her first questioner was a Tory backbencher, who asked her to give thanks for the Task Force and to agree with him that it was a fine moment for the country. 'I entirely agree,' she said, and went on to say she hoped we had let every nation know that we would defend our sovereignty. Mr Foot remained seated. A pro-Arab Tory asked her about the Lebanon. One or two Labour Members put questions about the sort of dreary economics to which our politics must soon return. One of them mentioned the Welsh miners striking in support of the health service workers.

When Mr Foot eventually did rise it was to ask about some United Nations 'special session' on disarmament which she was apparently to address in New York this week, though what was special about it was unclear. She replied by denouncing unilateralism. Labour bayed. The Tory Mr George Gardiner asked her to designate a Sunday soon as 'a national day of prayer and thanksgiving'.

Mr Gardiner is not noted for especial religious fervour or piety, except towards Mrs Thatcher. So, the left-winger Mr Bob Cryer shouted 'give over' and his friend sitting next to him, Mr Dennis Skinner, shouted 'Uriah Heep', or perhaps it was the other way about, though both shouts were well-deserved by Mr Gardiner. When the business moved on to the Prime Minister's statement on the latest from the Falklands, Mr Foot had to reply. On and on he went, like a barrel organ much-loved and capable of only one tune. When he eventually sat down, she rejected everything he had said.

And Mr Tony Benn? In the early days, he had told her to her face across the Chamber that she could not win, that Mr Reagan would stop her exactly as Eisenhower stopped Eden in 1956. I remember her staring at him palely as he said it – perhaps half fearing that it might come true. Yesterday he found some words to prove that she had not 'provided an answer to the problems of the Falklands'. Tremendously, she replied that he enjoyed free speech because of the sort of sacrifices which our forces had made. The Tories roared.

The Times

⊰ 18 June 1982 ⊱
Enoch Powell pays Mrs Thatcher a compliment,
but can anyone understand it?

Mr Enoch Powell, it will be remembered, drew attention in his speech in the Falklands debate on that fateful April Saturday to the fact that Mrs Thatcher had rather rejoiced in the name once given her by the Soviet Union: the Iron Lady.

And he added that in the weeks ahead we would see 'of what metal she was made'. As so often with Mr Powell, it was not just the words that chilled. It was the general Enochian carry-on. The gaunt features. The death-mask face. The black suit. The creepy Black Country vowels. Mr Powell is essentially the man who opens the door of the Gothic mansion to the travellers seeking refuge from the storm at the start of one of the many tales in the genre inspired by Edgar Allen Poe.

His words virtually pinned Mrs Thatcher to the back of her seat, at the time. Defiantly, she nodded agreement with him across the Chamber, we remember. Well, Mr Powell had the chance, when she proclaimed victory earlier this week, to give a ruling on her metal, and when he said nothing about it some of us thought it rather grudging of him. Could it be that like so many men of destiny, real or imagined, he is also a man of meanness?

Yesterday, Mr Powell rose during Prime Minister's Question Time. 'Is the Right Honourable Lady aware that the report has now been received from the Public Analyst on a certain substance recently subjected to analysis?' he began. 'I have obtained a copy of the report. It shows that the substance under test consisted of ferrous matter of the highest quality . . .' Members consulted one with another in some bafflement.

'. . . that it has exceptional tensile strength, is highly resistant to wear and tear and to stress and may be used with advantage for all national purposes.' Suddenly, Mr Powell was no longer the strange man at the Gothic mansion. He was now the mad scientist. But slowly, it began to dawn on the slower-witted among us. Mr Powell was saying that Mrs Thatcher had turned out all right. Furthermore, he was doing so in the form of a JOKE! Now, a joke from Mr Powell is never a laughing matter. That bit at the end about 'all national purposes' was presumably the SIGNIFICANT part. Ulster, standing up to the Common Market Commission, importance of nation-hood, that sort of thing. Anyway, Mr Powell sat down to a huge Tory cheer and cry of 'well said'.

Mrs Thatcher had become the first Tory Leader to win Mr Powell's approval for many years. Mr Edward Heath stared across the Chamber at him. He did not seem to think it at all jolly. Mrs Thatcher replied that she was grateful to Mr Powell. 'I agree with every word,' she added. A Tory backbench opponent of the Ulster Bill later asked whether Mrs Thatcher had fought any battles on Mr Powell's behalf in the Cabinet, for the opponents of the Bill believe that no measure produced by Mr James Prior can have Mrs Thatcher's real approval.

'I fight both the battles of war and the battles of peace,' she told Mr Budgen. But did she fight Mr Prior's battles? That was unclear. There was a more worrying problem about that answer, and about her agreeing with Mr Powell. In a word, hubris.

Mr Foot also was having difficulties in finding a peacetime role. At Prime Minister's Question Time yesterday, he once more called for negotiations. He was referring to the rail dispute. But for him the habits of the Falklands War die hard. Refusing him yet again, Mrs Thatcher said: 'This is a matter for the British Rail Board.' Mr Foot rose once more. Again she refused. The heart sank. Would Mr Foot be doing this twice a week throughout the rail strike? Would he produce another list of mediators, this time for the railways: ACAS, Lord McCarthy, an Independent Inquiry, the President of Peru? Undoubtedly.

Mrs Thatcher was defiant, sweeping out leaving Mr Foot shuffling his newspaper cuttings. For the Public Analyst had reported. Her metal was genuine. As the tabloids would say: Maggie An Old Battleaxe – Official.

The Times

Chapter 7

Winter 1982–1983

⊰ 16 October 1982 ⊱
**We knew that the SDP was losing momentum
but this was preposterous**

*The SDP was founded in 1981 as a fourth political party. In its democratic
infancy it had to shed the dominance of the Gang of Four and put in place a
one-member, one-vote democracy. In the first year, the SDP conference could
only consult so it rolled, metaphorically and actually, by courtesy of British Rail,
from north to south. Here Frank is writing about our second conference in 1982
mid-roll from Derby to Great Yarmouth, having started in Cardiff.*

*Frank was quite right in sensing that, on the platform in Derby, I was not
wholly at ease with the radical bearded vicar's speech about those 'certain
elements gaining ascendancy', as I thought it might be me he was hinting at.*

David Owen

'To those throughout the country distressed at Britain's
continued decline and fearful of our future.' Mr David Steel,
on behalf of the Alliance as a whole told the SDP conference at Great
Yarmouth yesterday: 'We say: Hold on, don't despair, our forces are
mustered; we are coming to your rescue.'

Anyone living in Great Yarmouth, and distressed at Britain's
continued decline and fearful of our future, would have been unwise
to wait up the previous evening to be rescued by these people. Several
of the most famous of the mustered forces had trouble coming to the
rescue, not of the country, but from Derby.

The rescuers spent a goodly part of the night aboard the famed
SDP special conference train, stationary in the silent East Anglian

countryside. The SDP, including Mr Roy Jenkins, Dr David Owen, Mrs Shirley Williams and Mr William Rogers, had made the elementary tactical error for a mustered force, of placing themselves entirely at the mercy of a ruthless organisation led by a notorious Social Democrat, code name Sir Peter Parker.

Or at least, if it is not certain that he is actually a Social Democrat, he is the sort of person who would be. It might have been expected that Sir Peter, inspired by the logistical challenge of getting the rescuers of Britain from Derby to Great Yarmouth, would be on more reliable form than usual, though it is true that he commanded the operation from British Rail headquarters in London rather than on the spot.

But, just over an hour out of Derby, the legendary conference train, drawn by one of the 'Spirit of Old Fashioned Keynesian Demand Management' class locomotives, began to slow down. Soon, progress became just a crawl. We knew that the SDP was losing momentum, but this was preposterous. Then it stopped completely.

The Gang of Four continued to ignore each other as if nothing unusual was happening. The SDP rank and file continued to bore each other rigid. We professional observers of politics continued to toy with the occasional medium sherry. Suddenly a guard appeared. 'We've failed,' he muttered. He was clearly the Keith Joseph of East Anglian railwaymen. Drawing on his experience as a former Secretary of State for Transport, Mr Rodgers commented: 'What's going on?' It was a brake that had failed, apparently.

Another railwayman appeared: 'We'll have a new engine put on in March,' he announced. Despair! Those throughout the country 'distressed at Britain's continued decline and fearful of our future' could not be expected to wait until March. Happily, he turned out to be referring to March, Cambridgeshire, rather than March 1983.

Not that this was much consolation, since at the time we were stuck outside Peterborough. The train lay becalmed there for some 45 minutes. It was a time for leadership so Mr Jenkins and Mrs Williams kept away from the rest of us and concerned themselves with writing speeches. As befitted a medical man, Dr Owen saw the importance of helping the more nervous among us to sleep through the crisis, so he talked about himself.

Mr Rodgers was likewise magnificent. Eventually a locomotive appeared at our rear and pushed us to March, from where, after another 25 minutes, a further engine led us through the flat, wet Brocklebank-Fowler country.

Around Norwich, Mr Jenkins emerged and carried out an inspection of the forward quarters. But by now we were making good progress. He is no fool. Sometime after midnight, an hour and a quarter late, Great Yarmouth, which must have given up hope, received its rescuers. Yesterday's proceedings were of little interest to those of us who had lived through such a night.

The Times

⊰ 23 November 1982 ⊱
Thatcher, the death of Leonid Brezhnev and an all-party spy

In November, Leonid Brezhnev (leader of the Soviet Union, 1964–1982), died. This coincided with the sentencing of Geoffrey Prime, an employee of the Government Communications headquarters at Cheltenham. He was charged with offences against female children and was found also to be one of the deceased's spies.

Mr Robin Maxwell-Hyslop, the Conservative backbench proceduralist, inquired of Mrs Thatcher, 'Has the Prime Minister noted the sad occasion of the death of . . .'

The heart sank. Tory backbenchers are compulsive payers of tributes to the deceased. They are obituarists by nature. They are masters of the patter that is employed on the occasion of a distinguished death. But surely they draw the line at Mr Brezhnev, even if he *was* a hunting man.

Mercifully, Mr Maxwell-Hyslop turned out to be referring to a much-admired officer of the House. 'One of the greatest Clerks of the House in living memory,' he said. But some of us suspected that many a Tory was quite prepared yesterday to go into action with the obsequies on the subject of a very different deceased.

A certain type of Tory is automatically reverential on the subject of powerful men. It matters not that the power be possessed by a communist. Labour members are fond of pointing out, undoubtedly with much justice, that on all-party delegations to communist countries it is often the Tories who are most effusive during the toasts and exchanges of compliments.

So the patter was all ready yesterday had it been required. 'Sir Leonid, one of the greatest proceduralists that the politburo has ever seen . . . a man who touched life at many points . . . remembered for his many personal kindnesses to new members . . . unfailing courtesy . . . is survived by his wife, though not by many of his critics.'

But there were no tributes in the House yesterday to Mr Brezhnev. Nor did it look as if there would be a memorial service at St Martin's-in-the-Fields to give thanks for his life and work. It seemed a sad way to go. No doubt somebody is arranging some sort of ceremony in the Supreme Soviet. But it will not be the same.

No death is truly distinguished until the chairman of the 1922 Committee has paid his respects. Not even those in the Labour Party who shared the deceased views put in a good word for him yesterday now that the old brute had at last gone to the place where, as Stalin's servant years ago, he helped send so many others of a less ripe age.

Mrs Thatcher was also silent on the subject of the bereavement. Like the rest of the world, she seemed to be bearing up remarkably well. But then, she and Leonid never did get on. Instead, Mrs Thatcher yesterday made a statement about the work of Geoffrey Prime, one of Mr Brezhnev's employees at the Cheltenham branch office.

The case of Prime would be referred to the Security Commission, she announced. The Commission was to be asked to advise whether any change in security arrangements was desirable or necessary. Members then began to fulminate on an all-party basis.

Why was not this man properly vetted? How many more of these spy scandals must we endure? Why cannot more information about these matters be made known to the House? (Because there are so many spies about, presumably.)

Labour Members were slightly hindered by the fact that Prime was active under the Labour as well as Conservative Governments. He was an all-party spy. Also, Labour likes spies to be upper-class homosexuals. Prime was a working-class child molester. To be consistent, Labour Members should yesterday have been raving about state school traitors. Understandably, they did no such thing.

The Tory backbencher, Sir Bernard Braine, frothed: 'It is more than a coincidence that the majority of traitors in this country since the war have been loners, perverts, or drunkards.' (A representative cross-section of society, really.) Sir Bernard demanded a vetting system, which would 'turn up quirks of character', perhaps having in mind something resembling the average Conservative constituency selection conference, with its unerring eye for loners, perverts and drunkards.

Mrs Thatcher replied that Prime's sexual proclivities were not even known to his wife. Mrs Thatcher was the most rational person in the place.

Mr Foot was rather subdued, perhaps because he still has to choose his ensemble for the Cenotaph on Sunday. Earlier in the week he wore a light brown suit and a yellow shirt. By yesterday, he was in dark blue. So some progress is being made.

The Times

⇥ 6 January 1983 ⇤
A visit to Dennis Skinner at Bolsover

It was with a degree of excitement and trepidation that I re-read Frank's piece on the trip around the Bolsover constituency on a January day in 1983.

He was very amusing when he wrote about my snooker exploits, social security tribunals and especially the lady attending hospital for a brain scan. He captured the spirit of the encounter.

I never felt uncomfortable in the few hours we spent together and yet I was with a right-wing journalist!

He was sharp, satirical, amusing and always readable – but most of all he was fair and could be trusted!

That's why I opened my door to him on that bleak January morning in 1983.

Dennis Skinner MP

Mr Skinner, who resides in this column throughout the parliamentary year, received me at his retreat: 86 Thanet Street, Clay Cross. It was as well I had not called the previous night, he said. For he had been at snooker. 'Beat a fella in three frames who is in the first team. They'll all be talking about it today, at least I 'ope they are.'

The spiritual leader of unnumbered, devout proletarians throughout the land wore simple, red carpet slippers. Protocol dictated that his wife, Mary, should offer me a cup of tea and that I, after seeking assurances that the kettle was not being put on especially for me, should accept.

The Skinners own the house. The architecture is 1920s council: Attlee Baroque. Not that it had ever actually been a council house for it would then have been unthinkable for Mr Skinner to have availed himself of Tory legislation and to have bought the property. Not long ago, in the Commons, some Tory backbencher made such a charge against Mr Skinner's election agent and it took Mr Skinner several heckles and a point of order to rebut it.

Mr Skinner did live in a council house. But on election in 1970, he thought it improper to continue to do so, now he was drawing an MP's, rather than a miner's pay.

He pointed to various trophies of his career, including two lamps for addressing the massed South Wales miners. You were only allowed to address them twice in any one lifetime, he explained. 'But how many times did Aneurin Bevan address them?' I inquired. 'Twice,' Mr Skinner assured me, 'same as me, same as anyone.' Then there was an engraving from Gateshead. 'I enjoyed speaking at that meeting because Horam had to move the vote of thanks.' (Horam, the then Labour Member for Gateshead, West, later defected to the SDP.)

A man in overalls, who had knocked on Mr Skinner's front door, was invited in. He had a relative with a problem. The relative did not live in Mr Skinner's constituency, but in another Labour one not far away. Yet he and the relative agreed that Mr Skinner was the man who could help. The problem was a slipped disc for which the relative was only getting 10 per cent.

'Final, or provisional?' Mr Skinner asked, displaying a practiced command of national insurance. The visitor was not sure. Ten per cent did not sound right to Mr Skinner. There might have to be an appeal. He explained that because it was not his constituency, he could not give advice officially, but suggested that the relative nonetheless telephone him. Mr Skinner's world is very much concerned with slipped discs, disability awards and sundry physical disasters. He has an almost romantic feel for the apparatus of the welfare state rather in the way that, say Mr Julian Amery, has for that of the Armed forces.

As we toured the constituency, a woman approached him and talked in detail about her various operations. There was not enough blood reaching her head, it seemed. So she was off to Sheffield that afternoon. 'For a brain scan?' Mr Skinner inquires, authoritatively.

Yes, apparently. 'Dr Davies?' Mr Skinner asked. 'I saw him for seven weeks after I fell off me bike that time. So I am the only MP with a certificate to prove that me brain's all right.'

'Get on with yer, Dennis,' the woman laughed as she contentedly got into the car taking her to Sheffield. Mr Skinner is in that category known as superb constituency MP. This is not a matter of ideology, examples are to be found among his enemies on the Labour right, and, for that matter, among Tories. It is a matter of temperament. Mr Skinner relishes tribunals and pension appeals.

He has always lived in Clay Cross. Was it true he did not own a passport? It was true. Had he never been abroad? Oh, aye. Where? Vienna. NUM delegation years ago. What did he think of the place? Didn't like it. The food, for one thing. It was all strudels or whatever they called it. He came back early at his own expense. 'But don't make too much of it because it might offend the people who took the trouble to send me.'

As we wandered around the superb, windswept moors and farmland in between the mining villages of his constituency, he was a Heathcliff figure – slim, younger than his 50 years, with thick dark hair and a long, handsome face.

He is melancholy too, given to such observations as: 'If you don't know sadness, you don't know happiness, d'yer?' But, as we went through a village called Creswell he was in good spirits.

'I appeared personally before the rent tribunal, representing 250 people 'ere, against the coal board. I selected the six best witnesses. "Have you actually seen the rats for yourself, Mrs Smith?" and, of course, her answer was: "Yes." We won.'

He started singing. He used to go round the clubs as a youth, imitating Johnny Ray, Guy Mitchell, Frankie Laine and Slim Whitman. Did I remember Slim Whitman? I remembered even less about Slim Whitman than about Walt Whitman. So Mr Skinner explained: 'High, whining voice like mine. Used to sing "Rose Marie".' Mr Skinner broke into song. The tune was 'Shall we Dance?' from *The King and I*, but the words were what he sang one year at the Labour conference revue, he explained, just after Mr Roy Jenkins had made that song about the SDP being like an aeroplane about to take off and all those right-wing Labour MPs were dithering about whether to join him.

Will they go – with a plane on the runway
Will they fly? Will they go –
Say au revoir when they really mean goodbye
But perchance, when the last drop of claret has run dry
Will they still cling together –
Lord George-Brown and Susan Slipman
Or will Steel come and take the show?
On the clear understanding
That they cannot make their minds up
Will they go
Oh, for Chrissake, let them go.

His Whitmanesque tone cut through the Derbyshire wind. 'Who wrote those words?' I demanded. 'I did, of course,' he said.

The Times

⊰ 8 January 1983 ⊱
And on to his neighbours at Chatsworth

R elations between the county's two great political dynasties have never been particularly close. Not much visiting goes on between them. There could be no question of intermarriage.

Mr Skinner, who describes himself in *Who's Who* as 'b. 11 Feb, 1932; good working-class mining stock', has two daughters, but they would be expected to make brilliant matches at the very highest levels of the NUM. The Duke of Devonshire was less restricted in his choice. He married a Mitford.

Truth to tell, Mr Skinner has very little time for the duke, especially since His Grace, who was the Minister of State for the Colonies in the Macmillan Administration, joined the SDP.

Mr Skinner is particularly proud of the defeat he inflicted on the duke a few years ago. As Mr Skinner tells it, the duke wanted the Commons to pass a private Bill enabling a marina to be developed at Eastbourne, a town in which the duke had much property. Mr Skinner opposed it, claiming some concern about the environmental damage to the Eastbourne seafront. 'The Tories thought we were going to talk about it for hours into the night and so they thought it was safe to go off to dinner,' Mr Skinner likes to recall. He enlisted the aid of Mr John Ryman, a barrister and Labour backbencher.

'I got Ryman to come in with a pile of books, so it would look as if he was going to talk for ever. Off went the Tories. Then we made sure there was a vote. That was the end of the Duke of Devonshire's marina.'

The visitor approaches the Devonshires conscious that they have suffered at the hands of the House of Skinner. Out of 1,000 acres of sumptuous parkland, the gleaming classical frontage loomed up. At last the SDP had shed that middle-class image.

The duchess followed the same procedure as Mrs Skinner. She immediately offered a cup of tea.

Through no fault of her own, she induces a certain initial reticence in people such as myself on this occasion, meeting her for the first time. For we cannot banish from our minds that it was her sister, Nancy Mitford, who decided what was U and Non-U.

So, for a while, one sat in terror that one would utter some terrible solecism, such as 'toilet' when of course one meant 'lavatory'. Though one can never be sure of these things, the visit seemed to pass off without a catastrophe of those proportions.

The duke was in London, unwell. But the son and heir, Lord

Hartington, was on hand. Mr Skinner's name came up early on. The duchess thought he was so brilliant. And a very good MP too.

That morning, she had been talking to the hairdresser about him. He had made the hairdresser laugh a lot over the years, she reported. 'And, in his way, he has this extraordinary charm,' I interjected, moving chameleon-like, into the genre. The duchess agreed. I resolved that this was about as far as we were going to get on the subject of Mr Skinner.

Why had the duke joined the SDP? 'I really shouldn't try to speak for him,' his son replied, 'but I think the unemployment had a lot to do with it.'

'And he's always been a great admirer of Roy Jenkins,' the duchess added.

Conversation turned to Chatsworth itself. Returning briefly to Mr Skinner, I asked what they thought a left-wing government would do about the place with its 175 rooms, a roof covering 1.3 acres, 17 staircases, 359 doors and 53 lavatories. Lord Hartington thought that such a government might want to get rid of his family, but that it would want to keep the house open, as it always had been, to the public.

It attracted thousands of visitors in the summer. It gave employment to local people, the parkland was free, since anyone could wander about in it.

But what such a government would not realise was that it was far cheaper to have the house run by a family than by some sort of a committee, or department. The ownership today already reposed in various charitable trusts. His family occupied only a small part of the house. 'We pay rent,' Lord Hartington said. 'Furnished rooms,' added the duchess.

Lord Hartington had huge enthusiasm for, and knowledge of the 'historic houses' business.

'What is your actual trade?' I inquired of Lord Hartington.

'Well, really, my trade is selling the idea of visits to Chatsworth.'

'It's called "the product" in heritage jargon,' the duchess said. 'The product is Chatsworth. He sells Chatsworth.'

So he was a heritage operative, I suggested. She agreed. He went to a lot of marketing conferences about the heritage, she added, amused by the concept.

For some reason, our conversation drifted around to the subject of standards of service in British shops. I expressed admiration for Harrods. The duchess preferred Marks and Spencer – much more professional service.

Based on his experience of giving good value at Chatsworth, Lord Hartington seemed to know a lot about good service. I suggested he should run Harrods. 'I wish he would. He would be so good at it,' the duchess said. 'Don't you think you would be, Stoker?'

Stoker? I had looked him up, and I felt sure he had a different name from that.

Why was he called Stoker? Well, despite his distinct likeness to his father, there was a family joke that he was the son of the painter and critic, Adrian Stokes. Furthermore 'my real name is Peregrine, and I don't really like being called Perry.' We agreed that it was therefore reasonable that he be called Stoker.

The Times

⊰ 15 February 1983 ⊱

Gerald Kaufman, the water strike and dead dogs in reservoirs

Members held an emergency debate on the water strike. Presumably there were loftier issues at stake. But, for Members on both sides of the House, the real emergency was the threat, not to the water supply, but to the vote supply.

Whose side are the voters on in this strike? Members had very little to go on. There are few guidelines as to the role, in British folklore, of water workers, for they have never been on strike before.

Either they could be the sort of citizens who are automatically feared or loathed by the country as a whole, such as car-manu-facturing workers, railwaymen, lawyers, journalists, estate agents, traffic wardens, and virtually anyone in Liverpool; or they could be the enviable category in which the miners found themselves in their first strike, 10 years ago – people the precise nature of whose work is sufficiently obscure to the rest of the populace for the work to have about it an aura of danger, self-sacrifice, indispensability, a kind of industrial romance.

Mr Reg Race opted for the latter belief. He is a left-winger. His name alone suggests that, combining as it does proletarian brevity and the Left's singly greatest preoccupation. The only name that could beat it for ideological purity would be, say, Ed Ethnic.

'We should have in mind what these workers actually have to do,' cried Mr Race. 'Water workers are not just people who purify the water we drink.' Whereupon he launched into the romantic conception of the water workers' role. 'They have to wade through raw sewage up to their waists to keep the sewers free and fish out dead dogs and dead bodies from the reservoirs, and maintain the filter base to produce clear water for everybody.'

He gave the impression that only people like him had knowledge of the water worker's life. Mr Race seemed overcome by the sheer beauty of what he was describing. Defiantly, he had announced at the start of the speech that he was a sponsored MP of NUPE, one of the unions concerned in the dispute.

A glance at *Who's Who* revealed him as having been 'senior research officer' of that body. 'Univ. Kent, BA (Politics and Sociology); PhD (Politics).' Not much fishing for dead dogs there.

But the public should remember that NUPE research officers and graduates in politics and sociology from the University of Kent have to wade through raw textbooks up to their waists, fishing out dead theories, to maintain the filter base that keeps the ideology pure for everybody.

The debate was opened by Mr Gerald Kaufman, the chief Opposition Spokesman on the Environment. 'I am a sponsored member of the General, Municipal, Boilermakers' and Allied Trades Union, and very proud to be so,' his opening announcement declared.

Actually Mr Kaufman over the years has made very few boilers. He has made a lot of steam, but has never required a boiler to do so, being chemically capable of creating hot air without assistance. His trades have been film critic, columnist of the *New Statesman* and now *The Times*, and writer of scripts for the once scandalous television show *That Was The Week That Was*.

That makes him a member of the Amalgamated Society of Satirists, Word Spinners and Allied Iconoclasts, which happens to be my own union.

Throughout the dispute, he has depicted the union's members as selfless souls who seek only to be allowed to carry on their ancient craft of wading through sewage, keeping an eye out for dead dogs and humans.

The Times

Frank actually reports the debate, something which is scarcely ever done by sketchwriters today, who regard their articles as a means of demonstrating their own wit, such as it is.

He ridicules the speaker – in this case, me – but very gently, and if I may say so, affectionately.

He shows Parliament as a legislative body, rather than inherently an object of derision.

Frank was not taken in by the pretensions of some Parliamentarians, quite possibly including mine. But he regarded the House of Commons as an indispensable institution of democracy, and his aim was to persuade his readers to value the Commons while not necessarily valuing its denizens. He was an avowed Conservative, but never allowed his politics to influence his judgement or his jokes.

He enhanced both democracy and journalism.

Gerald Kaufman MP

⊰ 22 March 1983 ⊱
Roy Jenkins (1920–2003) and Edward Heath (1916–2005), unemployed, look for jobs as world leaders

Mr Roy Jenkins, the SDP Leader, closed his speech in the Budget debate last night calling for 'world leadership'. Whereupon Mr Heath, an unemployed world leader, rose to speak.

Mr Heath is one of the long-term unemployed, one of the earliest victims of the Thatcher cuts. Nearly every week since Thatcherism made him redundant in 1975 he has come to the Westminster job centre. Any vacancies for a world leader? Sorry, no, is always the reply of the soulless people who run this place.

After years of that kind of thing, a man becomes demoralised. Special schemes have been set up to give such cases something to do. Mr Heath has been on several. One was called the Brandt Report. That kept him off the streets for a while.

Another was a think tank designed to sell to private industry some recycled opinions made by Mr Heath and Dr Henry Kissinger, an unemployed Metternich. But such is the pitiless nature of a world economy dominated by market forces, not enough consumers wanted to buy the tank's thoughts. The firm closed, with serious job losses, among elder statesmen.

For a man who had undergone such bitter experiences, Mr Heath was in remarkably good spirits last night. He stood confidently in the place especially built for long-term elder statesmen below the gang-way, hands thrust into his jacket pockets: statesmanning away with undiminished confidence.

But there is intense competition for the small number of jobs in the world leadership industry that are available. So worker is forced to compete against worker. Mr Heath for example, is forced to compete against Mr Jenkins. Both are world leaders seeking work in their old trade. But there they were last night competing against one another. It was another example of the way in which capitalism dehumanises.

Mr Jenkins, the first of the two to speak, set almost impossible standards of statesmanship and moderation. 'I certainly would not wish to stand on a rigid traditionalist position,' he said. (The precise matter, in connection with which he did not want to stand on a rigid traditionalist position, is unimportant.)

Mr Heath eyed him carefully. He had no intention of being caught wishing to stand on a rigid traditionalist position.

Next, Mr Jenkins said that Budgets were 'like toy ships engulfed by the waves of much greater movements in the economy'. Drawing on his famous supply of important-looking hand gestures, Mr Jenkins rippled his right hand across the air in front of him to indicate the waves of much greater movements in the world economy – or perhaps a toy sailing ship thereon.

Mr Heath stared across at him, confident that he knew about

sailing ships *and* the world economy, in contrast to Mr Jenkins who only knew about the world economy. There was nothing here that Mr Heath could not handle.

Mr Jenkins mocked the Government's alleged belief that there could be some kind of moral regeneration in the economy, and that 'the purification of the spirit can be achieved by mortification of flesh'. Mr Jenkins, we were sure, had no intention of mortifying any of the flesh comfortably, though not excessively, distributed about his person. He would go no further than the occasional visit to a health farm.

Later, Mr Jenkins discussed the PSBR [Public Sector Borrowing Requirement]. This he three times referred to as the PSRB. Another statesmanlike touch that: never show a grasp of petty detail. All in all, a difficult speech for Mr Heath successfully to follow. But successfully follow it he did.

He began with the homely matter of pensions in order to show that a statesman also hears the cries of humble petitioners. 'There is great confusion as to whether there is drawback or no drawback,' he said. One of those thus confused was Mr Heath, since the word is clawback. After that the speech soared to embrace the whole world. 'I am particularly worried about the position of Nigeria,' he observed eventually.

The next speaker was another craftsman, Mr James Callaghan. Unlike the other two, he is no longer looking for work. 'If I may intrude a personal historical note. When Giscard and Helmut Schmidt were going to set up the EMS [European Monetary System], we had breakfast together . . .' He mused on, as old men are wont to do, of the days when they perfected their skills.

The Times

Chapter 8

April–June 1983
The build-up to the election of 9 June

20 April 1983

Mrs Thatcher has election fever. The Queen has asked to be kept informed.

Mrs Thatcher had an attack of election fever in the Commons yesterday, the mystery disease which has had massive publicity for weeks and which can cause the premature death of entire governments.

Last night she was undergoing treatment from Dr William Whitelaw and Dr Francis Pym, two top physicians who have devoted their lives to combating the killer virus after the terrible outbreak of February 1974. And a warning went out to members of the public who live on the Conservative back benches to avoid contact with at least three men believed to be the 'carriers' of the disease.

One is Mr Norman Tebbit, who is understood to be connected with a bicycle business. Another is Mr Cecil Parkinson, a well-dressed, fair-haired former accountant from the Home Counties who is said to be a transmitter of the virus's lethal 'Conservative Central Office' strain. The third is Sir Geoffrey Howe, a Chancellor of the Exchequer from Surrey East about whom nothing is known.

Mrs Thatcher was taken ill after about five minutes of a routine Prime Minister's Question Time. Until then, she had been bullying Mr Michael Foot about nuclear war and raging at a harmless Labour backbencher who had accused her of causing unemployment in the West Midlands. She therefore appeared to be behaving normally.

Then Mr Foot asked her whether she had been correctly reported at the weekend when, according to Mr Foot, she had claimed that she would be the first Prime Minister to go to the country with a lower inflation rate than she had inherited.

He protested that her reported claim could not be true because Mrs Thatcher had inherited from the last Labour Government a lower inflation rate than the one she left to Labour as a member of Mr Edward Heath's Government.

The Prime Minister began her reply by saying: 'Assuming that the forecasts of inflation are reasonable, and even if they go up a bit in the coming months . . .'

At this, she was interrupted by Mr Denis Healey, a retired 1930s Oxford Marxist who was sitting on a bench opposite her. This man was heard to shout something like 'Cut and run'.

It was then that Mrs Thatcher had her seizure. 'Ooooh,' she cried, gesturing towards Mr Healey. 'The Right Honourable Gentleman is afraid of an election, is he? He is frightened . . . frightened . . . frightened.'

Above a great deal of noise, she had repeated the word as if in a trance. The symptoms were unmistakable. Those older Tory backbenchers who had been out East, and had experience of tropical diseases were in no doubt. It was the dreaded election fever. Panic gripped both sides of the House.

It looked as if Mrs Thatcher had been stricken by a form of the virus known as Psephologists' Tummy, since she appeared to have taken an overdose of opinion polls. Mr Heath was sitting only a few feet away from her, but was unable to come to her aid.

He contracted the fever in the winter of 1974. As a result, he called an election in the unseasonable month of February. It ruined his life. Now he lives in a twilight world below the gangway, emerging during debates on the Third World to tell his heartbreak story.

With considerable courage, Mrs Thatcher managed to pull herself together and resume haranguing Mr Foot and Mr Healey about inflation as if it were a day like any other. Mr Foot said he and his party were happy to have an early election.

This enabled everybody to start laughing as if nothing had happened. Life returned to normal. Mrs Thatcher left the Chamber shortly afterwards as if she were quite well. These periods of normality are quite common in this illness. They tell us nothing about the patient's chances of recovery.

Mrs Thatcher's condition last night remained serious. The Queen has asked to be kept informed.

The Times

⇥ 19 May 1983 ⇤
Mrs T. storms in to proclaim her manifesto

Conservative Manifesto Day at last. We shall never forget it. Not the manifesto. The day.

Hundreds of us were packed into a relatively small room at Conservative Central Office. Space ran out very early. In the corridor outside others of our profession clamoured for admittance. They were the lucky ones. Inside, a combination of the people, the television lights, and Mrs Thatcher talking non-stop at you for 20 minutes in a confined space, meant that conditions rapidly deteriorated.

The Prime Minister arrived through the throng accompanied by Mr Cecil Parkinson, Mr William Whitelaw, Mr Francis Pym, Sir Geoffrey Howe, Mr Norman Tebbit, Mr Michael Heseltine, Mr Tom King and Mr Denis Thatcher.

There was also Mr Ian Gow, her Parliamentary Private Secretary. He is her *eminence grise*, except that he is bald. Mr Parkinson, Mr Whitelaw, Mr Pym, Sir Geoffrey, Mr Heseltine and Mr King positioned themselves around her on the platform. Mr Gow *grised* away to one side.

Mr Thatcher took up the position of real influence, out of sight at the back of the hall. He fought a masterly campaign in 1979. When, on the first day of that contest, the then Leader of the Opposition cuddled a calf in a field in Norfolk, he was responsible for the best phrase to emerge from the Thatcher family during that campaign. ('If we're not careful, we'll have a dead calf on our hands.')

Now the only thing that stood between him and a second term in Downing Street was his wife. She had always been just that little bit too controversial for the wife of a public figure such as himself. But yesterday she was, so far as we knew, ahead still in every poll of which we had knowledge. Her confidence was unstoppable, as indeed was her conversation. All the indications were that her husband was fighting another winning campaign.

Mrs Thatcher's torrential opening, a 20-minute address to us explaining the manifesto, took in all topics at present known in British politics. She also promised to outlaw video nasties. A Labour Government would include within this legislation party political broadcasts by Mr Tebbit.

But Mr Tebbit was by far the colleague most in favour with Mrs Thatcher yesterday, and the only one who could come close to her inspirational tone.

Mr Whitelaw, the Home Secretary, elected not to make a statement at this stage, but to go for trial in the next Parliament.

'Can we have your questions?' Mrs Thatcher eventually demanded. It turned out that Mr Whitelaw, Sir Geoffrey, Mr Pym, Mr Tebbit, Mr Heseltine, Mr King and Mr Parkinson did not have any questions. This could explain how the Cabinet arrives at the Government's policies.

But it emerged that we had misunderstood her. *We* were the ones who were supposed to ask the questions.

Sir Robin Day inquired of an omission in the manifesto: any reference to the Trident weapon? Mr Heseltine replied that there was a reference to the deterrent, though not to Trident. 'I'm very grateful to you,' Mrs Thatcher whooped in the direction of Sir Robin. 'Have you got any more?'

Asked about the Falklands, Mr Pym implied that there could be negotiations if Argentina accepted an end to the conflict. 'On commercial links,' swiftly added Mrs Thatcher. 'The Foreign Secretary said quite clearly on commercial links.' Actually Mr Pym had not said it quite clearly at all.

Mr Pym, whose only intervention this was, drew his head back into those rather tortoise-like shoulders of his.

Someone asked if there would be a free vote on hanging in the new Parliament. She said yes. Suddenly, Mr Whitelaw stirred his large, much-loved, round features. 'Absolutely, and there are so many opportunities for doing it, I'm sure it will be done,' he said. This could have referred to hanging or voting. Someone else asked about the fall in industrial production. Sir Geoffrey began to answer. The questioner shouted something about the Chancellor's figures being to do with oil. 'Leaving aside oil,' said the Chancellor, and gently finished his answer.

'Why leave out oil?' crashed in the Prime Minister. 'It is a success for technology and for private enterprise.'

'Hear, hear,' muttered, at the back of the room, old oil man Mr Thatcher, a former director of Burma, who had dealt with many a blow out or gusher in his time.

The Times

⊰ **20 May 1983** ⊱

**Denis Healey and his former Cabinet colleague Roy Jenkins
flirt with constituents but not with each other**

Denis Healey was Deputy Leader of the Labour Party (1980–1983).

Out into the country yesterday to observe Mr Denis Healey, the man whose ex-officio title in this campaign is The Only One the Tories Fear – apart, that is, from Mr Edward Heath.

Mr Healey would be leaving London on the 10.04 for York, getting off at marginal Peterborough. Through the ticket barrier and King's Cross came the familiar figure. The only difficulty was that it was Mr Roy Jenkins. 'Where are you off to?' I inquired of his friend and counsellor, Lord Harris of Greenwich. 'Peterborough,' the peer replied. 'But Mr Healey is going to Peterborough,' I protested. 'So we understand,' said trusty Greenwich. There were the makings here of an incident.

The Jenkins faction installed themselves in a first-class carriage. Shortly afterwards, Mr Healey appeared, accompanied by two men of the sort described, in American political parlance, as key party aides. They chose the same carriage. We all set out for Peterborough.

After a while, Mr Jenkins, who was sitting a few seats ahead, rose and disappeared down the corridor. I inclined my head in Mr Jenkins's direction and smiled at Mr Healey. 'Who was that?' Mr Healey asked. I laughed. But it turned out that he genuinely did not know. 'Don't you realise who you're sharing a carriage with?' I asked. 'The same man you shared a Cabinet with.' 'Who?' I told him. 'Oh,' he said, 'you mean the David Frost of British politics.'

While I was still pondering the significance of that remark, we reached Peterborough. The two politicians carefully chose to get out from opposite ends of the carriage.

Awaiting Mr Jenkins were some Peterborough citizenry carrying SDP posters on the end of sticks, at least one television crew, and the microphones and tape machines of local radio. So Mr Healey could not avoid walking into the mêlée. Mr Jenkins turned and saw him. *The Times* pressed forward to record for history this uncovenanted poignant encounter. 'Hello, Denis.' 'Hello, Roy.' They shook hands. 'I wish you all the worst,' Mr Healey said. Mr Jenkins inclined his head with a smile.

Having intruded himself into the pictures of Mr Jenkins's arrival, Mr Healey moved off. 'That should bloody muck up his coverage,' muttered one of the key aides. The cameras and the tape machines now divided themselves between Mr Jenkins and Mr Healey and started to follow. Those citizens of Peterborough who had nothing better to do of a mid-morning, followed likewise.

I was carried along in the group behind my subject, Mr Healey. Soon we found ourselves across the road in an immense indoor shopping centre of glass. The politician was enjoying much success with a series of passing housewives. It was Mr Jenkins.

It is an error to assume that because he is not a man of the people, Mr Jenkins is at a disadvantage with housewives.

Once outside, Mr Jenkins moved to shake the hand of a woman at a bus stop. As she reciprocated, she transferred her cigarette from her right hand to her left, for she was not dealing with her old man now. She had moved from London. 'Do you feel a nostalgia for London?' Mr Jenkins inquired. 'Sometimes,' she said. 'The train service to London is very good,' he reassured her. 'The bus is better,' she said. 'Yes, it's cheaper,' he said. It was like one of the tense, early exchanges of small talk in *Brief Encounter*. A prelude to deeper emotions. Before long they had to part.

I caught up with Mr Healey being asked by local reporters what he thought about Mr Tebbit's saying he needed a sedative. Mr Healey replied that, if he needed a sedative, he would read Sir Geoffrey Howe's speeches.

At the big shopping centre, his way with women was different from Mr Jenkins's, but apparently just as successful. No fancy man from the scented salons of Brussels, he. ''Ullo, luv,' he greeted them. One woman expressed concern on his behalf at having heard Mr Tebbit on the radio call him a liar. He told her he would not lose any sleep over that. 'When I feel I might lose sleep, I just read Sir Geoffrey Howe's speeches,' he added, reworking, as we all do, some old material.

The woman stared at him uncomprehendingly. 'I suppose you get called a lot of names in your job,' she mused sadly. 'Oh yes, dear, yes,' Labour's Grand Old Name-caller replied.

The Times

⊰ 25 May 1983 ⊱
Mrs T. glares defiantly at socialist France from a lifeboat

Mrs Thatcher took her campaign down to Dover beach yesterday.

It will be recalled that, in his poem called by the very name 'Dover Beach', Matthew Arnold heard 'the melancholy, long withdrawing roar'. It was a metaphor for the decline of religion. Did Mrs Thatcher hear it amid the excitement occasioned by her arrival yesterday? If so it was a metaphor for the rival television camera crews kicking each other in the private parts or disembowelling one another with their vicious-looking sound equipment.

In the eyes of the politicians and their aides, these brutes are the most hated and most indispensable people in any modern campaign, even more so than the other parties. They form a heaving, cursing, Dantesque circle around the politician as he or she emerges from the vehicle that has deposited him or her in the regional constituency in question.

Marginal old ladies are thrust further to the margin. The terrifying entity made up of the cameramen and their hideous equipment begins to move slowly down the street with the politician inside it and smiling maniacally at the voters glimpsed outside.

Those crews which have missed a good shot of the Prime Minister cuddling a lobster, swinging from a chandelier, or whatever, plead with her public relation staff for her to do it again.

But this is not always possible. Whereupon, the television men wail and gnash their teeth as is the eternal fate of the accursed. Harsh words are spoken between them and the prime ministerial entourage.

Later, in the relative calm of the pub, or Conservative club in which we are all being victualled, the harsh words are forgotten. Diplomatically, the prime ministerial functionaries, knowing the dreadful expectance of home television, diplomatically blame the bad behaviour on the foreign crews.

It is generally agreed that it was all the fault of, say, any Scandinavians who might have been around, even though we all know they are gentler and less overwhelmingly manned than their British colleagues, and speak better English.

Either that, or agreed blame for all the pushing and shoving is directed at the Japanese, whose equipment and cameramen are half the size of the British. Honour is saved all round. All this adds to the general hilarity of being on the campaign trail.

On Dover beach, Mrs Thatcher glared defiance across at socialist-occupied France. But earlier, she took to the Walmer lifeboat, thus showing her first sign of doubt as to the result on 9 June.

The lifeboat, we were informed, had saved more than 100 lives. It was now about to save a redrawn marginal seat. Mrs Thatcher, having put on an orange nautical jacket, climbed up some steps and got into the vessel.

She laughed all the time. For the Thatcher campaign, apart from being immensely well-organised and so far triumphant, has about it a surprisingly joyous quality.

The vessel was poised on the slipway, and presumably capable of causing an international incident by being launched, armed with a monetarist Prime Minister, in the direction of French socialism. Mercifully, the vessel remained on the beach throughout her visit.

It was instructive to see the sort of people Mrs Thatcher would choose to share a lifeboat with her. Besides two lifeboatmen, Mr Michael Spicer, the Vice Chairman of the Conservative Party, had won a place which may have been a bad sign for Mr Cecil Parkinson, the Chairman who was back in London.

Then there was Mr Peter Rees, who is the plumply benign, very un-nautical-looking Minister for Trade. He secured a place in the boat for humanitarian reasons, being the candidate in the marginal seat. Then of course there was Mr Denis Thatcher.

For once, he did not want anyone to push the boat out. He engaged the lifeboatmen in vigorous conversation. One of them pointed to the horizon. Mr Thatcher looked rapt. The effect was reminiscent of 'The Boyhood of Denis'.

Finally, there was the daughter, Miss Carol Thatcher, so that the line could be continued. The Prime Minister stood in profile at the prow like a magnificent carving in a naval museum. Then, in response to the imploring cries of the cameramen behind she moved to the other end of the boat to adopt for their benefit, the stern approach.

The Times

⊰ 4 June 1983 ⊱
Back to the past for Mr Callaghan

It can be an elegiac sight – a former Prime Minister, now but a backbencher, canvassing in his own constituency in a general election where all is elsewhere.

Where once the photographers heaved and pleaded, there are now just a few faithful helpers. Pomp has fled. Now, he wanders the same streets that knew him all those years ago when the world did not. He should have an air of having learnt much on the intervening journey – of knowing things which those who occupy his former place have yet bitterly to learn.

But the setting must be right. In search of the last phase of Mr James Callaghan, I was led to a row of shops on the huge Llanrumney council estate in his Cardiff constituency. Rain beat down in straight lines. Big puddles formed in the undulations of the pavement.

Mr Callaghan stood bareheaded in a light plastic raincoat. Around him were about half a dozen women and two or three men with canvassing cards and rolls of Labour stickers. The dank streets were all but deserted. As a setting, perfect! For it must constitute as great a contrast as possible with the old statesman's time of grandeur.

Here, with rain dripping off his nose and glasses, was one who had not only been Prime Minister, but unlike any other Prime Minister of the century, had held the three other 'great offices of state': Foreign Secretary, Chancellor, Home Secretary. Perhaps standing there too was the last Labour Prime Minister.

We set out in a van to canvass. A capable-looking man with a London accent, whose employment seemed to be of a constabulary nature, remained at a discreet distance from Mr Callaghan at all times – sole reminder of power once wielded. One of his canvassers offered this man an umbrella. 'Thank you, but no. I prefer to keep both hands free when I'm working,' he replied, slightly chillingly.

Mr Callaghan's progress resembled that of a territorial magnate among his tenants, grandees of Old Labour such as Mr Callaghan being the last paternalists. In between calls, he reflected on the state of the world. The whole effect was of a proletarian or lower middle-class version of the Third Marquis of Salisbury – wary, experienced, loathing ideological fervour. Mrs Thatcher would see the world this way, in the end, he no doubt believed.

The few people who were out in the rain tended to call out their support to him. 'People here are uprooted,' he said, 'They come from the old, poor communities, but they were communities. These are not – though we are trying to build communities in some of our new schemes. Often people live in the past. Perhaps it is not for me to say it, but they see me as part of the past.'

Mr Callaghan was both moved and moving. The rain kept on. A passing bus set up a tidal wave across the pavement. Canvassers canvassed, Mr Callaghan, myself – a not unpleasant melancholy settled on us all.

As we reached the end of the road, I asked him: 'Why are you carrying on?' 'We're not, we're going back in the van now,' he replied. 'No,' I said, 'I mean carrying on in Parliament. You've been in since 1945. You've been everything. Why continue?'

'I can give you a priggish answer, which is that I want to try to do something to help, to stop things I'm against. The unpriggish part of the answer is that I enjoy it. I'm fit. Why not?'

I said I wanted to ask him one difficult question. Did he think we were right to sink the *Belgrano*? 'I don't want to say anything about that,' he replied. 'ITN and BBC have been chasing me to say something about that. But it's not part of my campaign. I have my views about it. You know I have my views. You remember . . .' But he was now interrupted by another well-wisher. He extended his hand, and we parted.

The Times

⊰ 7 June 1983 ⊱
Mrs T. takes a marzipan factory by storm

One of the happiest moments of Mrs Thatcher's election campaign of 1979 was her visit to the Cadbury's factory in a Birmingham marginal.

There, balancing on the brink of successive vats of whirling chocolate with the crush of photographers threatening to propel her downward at any moment, she narrowly missed being incorporated in a range of delicious walnut whips. The history of Britain of the last four years could have been so different.

Many of us interpreted that visit as the turning point of the 1979 campaign – there being more pigs among the electorate than joggers.

Yesterday, just over four years later, she kept faith with the pivotal 'fat vote' by visiting a marzipan factory in a south London marginal.

'10:00. Arrive John F. Renshaw Ltd, Lock Lane, Mitcham, manufacturers of marzipan', said the sheet of paper issued to those of us travelling with the Prime Minister. 'Please note: very limited press facilities because of hygiene regulations.'

This was rather offensive since some of us reporters are a good deal less filthy than some politicians.

Three coaches, one of them containing the Prime Minister, descended on the factory. Then, as in Act Two of *The Nutcracker*, we children were led by her through the Kingdom of Sweets.

The elegant Mr Denis Thatcher was characteristically reliable in the role of the Prince. The photographers were of course the rats. Opinions will differ as to whether the Prime Minister was dancing the role of the Sugar Plum Fairy or the Wicked Fairy.

Balletomanes will note that, if it was the Wicked Fairy rather than the Sugar Plum Fairy, then the ballet must have been *The Sleeping Beauty* because *The Nutcracker* does not have a Wicked Fairy, so it would be best if this balletic metaphor were abandoned. Anyway, there were a lot of sweets.

The machinery clattered, The marzipan churned and gurgled. Women continued to stuff chunks of it into brown boxes. Mrs Thatcher started to make full use of her gift of being piercingly interested in whatever is being explained to her on an election tour.

Unlike the sadly limited Mr Foot, she has many roles which, depending on the role of the person whom she is addressing, she can assume at will – politician, wife, mother, shopper, marzipan-maker.

On this occasion she was all five. 'Making marzipan with almonds is a brute of a job,' she told a group of the women, referring to her own experience of the process.

Meanwhile, Mr Denis Thatcher, whose mastery of factory-visit conversation is now the equal of the Duke of Edinburgh's, could be heard in the background working away at the firm's executives: 'Do you buy your almonds from the almond people overseas? . . . I see, yes . . . you make the cherries, d'you?' Back to the Prime Minister, still working the women. 'I don't like too much of it because it is VAIRY VAIRY rich . . .'

Clatter-clatter, continued the machines. Gurgle-gurgle, continued the marzipan. The Prime Minister sat down at a conveyor belt with some more women and joined in the sorting of dark almonds from light. Whereupon the photographers started climbing up the adjacent walls, and indeed each other.

'By law, you can only make marzipan with almonds,' an executive was at the same time explaining to Mrs Thatcher, 'which is in itself an astonishing piece of information.'

Excitement mounted. 'You skin them and grind them yourself,' the Prime Minister could be heard bafflingly telling some of the executives at one stage. This turned out to be a further reference to her way with nuts, when marzipan-making, rather than to her way with Cabinet colleagues.

A joyous occasion, then. Sadly it was time to go.

Reluctantly, we took off the long white coats, and the white hats, which all of us – including the Prime Minister – had had to wear for hygiene reasons.

Mr Thatcher had looked like a reassuring surgeon in a private hospital catering for senior businessmen.

'Nothing wrong with a medium sherry now and then, old boy,' one could imagine him advising after an op. 'But I'd go easy on stuff like marzipan if I were you.'

The Times

⌐ 9 June 1983 ⌐
Electioneering in safe territory where plump
chartered accountants graze

And so to the last day.

Labour having been dealt with to her own satisfaction, the Prime Minister devoted her energies to constituencies where the issue lay between the Conservatives and the Alliance. That meant a descent on the cream-tea-and-scone belt of the outer Home Counties. It was a welcome journey for those of us who take the anti-Orwell view that this part of England is no less 'real' or 'warm' for not being in the industrial north.

Out along the line of the A3 flew the Prime Minister by helicopter with journalistic escort, as the proud names passed below: Esher, Cheam, Bagshot, stretching away to Guilford itself, the Queen of the

South, a place whose impenetrable one-way system is fully worthy of a town whose previous and probably next MP is the Secretary of State for Transport. Happily we were in the air yesterday,

Prosperity burgeoned below us, antique dealers, chartered accountants, estate agents: the simple folk who are the backbone of England. On went the names: Leatherhead, Godalming, Basingstoke. We were in a traditionally patriotic region. Selflessly, it yields up the finest of its daughters for service in the typing pool at Conservative Central Office.

Whole careers in the Labour Party have been founded on the simple desire to impoverish regions such as this. No wonder one instinctively felt a sense of solidarity with the people living below.

The Prime Minister turned west towards Wiltshire. The grazing cows were plumper. So were the grazing chartered accountants.

One of them, called Mr Key, was the Conservative candidate in Salisbury, the town near which we landed. Here the Liberals were said to be reorganised.

The Conservatives, it was emphasised, had to be on their guard against complacency. But it all seemed Tory enough to me. Matrons in spotless floral dresses with stiff white collars, cooed and ahed at the Prime Minister's approach and told each other that she was lovely.

Exquisite children presented bouquets. The sun shone. The candidate, Mr Key, turned out to be a typical sturdy, jovial specimen of Home Counties stock. He even had a wife called Fiona. All seemed under control.

From the helicopter port at Old Sarum, yes, the small hill which was once an entire parliamentary constituency before the Tories were forced by extremists to accept changed methods of reselection, we were bussed to Salisbury's fine market square.

A large crowd had gathered. The great majority were loyal. But there was quite a large disloyal element, who booed and shrieked defiance. 'You stand there shouting,' Mrs Thatcher shouted back. 'How pathetic you are, haven't got an argument left.'

I retreated out of earshot to the edge of the throng. After four weeks on the trail, diverting though it has all been, there comes a time when the old brain can take no more. The din must have been particularly disturbing for those of one's colleagues who had apparently celebrated the end of the Thatcher tour with an epic number of *digestives* late the previous night.

Mrs Thatcher brought her campaign to a climax by landing on the Isle of Wight, the British possession which she regards as having been illegally occupied by the Liberals since 1974. The launching of the attack from Salisbury was a complex operation involving helicopters, Wallace Arnold coaches, and a hovercraft. It was surprising there were so few deaths.

The journalists swarmed ashore from the helicopters in advance of the Prime Minister, though, from the sound of the previous night's debaucheries, their regiment was Too Paralytic rather than 2 Para.

Mrs Thatcher arrived in the shape of the prow of the hovercraft. At Cowes she met some resistance from forces loyal to the Liberal sitting candidate, Mr Stephen Ross. As she approached the site of her open-air meeting, jeers and boos greeted her as well as applause. But she overwhelmed them with her superior firepower, and left for London with the Tories confident that the Alliance everywhere will be seen off by the Isle of Wight factor.

The Times

Chapter 9

September 1983–
October 1984

From 1983 to 1988 Frank continued to write for The Times, *no longer as sketchwriter but as political correspondent in Paris and then Bonn. He would occasionally return to England to sketch the conferences, as he did on that fateful day when the IRA bombed the Grand Hotel in Brighton – described in the last article in this chapter.*

⊰ 13 September 1983 ⊱
David Owen is banned from the Cenotaph

D r David Owen yesterday made his first big speech as Leader of the Social Democratic Party. He was addressing the second day of the party's annual conference at Salford. Never a man to disdain a cliché, he began: 'Let us look to the future,' for he had to start the speech somehow. It was the future, he might have added, which lay ahead of us.

Happily, the speech recovered from this start. He settled down to a perfectly respectable explanation of how, given the chance, he would sort out the economy, central America, the Middle East, nuclear proliferation – the usual topics.

But then he turned to humanitarian issues and, in doing so, launched an astonishing personal attack on the Prime Minister, accusing her in effect of lacking compassion. 'She manoeuvred to exclude the Social Democratic Party from the political broadcasts we are entitled to this year after our election result,' he protested.

This was very much the idealistic Dr Owen, moved by social concern. Mrs Thatcher could of course only increase the SDP's popularity with the television viewing public. But Dr Owen did not see it in this way.

Instead, he used her heartless policy on political broadcasts to begin his dossier of shame on Mrs Thatcher's Britain. 'She refused to appoint a single Social Democratic life peer,' was his next item.

We were left to assume that the figures for our inner cities showed that there were scores of Social Democrats being denied the life peerages to which they had a right – men and women who would never know what it was like to get togged up in ermine or, by mentioning their titles, secure instant telephone reservations in restaurants.

In Kensington alone, there was Mr Roy Jenkins.

From Dr Owen's point of view, there was worse to come. 'She refuses to rearrange the procedure of the House of Commons and conspires to allow the Labour Party control over every day available for debate to criticise the government and to bring the issue to the vote.'

Dr Owen concluded his heartbreak list with the revelation: 'She appears ready to exclude the representation of three and a half million SDP voters at the Cenotaph ceremony.' What he meant was that she appeared ready to exclude *him* and his wreath from the Cenotaph ceremony.

But Dr Owen sees himself as the spiritual leader of the three and a half million SDP voters. So from his point of view, at the Cenotaph ceremony, his presence and theirs would be synonymous.

To his great credit, Dr Owen understood this yesterday and sat down abruptly in mid-ovation having secured of course the necessary few seconds of adulation for that evening's cameras.

The Party President, Mrs Shirley Williams, who chairs the conference, said something about Dr Owen having to accept standing ovations with more grace. But lest she thought we thought she meant it, which no doubt she did, she quickly added that the ovation was deserved because it was such a fine speech.

An interesting human incident, this. Significant, certainly. Significant of what I have no idea. Perhaps we will find out in the dreadful struggle in the party over the years to come.

Elsewhere during the proceedings, it was minorities day. The conference accepted a motion taking note 'of policy document No.9 on urban policy and policy document No.10 on citizens' rights and endorses their central principles, in particular . . .'

These central principles embraced most minorities and progressive policies thereon. But, as at the Edinburgh Festival, it is the fringe events which are proving the most creative.

At lunch time alone, there were, among other attractions, the Gay Social Democrats with a meeting entitled 'Homosexuals Are Citizens Too', addressed by Miss Neuberger who is not only a woman but is also reputedly Britain's only female rabbi. So, by taking in that meeting, the diligent progressive could bag at least three minorities – four if you include female rabbis as a minority in their own right.

What both the conference and its fringe had lacked, however, was an extremist. Whereupon Mr Kenneth Livingstone suddenly materialised. He arrived on the pretext of addressing a meeting last night on the Tory threat to the Greater London Council – the same excuse he is giving at all this season's conferences.

A huge and excited audience crammed one of the lecture theatres. Mr Livingstone spoke with restraint and moderation, thus confirming his critics' belief that there is no trick to which he will not stoop.

The Times

⊰ 7 October 1983 ⊱
Neil Kinnock and great billows of sound

Kinnock's first conference speech after becoming Leader of the Labour Party (1983–1987).

'If you want a short word for it,' Mr Kinnock said yesterday, concerning what the Tories had allegedly done to the economy, 'it is a grand-scale act of profound economic treachery.'

That was no short word. It was half a dozen words, including three quite long ones, plus a hyphen. Commonplace though it now is to describe Mr Kinnock as a Welsh windbag (even the healthily-self-mocking Mr Kinnock does so, it is said), it must be stated that this man yesterday showed the sort of form, in his first big speech to a Labour conference since winning the leadership, that has taken him at the age of 41 to the top in British windbaggery.

He is in a great tradition. Most of our major windbags, like most of our good opera singers, have been Welsh. Admittedly, Mr Foot has no real connection with any of the valleys. Well, he had – but the valley is on Hampstead Heath. Yet he is a naturalised Welshman.

What is it about this gifted race that enabled them to pluck, as if from the air they breathe, phrases such as 'That is how poverty becomes a raging world infection' (Mr Kinnock yesterday)? The precise process by which something or other achieved the status of raging world infection was unclear.

Mr Kinnock is an orator – not an economics textbook. He sends up great billows of sound. When he reaches a climax, everybody cheers and applauds. Through the clapping you can pick out words as he surges on. Clap, clap, clap. 'Hypocrisy'. Cheer, cheer, cheer. 'Stupidity'. Clap, clap, clap. 'World starvation' (laughter).

Mr Kinnock's trainer, the old crowd-pleaser Mr Foot, looked on admiringly. He taught that boy all he knew. Mr Kinnock had been in training for this big one all week.

By yesterday morning, his handlers were quietly confident. Early on in the speech he told a complex joke involving the National Health Service, private medicine, a sex clinic in fashionable London about which he had read in the popular press that morning, monkey glands and the Tory Cabinet.

He was going to be difficult to beat. Minutes after that, he was deep on to the nuclear holocaust, the Third World, the British Economy and Mrs Thatcher's responsibility for all such problems.

At the end, he was rewarded with a sort of genuine standing ovation that the conference had only ever given to Mr Lansbury (in prehistoric times) and Mr Michael Foot. These were the only two previous leaders who have had what it takes to win over a Labour conference: complete inability to win over the electorate.

Happily, that problem lay long in the future yesterday. Mr Kinnock allowed his triumph to surge over him. He smiled and waved. He said lots of things which would make him look excellent in brief clips on television news.

Urging his party to prepare even now for victory in five years' time, he ended the speech by urging them to 'go to it' – an injunction of such Attlee-esque terseness as to endanger the reputation which Mr Kinnock had built up over the previous 40 minutes and previous 40 years.

Sadly the charm of the delightful Mr Kinnock was followed by a charmless debate on Northern Ireland. Although himself a member of the national executive, Mr Wedgwood Benn made mischief by moving a motion opposing the executive's policy that the border can only be abolished with the consent of the Northern Irish population.

The Times

⊰ 22 November 1983 ⊱
The Elgin Marbles, William Waldegrave,
and the Curse of Foot

Melina Mercouri, Greek Minister of Culture (1981–1989), had been campaigning for the return of the Elgin Marbles to the Parthenon. Here, the Labour Party takes up her cause.

The Hellenic wing of the Labour Party, much in evidence last week on the occasion of the Turkish Cypriot announcement of independence, went into action again yesterday on the more emotive issue of the Elgin Marbles.

No doubt on behalf of Kentish Town, Haringey and all those other parts of north London where Greek is widely spoken, and Labour widely voted, the party demanded the departure of the marbles from the British Museum in alien Bloomsbury. Ideally, the Opposition would doubtless like the marbles to be sent to Kentish Town or Haringey or at least Cyprus, which is where their voters come from. But as an intermediate step, the demand yesterday was that they go to Greece.

The great moment of the rather passionate exchanges came when Mr Michael Foot, the former Leader of the Labour Party, intervened. It nowadays takes an eccentric cause to draw Mr Foot out of retirement.

Yesterday he assured Mr William Waldegrave, the minister responsible in the Commons for the arts who was stalling at the Dispatch Box as best he could: 'The circumstances and manner in which the Elgin Marbles, so-called, were taken from Greece, was bitterly denounced by most English people at the time, headed by Lord Byron, and he pronounced a terrible curse on those engaged in the transaction. Will Her Majesty's Government look seriously at this request from a friendly, democratic government?'

Across the gangway, Mr James Callaghan, the other former Labour Leader extant on the back benches, gazed up at Mr Foot with what seemed like a look of wonder.

Lord Byron appeared to have laid a curse on Mr Waldegrave. There must have been some doubt as to whether this was in order, but the Speaker allowed it.

There was no point in seeking to disguise from Mr Waldegrave the seriousness of his position. The last time Mr Foot laid a curse it was on the Labour Party. He became its Leader. The curse proved fatal.

At the subsequent general election, hundreds of Labour MPs and candidates disappeared in mysterious circumstances. They included one of the most famous men in the country, Mr Tony Benn, though he was lately reported wandering in the area of Chesterfield, a town with which he had no previous connection. So the Curse of Foot, as well as precipitating his disappearance for months after the election, now seemed to have unhinged his judgement.

Despite these precedents, Mr Waldegrave remained calm. 'Lord Byron may have been against it,' he said, deciding to humour this strange, white-haired old man who had just laid a curse on him. But a select committee of the House had looked into the matter, he added, a select committee being the traditional means by which the House deals with curses. This committee, he said, had believed that the marbles had been legally acquired and had expressed the view that if the marbles had not been taken away by Lord Elgin they would have been more seriously damaged.

The matter of the marbles had originally been raised yesterday by a Tory, Sir David Price, of Eastleigh. Mr Waldegrave told him that the Greek government had now formally asked for the marbles' return.

In a magnificent supplementary question, Sir David demanded: 'Will the minister remind the Greek Government: "No Elgin, no marbles, and no British Museum, no marbles." The present level of sulphur dioxide in the Athenian atmosphere is as destructive of what remains of the Parthenon as Turkish gunfire, Turkish gunpowder and the vandalisers and marauders among the Greek people themselves,' all of which presumably meant that the Byron–Foot Curse was now laid on Sir David Price.

It was unclear whether Sir David expected Mr Waldegrave to say all that about the vandalisers and marauders among the Greek people directly to the face of the terrible Miss Melina Mercouri. If Mr Waldegrave is careful, he will get our Ambassador in Athens to say it to her.

In a reply to Sir David, Mr Waldegrave mused: 'Worst of all were those who converted it (the Parthenon) to a church in AD 450' – a shrewd bid for the pagan vote.

The Times

↤ 13 October 1984 ↦
The Brighton bomb

Thursday having been reached, the clock having passed eight in the evening, it was time once more for all of us whose business in Brighton was politics, whether practitioner or observer, to face the joys and rigours of a Conservative conference's final night of socialising.

The day's writing done, off then to the beloved Grand: the superb wedding cake of a hotel on the seafront. This is the building which for years has divided with the Blackpool Imperial all the folklore and intrigue of the British party conference. Here is the place to see and be seen: for journalists to demonstrate their acquaintance with rulers, and rulers, more selectively, to demonstrate theirs with journalists. All the waving, nodding, hullo'ing and bantering swirls amid a

Frank, aged 30, when he started work as a sketchwriter on the *Daily Telegraph*.

Left: Frank as a junior reporter, aged 18 covering the 'Wood Street Walk' – a yearly event through the East End of London – for the *Walthamstow Post*.

Right: Frank, Marcia Falkender, Jeremy Robson and Simon Hoggart at the joint launch in 1982 of Frank's book *Out of Order* and Simon's *On the House* drawn from his column in *Punch*.

The Queen and the Duke of Edinburgh visit the *Daily Telegraph* in February 1976. Behind the Queen is the proprietor Lord Hartwell; Bill Deedes, the editor is at his desk; Frank is perching on a table in the middle and just in front of him is Peter Eastwood, the managing editor.

Frank followed Roy Jenkins in the run up to the General Election of June 1983. Roy ended his battle bus tour of Britain by declaring that a move towards the Alliance was coming 'almost like a tidal wave'.

"SHALL WE HAVE A SHORT THIRD ON THE FARM PRICE REVIEW?" or 'Let me see — who wrote yesterday?'

A Nicholas Garland cartoon depicting a leader writer conference at the *Telegraph* in December 1974 where everyone was always trying to get out of writing the leader. From left to right: Eric Frances, Frank, John O'Sullivan; Colin Welch; Tom Lindsay; Maurice Green; Michael Harrison; Peter Utley; Reg Steed; Michael Hilton; Ian Colvin.

Paul Johnson, historian and former editor of the *New Statesman*, with Frank in Rome.

A dinner for Charles Moore, as he leaves the editorship of the *Daily Telegraph* in October 2003. The cast includes: Craig Brown, Boris Johnson, George Jones, Harry Mount, Daniel Johnson, Alice Thomson, Rachel Sylvester, Caroline Moore, Frank, John Keegan, A.N. Wilson, Sarah Sands, Kim Fletcher, Dean Godson, Bill Deedes and Michael Kallenbach.

A photograph taken to commemorate the bicentenary of the day journalists were officially admitted to the House of Commons. They were granted the back row of the old Public Gallery by the then Speaker Charles Abbot in May 1803. From Left to right: Simon Hoggart; Frank; Quentin Letts and Ben Macintyre.

Frank, Jessica Douglas-Home and Daniel Johnson at the wedding of Lucy Lambton and Peregrine Worsthorne, former editor of the *Sunday Telegraph*.

Left: The official portrait of Frank on becoming Editor of the *Spectator* in 1995.

Right: Puzzling over a joke with Quentin Letts at the office of the *Daily Telegraph* in the House of Commons in 2002.

Left: An alfresco lunch at Saltwood as a guest of Alan Clark. From left to right: Alan Clark; Richard Ryder; Frank; Tristan Garel-Jones and William Waldegrave.

Left: Taking tea on the terrace of renowned Italian composer Gian Carlo Menotti at the Spoleto Arts Festival in 2003. From left to right: Michael Kennedy, former Northern Editor of the *Daily Telegraph* and music critic; Frank; Virginia and Gian Carlo Menotti.

Right: At dinner in the gardens of Palazzo Campello in Spoleto with Nicolai Ghiaurov, the Bulgarian bass, after his performance with his wife, the Italian soprano Mirella Freni.

Left: Gian Carlo Menotti, composer, librettist and founder of the Festival of The Two Worlds in Spoleto and Charleston USA.

Left: Frank aged 6.

Right: Frank with his niece and nephew, Jenny and Kevin Collins of whom he was inordinately proud, Xmas 1982.

Left: Our wedding in December 1998 with Frank's sister Peggy on his left. It was the day of Peter Mandelson's first resignation, announced during lunch after the ceremony, at which most people dropped everything and dashed out.

Left: At Honor's wedding in 2004 Frank made a speech about the making of hip hop films, part of my son-in-law's profession. Even this subject failed to defeat Frank.

Above: Frank breaks from his work at the House of Commons to watch my son Jack's school team win the Devizes to Westminster canoeing race in 2002. Bernard Worth piped the team on as they raced under the bridges of London.

Above: At a fundraising dinner for Orlando Fraser's election campaign. From left to right: Harold Pinter; Tessa Keswick; Frank; Antonia Fraser and Orlando Fraser.

Right: Frank, always glued to a book even going down the Grand Canal in Venice in a water taxi, is guarding his holiday reading from a group of friends.

Left: Peter Oborne putting the finishing touches to his book in the garden of our house in Languedoc, amongst the vineyards.

Right: An operatic moment at lunch when historian Andrew Roberts stayed with us in France.

Left: John Casey, the Cambridge don, would visit every year.

Right: One of Napoleon's avenues of plane trees on the road to Pezenas, our nearest town in the Languedoc.

The Travel Club set up by Frank and others explored the cities of Europe on long weekends. The cast of friends, often journalists and historians fluctuated. Here from left to right in Venice are: Gina Thomas; John Casey; Robert Hardman; Petronella Wyatt; Frank; Andrew and Camilla Roberts and Santa and Simon Sebag Montefiore.

Frank at the wedding of historian Simon Sebag Montefiore talking to Aurora Dunluce.

Left: At The Royal Opera House, Covent Garden, Frank leads the pirates onto the stage in *Carmen.*

Right: The pirates try hard to pick up some musical cues from the pianist during rehearsal. Frank is in the middle.

Left: Frank described in his piece in *Opera* (magazine) in 1982, how Maria Callas clasped him to her bosom as a small boy in the opera *Norma.*

Left: More operatic moments with Camilla and Andrew Roberts in Venice.

Right: And still more in the garden of the doyenne of literary editors, Miriam Gross.

Left: Frank and I in Scotland in 2003.

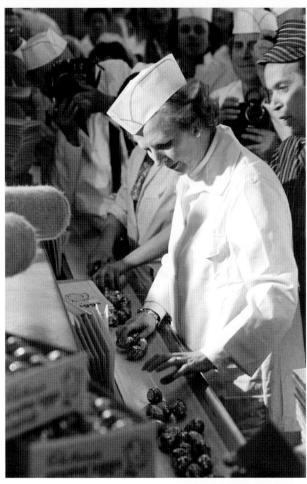

Left: In 1979 Frank wrote a funny account of Mrs Thatcher electioneering in a chocolate factory. This election broke new ground. It was the first ever to be televised.

Above: Passing by chance near a village called Montoire-sur-le-Loir, (a tributary of the Loire) we discovered that it was the same village where Hitler and Petain shook hands on the one and only occasion they ever met. Frank had to write about it.

Right: Peter Falk as Columbo, the Los Angeles TV detective, was a great favourite of Frank. In one of his articles he analyses the formula that Columbo invariably adopts to solve the murders.

Left: The Wolf's Lair, Hitler's wartime headquarters in Poland consisted of 80 buildings including a cinema, a railway station and a sauna. It accommodated up to 2000 people. The conference room in this photo was destroyed by Stauffenberg's bomb. We visited the ruins in 2004, an account of which is included.

Right: Saddam Hussein is toppled and Baghdad falls in April 2003. Frank describes the House of Commons' reaction to this momentous news.

'White-haired, courtly, still with his wits about him, though occasionally a little forgetful, this was no ordinary leader of the Labour Party. This was Mr Michael Foot.'

throng of the constituency humble, of unknown backbenchers, PR men, pretty and treacherous girls from gossip columns out to lure the mighty into indiscretion.

Treading warily through the crowd, eyes ever watchful for bores, I felt a shove at the shoulder and turned to find with delight that the shover was Norman Tebbit. It so happened that I had just finished writing about his success on the platform that day. Bantering ensued. He mocked me from out of a ring of what looked like admirers from the constituencies. Perhaps his wife was at his side. I cannot remember. What he said I soon forgot. I was not to know that the outside world would want to learn of his every word and act this evening.

I answered back something suitably fatuous about his speech having been deplorably elevated in tone and about how he might turn out to have been a wet all along; he threw his head back with a scoff, and wished me a convivial night out. He knew he had enjoyed a deserved success that day. At ease among his admirers, glass in hand, he was enjoying what, for any politician of his ambition, was a rare moment of serenity before further struggle.

Off then to something called the Starlight Room of the rather less-than-beautiful Metropole next door. At the table in front of us, Mr Edward du Cann was giving a dinner party which included Sir Robin Day and Mr John Wakeham, the Chief Whip, and his wife Roberta, she in the last hours of her life, he within hours of his ordeal under the rubble. At the table behind us, presided Mr John Gummer, Chairman of the Conservative Party, and his wife Penelope. The various gatherings merged as they got up to leave.

On through the crowd. The Tebbit circle disappeared behind me. Soon we were all plunged into the nightly conference ritual of the rendezvous for dinner.

There was much jostling. A slender young woman called Alison Ward from the Gummers' table came over to say that what we all had to decide was whether to go to the conference ball or to drink champagne with Lord McAlpine, Treasurer of the Conservative Party: a host of fabled generosity whose suite in the Grand was a few windows from where the bomb was to do its work.

We all agreed that politics was full of these terrible dilemmas. Miss Ward had been one of Mrs Thatcher's secretaries. Since the general election she had had a job which placed her still more at the centre of things: special assistant to Mr Wakeham. We agreed, that after the punishing course that was the Young Conservatives' Ball the night before, Lord McAlpine's hospitality was irresistible.

Back to the Grand. Lord McAlpine dispensed champagne. Mr Denis Thatcher arrived in evening dress. Just been to the Conference Ball with the PM, he explained. Very noisy band, difficult to dance. PM back working on her speech. It was now well past midnight.

Mr Gordon Reece, special adviser to the Prime Minister, a hugely genial man quoted with working many wonders on her mastery of television, reported that work on the speech was still going on.

Mr Wakeham was there. So too were various magnificoes from the mysterious National Union of Conservative Associations. Mr Thatcher, in expansive mood, delivered strong views on the television licence. Eventually, it was time to return to Wheelers Hotel on the seafront, a few hundred yards from the Grand, and sleep the sleep of the well victualled.

A friend and I came upon Sir Anthony Berry, MP for Southgate, returning his two small dogs from a walk, and rejoining his wife in their room off the Grand's third-floor landing. 'We must have lunch soon,' he said. His wife was to survive; he was not.

After some indeterminate period of slumber, the telephone rang. The woman at the switchboard said I might like to know that a bomb had just gone off in the Grand. I had heard nothing. Was it serious? Surely not; I dozed for five minutes. Sirens sounded outside. I pulled on some clothes and went downstairs where a youth was sobbing hysterically face-down on the reception counter, repeating that it was terrible.

My friend Alan Watkins of the *Observer* and I reached the back door of the Grand at the precise moment at which a black Jaguar swept out containing the Prime Minister. It was 3.21am.

Mr Peter Morrison, Undersecretary of Employment, suddenly appeared on the pavement in his shirtsleeves. He had been fast asleep he said, after working on his boxes 'like a good boy'. Then the bells went off. Bloody Young Conservatives playing a boring prank, he had assumed. Then there were people banging on his door and telling him to come out, and here he was. Must have been a fire. 'Did you hear the bomb?' I asked him. 'What bomb?'

'I think, dear boy, that I know more about this crisis than you do,' I remember telling him. He expressed appropriate astonishment at news of a bomb.

Round to the front of the hotel, or as near to it as we could get, which was behind police cordons 50 yards away. Lord Gowrie could be seen bringing deck chairs up from the beach into which he assisted various, extremely calm Conservative ladies. Sir Keith Joseph was sighted wearing an immaculately tied dressing gown from which protruded rather chic, cream pyjama legs – the whole effect resembling Sir Noel Coward at his most characteristic.

Sir Keith sat on an upturned red dispatch box on the promenade. Similarly seated, nearby, was the Solicitor-General, Sir Patrick Mayhew, fully suited. A bright moon hung in a dark blue sky on a night exceptionally warm for the time of the year. A beautiful light was thus cast over the terrifying scene of a tall stretch of the Grand's façade collapsed like Ronan Point.

It was hours before we learned how many people had been injured or how serious it all was. But many good friends could be seen safe on the promenade in diverse forms of nightwear. Despite the terrible look of the Grand, a lot of us wanted to assume the best. We did not know that, during all these hours, firemen were working to free Mr Tebbit and Mr Wakeham, and that Mrs Wakeham was dying. The neighbouring Metropole took in the refugees. A Tory lady could be heard giving some magnificent advice to another: 'We'll ring up the managing director of Marks and Spencer, get him to open early so we can all get kitted up properly for the conference.' And, indeed, at daybreak, the incomparable Lord McAlpine had arranged just that.

He was safe, though forced to flee the hotel without his Garrick Club tie which, for some reason, he regards as his only correct neckwear. He insisted on borrowing a journalist's Garrick Club tie for the remainder of the day. Sir Robin Day had been forced to abandon in the Grand all his clothes, his spectacles and all his supplies of bow ties. What the nation would want to know, I remember musing, was (1) whether he was safe and (2) what he wore in bed. The answer to the first was, yes, and to the second, paisley pyjamas under a sky blue dressing grown with dark stripes.

At 6:30 the throng gathered around the Metropole's television sets. Never had BBC breakfast television had such an audience. On to the screen came horrifying images accompanied by a superbly lucid report by a BBC political reporter, John Harrison, in a firm voice free from hysteria which revealed to most of us the horror of the event for the first time.

With the dawn came a realisation of the awesome nature of the crime. Attempts had been made to murder the rulers of a free people. We had all been close to a great and terrible thing.

The Times

On the night of the Brighton bomb, my wife and I were staying in the fateful Grand Hotel as I was a member of the Cabinet. I was also the most junior member so we slept at the back and were safe. Hobbling about outside, dazed and anxious, we ran into Frank and spent the rest of that beautiful and dreadful dawn with him. After a while we went to his hotel room as he needed to scribble then file his copy. I had run into Keith Joseph earlier and supplied the Noel Coward joke. The piece is vintage Frank as it understands how human life combines comedy and tragedy simultaneously, in the way of a Mozart opera.

Grey Gowrie

Chapter 10

October 1986–
March 1987

⊰ 8 October 1986 ⊱
**Mrs T., it is rumoured, falls into a manhole.
The wets and the dries plot.**

The afternoon session of the Conservative Party conference was getting smoothly under way yesterday when word filtered into the hall that the Prime Minister, while returning from a lunchtime meeting, had turned to wave to the crowd, and fallen down a manhole.

The dries thought it outrageous that, amid all this security, someone had left a manhole uncovered. The wets thought it vital that, with the woman safely gone at last, now was the time to cover the hole. But what both sides needed, in these crucial minutes after the first reports of the incident, was hard information as to what had really happened. Otherwise, people might do things which would look embarrassing if Mrs Thatcher were to climb back up.

Zealous Thatcherites – motivated either by genuine patriotism or fear of what the fall of the regime would mean for them personally – hurried about the hall, doubtless assuring anyone who would listen that Mrs Thatcher had survived, and would be broadcasting to the nation as soon as possible.

They assured us that this deed was the work of a defeatist group of Cabinet Ministers and other discredited Privy Councillors who were wholly unrepresentative of our nation and our party. Rather than defend British women and children against atheistic Kinnockism at the general election, they were prepared to revolt against the leader and try to make a separate peace.

The names of those responsible, and of their defendants, would be ever accursed, and made synonymous with treason. But one thing was certain. The minister, and former ministers, responsible for this outrage would be hunted down and handed over to the Whips.

But who were the perpetrators? Prior? On Monday night, there had been a publisher's party in London, attended by journalists and other freeloaders, in connection with his disloyal memoirs. The trouble with that theory was that, at the time Mrs Thatcher neared the fateful manhole yesterday lunchtime, the party would still have been going on. Had he been involved, Mr Prior would surely have been seizing the radio station or doing something similarly useful.

Heath? He had recently moved into a new house in Salisbury, not far inland from Bournemouth, where he is said to be giving dinner parties this week for anti-Thatcherites ferried in from the conference resort. Suspicious.

Pym? No one had heard of him for months. Interesting.

Gilmour? He made some anti-regime pronouncements in the *New Statesman*. Tories don't read the *New Statesman*. Exactly. But the crucial thing was that the plot had failed. Thatcherism had been saved.

Some of the wets seemed to be equally active in the hall. Clearly, they were assuring the wavering rank-and-file that the dries were bluffing, and that the Thatcher regime had indeed fallen. Now was the time for anti-Thatcherites to proclaim a Government of National Reconciliation and Renewal.

Despite the tense situation, and the absence of any definite news, Mr Kenneth Baker went ahead with his planned speech in reply to the debate on education. Mr Baker has long been thought of as a wet candidate for the leadership should Mrs Thatcher ever fall down a manhole.

But, assuming that such an event was long delayed, he had planned to make a dry speech. Just his luck to be dry at the very moment of the wets' triumph. But it was no time to take chances. He made the speech as he had planned it, although – in the event of a Wet Restoration – he could always draw attention to the absence in the speech of any promise to bring back corporal punishment to our schools, or indeed capital punishment.

Eventually, we learnt that Mrs Thatcher had merely tripped on the manhole. She was in the best of health. The wets, however, were not.

The Times

A rumour had swept through the feverish atmosphere of the conference that Margaret had had an accident. It was of course false but Frank couldn't let the moment pass without bringing out the wets' 'joy' and the dries' 'anxiety'. The 1986 conference was the launch pad for the 1987 election and Norman Tebbit, the Chairman, had instructed all ministers to come up with specific promises and proposals. I announced City Technology Colleges which became Blair's Academies. The Tory wets didn't like them but the electorate did.

Kenneth Baker

⇥ 13 November 1986 ⇤
The State Opening of Parliament – or is it
the State Opening of Dimbleby?

The morning of the State Opening of Parliament seemed a good time to read a mischievous-sounding book, now in paperback, called *The Invention of Tradition*.

This turned out to be a set of essays arguing in effect that most British traditions, such as these royal ceremonies, are not hundreds of years old, but were invented – in historical terms – only the other day. One of the book's editors is the Marxist, Professor Eric Hobsbawm. He often gets himself written up as an adviser to Mr Kinnock, although that too may be a recent invention. He seems to think that European monarchies, including ours, were invented some time between 1870 and 1914. This theory is applied to ours in a fine essay by the less politically contentious figure of Mr David Cannadine, a Cambridge don. He says that our royal ceremonial is now so good that we have been able to persuade ourselves that it always has been. But as recently as 1861, the third Marquess of Salisbury – after watching Victoria open Parliament – wrote that it was not the sort of thing we were good at. Some 'malignant spell' always 'inserts some feature which makes them all ridiculous'.

It was only much later that we became good at it. Mr Cannadine also points out that not all of it is particularly old. 'Old ceremonies have adapted and new rituals invented,' he says. He also quotes approvingly a biographer of the late Richard Dimbleby, who said 'that great man did more than any other individual to secure the position of the monarch in the affections of British people'.

Good though the book is, we of the broad masses did not need dons to tell us that. Those of us of a certain age derive all our traditions from the late Mr Dimbleby. That is why even those of us with access to Parliament always watch the State Opening on television. And so yesterday morning we sat rapt before the ancient ceremony which goes back to 1958, which was when it was first televised. The familiar symbols were paraded before us: the Sword of State, the Cap of Maintenance, and above all, on the BBC, the great Crown Headphones handed down by Dimbleby to his eldest son, David, who conducted the Commentary of State as he has done since time immemorial, or since about 1975. Not only is the ceremony old, or young as the case may be, it is traditionally incomprehensible, and long may it remain so. 'The Cap of Maintenance,' said Mr Dimbleby, 'carried by Lord Belstead.' The Crown. The Sword of State. Symbols of authority, escorted by watermen? Did their union use intimidation to keep these manning levels? Wisely Mr Dimbleby did not go into the matter.

We switched to the other channel to check up on the parvenu Sir Alastair Burnet. 'The great sapphire, said to be worn in a ring by Edward the Confessor . . .' A likely tale! The upstart Sir Alastair was blatantly competing with the House of Dimbleby, which had ruled this country well since the royal funeral of 1936. But then, while explaining the background to some of the regalia, he began to discuss the origins of the Cap of Maintenance, something every Dimbleby is brought up never to do. 'The Cap of Maintenance is something else again,' he said, 'and everybody takes their pick.'

We immediately switched channels in protest. It was under a Dimbleby that yesterday we watched once more such rightly unexplained figures as 'the Duke of Norfolk, who is Earl Marshal of England and the Chief Butler of England' in which latter capacity he may, for all we know, have to hand round the After Eights of State at grand functions in Dimbleby House.

There was also Lord Whitelaw, who has just been made chairman of the Cabinet committee on AIDS and who was happily without the Great Condom of State – although it could come to that in the end, since all rituals are constantly being invented, as that don said.

But Mr Dimbleby, like all constitutional rulers, has to take account of a certain amount of modern scepticism. At one stage, he allowed himself to muse: 'As with all this ceremonial, nobody quite knows. Did Edward the Confessor really wear that ring?' Or does it date from Alastair the Commentator? Some of us don't wish to know.

The Times

Of course Frank had us bang to rights. There are parts of the ceremonial that no one understands so everyone just makes it up. Not just broadcasters but the experts in the Houses of Parliament too, who can never agree. The official guide to the House of Lords says one thing, the clerks and librarians another. The Earl Marshal has his views. Maybe the Queen knows what is going on.

The Cap of Maintenance was always a special pleasure: 'given to Henry VII by the Pope' it is said. Carried on a staff and called 'the squirrel on a stick'. Worn under the Crown to stop it scratching. No one knows.

Frank Johnson on the State Opening ended up being part of the ritual himself. I used to relish the challenge each year to introduce some new arcane detail knowing that he would pick it up next day. How about this: the wives of peers are only at the State Opening because a Royal Commission on ceremonial, appointed after Queen Victoria's death, decided they were 'decorative'. You would not get away with that today. Or rather, you would, because Frank is not around any more.

David Dimbleby

⊰ 11 March 1987 ⊱
Edwina Currie conducts a flirtation at the Dispatch Box

In this sketch, Edwina Currie, MP for South Derbyshire, is
Undersecretary of State for Health. In 1988, having sparked outrage
amongst egg producers and farmers by stating that most eggs in the
UK had salmonella, she was forced to resign.

Mr Frank Haynes (Lab. Ashfield), a former railwayman and coalminer, yesterday prefaced a question to Mrs Edwina Currie, the Undersecretary of State for Health and Social Security, by asking: 'Is the Honourable Lady aware how attractive she looks today?'

Mr Haynes' remark will be seen in the context of the campaign by Mr Kinnock and the party Establishment to dissociate themselves from the gays, lesbians and militant feminists who are thought to be damaging the party in the eyes of its traditional supporters. The aim is to convince voters that the extremists are not typical, and that Labour remains the party of ordinary, decent sexists. The answer to the question of whether Mrs Currie was aware how attractive she looked yesterday was of course: yes. The rituals of courtship prevented such an answer. So she contented herself with raising a vast peal of laughter from both sides of the House by saying of Mr Haynes: 'I think he looks pretty cute today too.' Mr Haynes, aged 60, was wearing a grey suit and matching accessories. It was heartening that Mr Haynes and Mrs Currie were able to find one another and snatch a moment of old-fashioned, pre-AIDS romance, amid a Social Services Question Time in which the major issue was the connection between AIDS and homosexuality. Mr Haynes and Mrs Currie were the only couple referred to all afternoon who were of the opposite sex from one another.

Mr John Townend (Con. Bridlington) and Mr Patrick Nicholls (Con. Teignbridge) suggested that the Government had minimised the extent to which the spread of AIDS had mainly come from homosexuals. Mr Fowler assured the House that the next phase of the Government's anti-AIDS advertising campaign would be directed at drug abusers and homosexuals. This was welcomed in many parts of the Chamber, since the present phase of the campaign seems to be directed at stonemasons, do-it-yourself electric drill users, and Arctic explorers.

Mrs Currie was not involved in any of the questions about AIDS. But she has a tendency to dominate Social Services Question Time. Labour members drag her name in at the slightest opportunity because they make the probably erroneous assumption that she is unpopular in the country. The progressive classes made the same mistake about Alf Garnett.

Yesterday, Mr David Winnick, (Lab. Walsall North) asked Mr Fowler whether the Prime Minister had a grudge against him and wanted 'to punish him by putting such a publicity-crazed person into the Department of Health and Social Security'.

Without hesitation Mr Fowler replied that a successful politician such as Mrs Currie says 'what everybody is thinking. While unsuccessful ones like Mr Winnick say what nobody is thinking, nor would think.' (Much laughter, including from Mr Winnick.)

Mr Fowler reeled that off so unhesitatingly because it is perhaps from the standard reply prepared by his Ministry to be sent to people who submit rude letters about Mrs Currie. A whole floor in the Ministry is probably devoted to this important work.

The Times

⊰ 13 March 1987 ⊱
The election of the Chancellor of Oxford University
and the direction of the High Table camembert

Mr Peter Walker, the Secretary for Energy, yesterday consented to the Sizewell B nuclear power station. He was denounced by those Labour Members who traditionally receive the votes of the coalminers.

Mr Richard Luce, the Minister for the Arts, defended the level of spending on the arts. He was denounced by the Labour Members who traditionally receive the votes of the museum directors, subsidised poets, post-modern choreographers, regional opera administrators, and Sir Peter Hall: workers in an old industry who had so often held the nation to ransom in the past, but who have been bravely resisted by Mrs Thatcher.

Election fever, then, was all about us. Less than 60 miles to the north, Oxford was already voting. A new Chancellor was being chosen – one rarer than any from an Exchequer or a Duchy.

Oxford had until Saturday afternoon to make a choice which could affect the direction of British politics, and certainly the direction of many a High Table camembert. Oxford is fortunate to have a choice between two such men. Both have eaten for Britain in Europe. For the voters, it is a difficult decision.

One of the candidates, Mr Roy Jenkins, had last been seen in the House the previous afternoon. In his unconvincing disguise as Member for Glasgow, Hillhead, he had appeared at Scottish questions, perhaps in a last-minute bid to clinch the ethnic vote. Trevor-Roper, and Dacre of Glanton, are said to be Border country names, or at least Northumberland. But both are reported to be voting for Mr Edward Heath.

Tactical voting is what this election is about. For the winner, the tactical eating will come later. Between yesterday and Saturday, crude electoral considerations dominate. In the bruising campaign, Mr Jenkins has emerged as the Deirdre Woods of moderation – the candidate of the 'loony centre'. Half the stories in the tabloids about his moderation are exaggerated or simply made up. But the tabloids are the only papers which most Oxford MAs read on the subject of politics. Most of the electorate is probably convinced that he is a raving centrist. So the question is: who should the ordinary, decent extremists vote for?

Here, the Thatcherites may have made what could be a great mistake. They – or at least Mr Norman Tebbit – are reported to be urging their people to vote for Mr Edward Heath. In the Commons, Mr Heath sits in the first seat below the gangway – motionless, staring ahead, unsmiling. When he speaks, it is often to lecture about the Third World. A combination of motionlessness, no laughs, and the Third World amounts to grim company at High Table. From the seat below the gangway, Mr Heath has kept all three up since 1975. He could stay as long at High Table.

By urging Tories to vote for Mr Heath rather than Lord Blake (the other candidate who is a Tory) Mr Tebbit could be condemning generations of dons and undergraduates to the dreaded Chancellor's Silence – punctuated by gruff observations about Mexican debt, what it was like to negotiate with Pompidou on sterling as a reserve currency, and 'that woman'. But if the MAs take Mr Tebbit's advice, so be it.

This seemed to be the view of most of the Commons as they waited for the results. As well as the above-mentioned nuclear power, and the arts, members whiled away the time before the Oxford result by studying the climactic written answer by the Leader of the House, Mr John Biffen, on Cabgate. This was the scandal, which came to light last week, involving an attempt by the clandestine accommodation sub-committee, a tiny all-party group of MPs, to ban non-MPs and non-peers from queuing for taxis at the Members' Entrance. Since the ban would have excluded journalists from the queue, it was seen as an attempt by queuers from the legislature to bypass a free press.

Mr Biffen's written answer was a triumph for the egalitarian Mr Eric Heffer (Lab. Liverpool, Walton) who revealed the scandal. Mr Biffen said the scheme had been postponed for three months. He distanced himself by implying that it all happened on the initiative of the sub-committee. With this written answer to the nation, the Biffen leadership pledged itself to a new beginning. Let us hope it is not too late.

The Times

Chapter 11

1990–1999

In 1988 Frank left The Times *and returned to the Telegraph Group. He became associate and then deputy editor on the* Sunday Telegraph *under the editorship of Peregrine Worsthorne and continued as deputy when Charles Moore was made editor. In 1995, he was appointed editor of the* Spectator *where he remained until 1999. During this period, when not editing, he was writing longer commentary pieces rather than sketches.*

Mrs Thatcher resigned in 1990 and John Major, elected Leader of the Tories, became Prime Minister. In the general election of 1992 the Conservatives won more votes than they had ever done before.

⊰ **20 September 1992** ⊱
Out of the ERM: Trusty Tebbit, Mistress Hogg and Lamont pleading to be spared the block

Britain had joined the ERM – the precursor to the euro – on 5 October 1990, when John Major was Chancellor of the Exchequer. By the summer of 1992 the country was in the grip of a severe recession with rising unemployment and high interest rates. The pound was also coming under pressure on the foreign exchange markets. On 16 September, amid scenes of panic and chaos, the Chancellor, Norman Lamont, announced that the pound was leaving the ERM. This day quickly became known as 'Black Wednesday', though in fact it marked the beginning of economic recovery, and was soon described as 'White Wednesday' by critics of the ERM.

As with the Kennedy assassination cliché, and with Mrs Thatcher's resignation, we all seem likely to remember where we were when we heard that we had left the ERM. I like to think that, on these exceptional occasions, we are all doing things with which we are especially associated, or associate ourselves. Some famous men, clad in the strip of their favourite football team, were safely with their mistresses. Some famous mistresses were lucratively with their public relations advisers. I was at the opera.

It was the first night of the English National's new production of *The Force of Destiny*. We must have floated the pound at around the moment when the tenor came through the window to elope with the soprano just before accidentally shooting dead her father and making her brother follow him wherever he went – the tenor, that is – for purposes of revenge, eventually tracking him down to a monastery in a cave near where, unknown to either the tenor or the brother, the soprano had also taken refuge, eventually dying, although not before receiving a knock on the door from the tenor seeking help after having killed the brother in a duel. Immersed in this perfectly believable story, hardly anyone in the theatre was aware of the implausible tale being enacted outside.

Home too late for *Newsnight*, I fell asleep unaware that I had become one of a relatively small number of Britons who had pronounced against membership of the ERM from the start – as opposed to just the last few weeks or months when it became obvious that it had gone wrong – and had been proved right.

Around midnight, the telephone awoke me.

It was a Thatcherite friend now in America. 'What do you think's going to happen now, then, eh?' he inquired.

'Well,' I dozed, 'I think they're going to have to come out of the ERM.'

'They already have,' he informed me. There followed a period of mutual gloating lasting no more than about three-quarters of an hour. We should never trust anyone who says they do not gloat, any more than we should trust anyone who says they do not gossip. It is a denial of nature. We then discussed how ministers would go about blaming it all on Lady Thatcher.

As it happened, they blamed it on the Germans. Had they realised it, that was another confession of failure. One of the complaints against

Lady Thatcher at the time of her fall was that she did not get on with the Germans. Almost Mr Major's first act, on becoming Prime Minister nearly two years ago, was to fly to Bonn to get on well with Herr Kohl. Now, at first disaster, he plays the anti-German card.

It was an example of how those who want to be 'at the heart of Europe' are not automatically better Europeans than the rest of us. I admire the Germans. In a faltering, blundering way, I have made some efforts to appreciate their culture, more so, I suspect, than Mr Major has. When it is of no cost to himself, Mr Major just wants the Germans to like him, just as, when it is of no cost to himself, he wants everyone to like him. To him, the Germans are in the same category as a deputation of gays, dropping in at Number 10, under the leadership of Sir Ian McKellen – another chance to show that he is 'nicer' than his predecessor.

Admiring the Germans, and wanting to understand their civilisation, does not mean that one should also sign up for a Europe of which they are the largest part. Such a Europe would be bad for them, as well as for us. Everything that goes wrong will be blamed on them, as Mr Major and Mr Lamont are trying to do now.

I consider myself a better European than either of that pair. I would not be so shameless as to blame Germany for what happened last week. The Germans are not responsible for our exchange rate or for the failings of our economy.

Not that Lady Thatcher escaped all censure. 'Just remember who was Prime Minister when we went into the ERM,' the creeps have been muttering since Wednesday night. Given the state she was in at the time, it was like saying that Mr Gorbachev should accept collective responsibility for the coup against him. But, in a way, it was a tribute to the politician whom every time-serving Tory also insists is 'finished' and 'totally discredited'.

It is as if they fear Lady Thatcher, like William of Orange at Torbay, landing at Clacton, on the shore of the county most identified with her cause. The Thatcherite barons ride to greet her. Lord Tebbit, hot-foot from Epping, assures her that all Essex is rallying to her side. 'What news from London, trusty Tebbit?' 'My Lady, the ministerial curs have fled the ERM. They inflame the rabble 'gainst the Teuton. Major a virtual recluse. Lamont pleading to be spared the block. Mistress Hogg still insisting that the parity was the right one, just as she wrote in 1990 when employed by the *Daily Telegraph* sheet. How they cower before the repossessed of Basildon.' 'And the jackal Heseltine?' 'He bides his time, my Lady. 'Tis said he seeks an alliance with us.'

A familiar whiff of Brylcreem scents the morning air. Enter Lord Parkinson.

All advance on London. The trouble is that Mr Major would say he looked forward to working with them.

Sunday Telegraph

⊰ 27 September 1992 ⊱
John Major's Government of Pals

This included Norman Lamont, Richard Ryder, Tristan Garel-Jones and David Mellor, Secretary of State in the Department of National Heritage or, as the press preferred, 'Minister of Fun'.

Since no one else is likely to do so on this column's behalf, the column hereby claims copyright for the theory that this is a Government of Pals.

Two Sundays ago it was argued here that in 1990 a group of pals made one of their number, Mr Major, Prime Minister. He in turn gave them jobs.

One pal, Mr Richard Ryder, was made Chief Whip; another, Mr Garel-Jones, Minister of State at the Foreign Office; another, Mr Lamont, Chancellor. Yet another, Mr Mellor, became the Secretary With the Silly Title. Mr Major became primus inter pals.

None of this was said too censoriously. If I were told to look for a new job, I would expect my pals to rally round and find me one. But it was also argued here when the pals got into difficulties, either individually, as in the case of Mr Mellor, or collectively, as in the case of the pals' adhesion to too high an exchange rate, their instinct was to 'tough it out' together, as pals should. This was not good for the country.

Over the past week or so Mr Alan Watkins, the *Observer*'s political columnist, Mr Michael White, the *Guardian*'s political editor, and

Mr Paul Johnson in the *Daily Mail* have all called this a 'pals' Government – sometimes varying it to 'chums'.

But at the moment of its general acceptance, the theory seems to have been undermined by events. One of the pals has been, as the grim, fashionable phrase has it, thrown off the sled. Or he threw himself off – disclosing a hitherto unnoticed capacity for self-sacrifice in the interest of others. Or he fell off, and – amid the storm, ice and driving snow – the other pals did not notice until it was too late.

'Where's Dave?' one of them might have asked, several miles on.

'Dunno. Isn't he still aboard? Christ! He must have gone over the side. What the hell are you doing now, John?'

'I'm trying to turn this bloody sled round. Presumably, you want us to go back and find him, don't you, Richard?'

'Of course not. There are wild animals out there. The executive of the '22 would have eaten him by now. We've got to get out of this blizzard before we all start falling off. As it is, Norman's looking none too good. Do y'wanna get us all chewed up? Just get us all to Brighton in one piece by the second week in October.'

Sadly, the Prime Minister would have resumed the sled's course, perhaps muttering to himself: 'Sorry, Dave.' That night, over cocoa at base camp, the pals would have brooded: 'Bloody good bloke, Dave. Miss him already.'

However it happened, Mr Mellor is supposed to be discussing the economy. But, in the bars and the smoking room, they were also discussing Mr Mellor. He went before the 1922 executive had a chance to make him. So, the pals were beaten by the suits. It is the first blow to pal power since pallyness became the ruling ideology of our country on the fall of Mrs Thatcher.

But Mr Lamont has so far survived, and he is one of the pals. Mr Lamont, however, survives because there is a Government split, and Mr Lamont has taken the anti-ERM side – the one backed by majority back bench opinion. Mr Major does not know whose side to take. On the Tory back benches there is, therefore, more admiration for Mr Lamont at the moment than for the Prime Minister. Also, Mr Lamont made a brilliant speech in the emergency debate, and Mr Major did not.

Sunday Telegraph

⊰ 15 September 1994 ⊱
A Tory vote, the vote that dare
not speak its name

Only 56 per cent of voters who told the latest *Daily Telegraph* Gallup poll that they would vote Conservative at a general election said that they would be prepared to admit it to a friend or colleague. This finding poignantly draws attention to the twilight world of the Tory voter.

Their plight is reminiscent of the secret lives which certain minorities were forced to lead before the 1960s liberal reforms. How do they live? What sort of jobs do they have? Is it true that some even marry and have children?

How do they meet one another? In private clubs? (Gossip has it that there are such places, and that they have suggestive names such as 'the Carlton', and even 'Pratt's'.)

And at the risk of sounding crude, when they get together, what do they actually do? In the bad old days, members of those earlier minorities, when brave enough to be interviewed on television, used to have their faces blacked out.

In fact, I am in a position to offer a certain amount of information. I do not wish to sound an exhibitionist, but I am prepared to admit that I am a Conservative voter. I first realised it at school. I felt somehow different from the other boys.

It was in the 1950s. Labour had not long ceased to be in government, and were still an impressive Opposition. So the other boys drooled over pictures of, say, Aneurin Bevan. But I was strangely attracted to, say, Selwyn Lloyd.

Occasionally, another boy would admit to me that he had the same feelings. But it was only when I left school that I realised that there were plenty of other men like me.

But it is hard for us at the moment. There is tremendous pressure on us to behave in accordance with a particular bourgeois stereotype (Tony Blair).

But society tried to force us to conform at the last general election. Then, many of us told pollsters that we would vote Labour, but in the privacy of the polling booth – as next time – we still cast the vote that dare not speak its name.

Daily Telegraph

-ᵊ **12 December 1998** ᵇ-
The Brown–Mandelson dispute
is of immemorial antiquity

Violence flared again this week between Gordon Brown and Peter Mandelson. They reportedly clashed over Post Office privatisation. But the subject of the dispute does not matter. All that matters is the dispute. Yesterday, as tension rose, it was reported that Tony Blair had ordered Mr Brown and Mr Mandelson to stop the violence and resolve their differences peacefully.

This was another worrying example of the Prime Minister's ignorance of history. He should stick to solving Northern Ireland or the Arab-Israeli dispute. The Brown-Mandelson dispute is of immemorial antiquity.

All who have studied the conflict – in the universities, at Chatham House, in the US State Department, the Foreign Office and the Quai d'Orsay – agree that Mr Mandelson and Mr Brown once lived peacefully side by side, in the way that anti-Zionists say that Arabs and Jews lived peacefully together in the Holy Land before the threat of an Israeli state.

They fell out only after Mr Mandelson decided to support Mr Blair, and not Mr Brown, as Labour Leader. (I speak as someone who came up through the Brown-Mandelson Department at the *Spectator*.)

Much of the low-level violence is by stone-throwing youths described as Mr Mandelson's 'political advisers'. They seek to tempt Mr Brown into over-reaction, and thus get on to the world's television screens.

But both sides also have sophisticated weaponry: mobile phones, faxes, pagers. These sometimes hit the innocent. I myself have occasionally been struck on the head by Mr Mandelson's complaints about articles that might make him look less dignified or powerful than Mr Brown.

Mr Blair has embarked on a peace process. That may work with Benjamin Netanyahu and Yasser Arafat, or with David Trimble and Gerry Adams, but with Mr Brown and Mr Mandelson, the world is confronted with two leaders who hate each other.

My own solution is, I am unashamed to say, the saloon bar one: I am now in favour of British withdrawal. I say, a plague on both their pagers. I do not see why British taxpayers should have to foot the bill for this intractable struggle. The Department of Trade and Industry's telephone bill, for all those calls to journalists and editors – trying to outspin Mr Brown – must run into millions.

There is talk of a Christmas ceasefire. Some idealists say that, given a modicum of goodwill on both sides, it could become permanent.

Ha! Where do such woolly liberals think they are? Northern Ireland? They know not of the past – the past which, such is the human condition, mankind is forever condemned to repeat.

Daily Telegraph

⊰ 20 November 1999 ⊱
An encounter with Mr Al Fayed at Harrods
and his gift of a teddy bear

I met Mr Mohamed Al Fayed just once. I was entertained by him: entertained in both senses of the word. It was at a time when he was being much mentioned in these pages by several regular contributors. The mentions were all unfavourable. His famous public-relations man, Mr Cole, who has now left his service, would usually be the one who replied in Letters to the Editor, but on a couple of occasions a letter arrived signed by Mr Al Fayed himself. (I shall persist in including the 'Al' in his name. I realise that many, including Mr Hamilton and his lawyers, deny his right to it, arguing that it is a Middle Eastern title which has to be bestowed by some higher authority, or inherited, and that he is entitled to it on neither account. But I believe in addressing people as they wish to be addressed. He could call himself King Fayed for all I care. I might draw the line at Duke Fayed, but then the principle would be no different – as in Duke Ellington.)

We at the *Spectator* were especially delighted when the letters bore Mr Al Fayed's signature. It is no disrespect to Mr Cole's vast collected letters on his behalf to say that Mr Al Fayed writing, or at least signing personally, was an exceptional attraction from our point of view. After we printed a few, I wrote to Mr Al Fayed, to say that he had provided us with so much lovely, free material that the least we could do was ask him to lunch at the *Spectator*. He replied that he would be delighted to have lunch with me but would rather it to be in the restaurant at Harrods. He added that the meal would, of course be Egyptian, or Maghrebian, with much couscous. But he quickly explained one sentence later that he was only joking and that I would be offered the roast beef of old England.

Someone with knowledge of him explained that he declined our offer of lunch on the grounds that he wanted to avoid being poisoned. I replied that our food was not that bad. Indeed, most of our guests admired it. No, really poisoned, it was further explained. He thinks that there are a lot of powerful people out there trying to poison him. I was, of course, flattered. It is always agreeable to be thought powerful.

The lunch duly took place at Harrods: Mr Al Fayed, Mr Cole and me. Very early in the conversation he dismissed a prominent British politician as a 'fuckhead'. I think it was the then Prime Minister, Mr Major. But Mr Howard, the then Home Secretary, was soon called a 'fuckhead' too. So were successive Chancellors of the Exchequer and Foreign Secretaries. Eventually even Lady Thatcher qualified. Then we got on to journalists. Quite a few of us were also 'fuckheads'. The worrying thought crossed my mind: at his next lunch, will I be one too?

After a while, I interrupted to say that, admiring though I was of his command of English, I thought the word he must really have in mind was 'dickhead' not 'fuckhead'.

'So sorry, thank you,' he replied with impeccable courtesy, capping one side of his head with the palm of one hand. 'Thanks for correcting me.' His tone was as if I had put him right about a point of grammar or a line of English poetry: 'A host of golden *daffodils*, Mr Al Fayed, not chrysanthemums.'

I then mused to him that the term of abuse in question, 'dickhead', was of relatively recent usage. I had first heard it only about a decade before, from the lips of the young. In due course, I had heard Mr Tony Banks, a Labour politician who likes us to think that he has a command of the demotic, use it in the Commons.

'Really!' said Mr Al Fayed in a scholarly tone. It was clear that Mr Al Fayed also liked to keep up with the demotic, and I had contributed to his impressive command of this branch of our language. When we parted, he gave me a Harrods teddy bear. Back in the office, colleagues debated whether, in order to save me from myself, they had better perform surgery on it to ensure that it contained neither a tape recorder nor pound notes. A carving knife was fetched from the kitchen. I seized the beast and ran off with it into the night, presenting it eventually to a friend's child.

Spectator

⊰ 27 November 1999 ⊱

**Hamilton v. Al Fayed: Will a dozen
red-bearded dwarfs appear . . . ?**

In November 1999, Frank sat in on a libel action brought by former Conservative minister, Neil Hamilton (MP for Tatton 1983–1997) against Harrods owner, Mohamed Al Fayed – brilliant theatre.

Though no lawyer, I assume that all precedents and points of law touching upon Hamilton v. Al Fayed are to be found in Jarndyce v. Jarndyce, or better still, Beachcomber's lengthy Case of the Twelve Red-Bearded Dwarfs. Beachcomber, for the benefit of younger readers, was for decades the surreal columnist of the old *Daily Express*. On leaving the High Court one evening this week, I consulted Michael Frayn's useful Beachcomber anthology. 'A Mrs Tasker is accused of continually ringing the doorbell of a Mrs Renton, and then, when the door is open, pushing a dozen red-bearded dwarfs into the hall and leaving them there.'

The details of that case need not, as the lawyers say, detain us here. Its resemblance to Hamilton v. Al Fayed resides, apart from its picturesque implausibility, in such passages as: 'The first sensation came when Mrs Tasker submitted a list of 7,000 people whom she wished to call as witnesses.' The judge asked, 'Surely they cannot all be connected with the case. For instance, I see here the name of a Cabinet Minister. Also, a well-known film actor. And that distinguished sailor Rear Admiral Sir Ewart Hodgson?' Counsel: 'I understand he knows one of the dwarfs.'

Sitting in the High Court for the past week or so, one asked oneself, 'Surely they cannot all be connected with the case?' But they must be. Otherwise, as name after famous name falls from Mr Al Fayed's lips in the witness box, the judge presumably would have stopped him. Mr Al Fayed did not mention a distinguished sailor. But he had at least one Cabinet Minister. And, as his days of cross-examination passed, he submitted the names of the Duke of Edinburgh in his capacity as organiser of assassination; the late Mr Tiny Rowland as payer of bribes; Mr Hamilton as homosexual; Mr Hamilton as sexual prostitute; Lady Thatcher, not necessarily as either of the latter, but certainly as a conspirator against Mr Al Fayed; and, just to be bipartisan, Mr Jack Straw as refuser of Mr Al Fayed's fabled British passport on the orders of MI6 and, indeed, MI5. At the time of writing, Mr Al Fayed is still in the witness box, and so this may not be the exhaustive list.

An unusual case, as Beachcomber would say; and a gripping one. As the days lengthened in Court 13, the outside world had no reality or significance, except insofar as it affected our case, the case by which all of us in the press seats and Public Gallery were by now hypnotised. But, as always for us laymen, we can follow only the non-technical stuff. Every now and then, judge and two leading counsels talk and dispute among themselves in their learned tongue. The rest of us are cast adrift.

'My Lord, this is *contrary* to Phipson,' said Mr George Carman, for Mr Al Fayed, interrupting Mr Desmond Browne's cross-examination of the owner of Harrods. 'Yes, Phipson is clear,' commented the judge. Mr Browne, reflecting, does not *think* he is doing anything in the contrary to Phipson. But he seems to think Phipson has to be borne in mind. We press on. An hour or so later, Mr

Carman was up again, refreshing his learned friend's memory of Phipson. No one answers the question that is by now on all our lips: who is this Phipson? He cannot be famous. Otherwise Mr Al Fayed might have mentioned him. On the other hand, perhaps he is famous in his field, like that distinguished sailor Sir Ewart Hodgson. Another possibility is that he is famous, but has not conspired against Mr Al Fayed, which would make him an unusual figure in this case.

By a process of elimination, we deduce that Phipson was (is?) an important lawyer. His rule has something to do with whether, in cross-examination, counsel can mention a document or an exhibit which the cross-examinee does not admit to have seen. I am sure it is more complex than that. But it seemed to prevent Mr Hamilton's side mentioning in detail a lot of things it wanted to. Perhaps Mr Al Fayed began to think after a while that this Phipson sounded like a great guy, worthy of a Harrods Christmas hamper.

Still, Mr Browne, in pursuit of Mr Al Fayed, was able to drag in quite a lot. For example, he got in a taped telephone conversation between Mr Al Fayed and the late Tiny Rowland. Mr Browne had asked Mr Al Fayed whether it was his practice to tape his own telephone conversations. Mr Al Fayed replied that it was not. Mr Browne produced his tape, presumably supplied by forces hostile to Mr Al Fayed. On it, Mr Rowland asked Mr Al Fayed whether the conversation was being taped. Mr Al Fayed replied that it was not. When the tape ended, Mr Al Fayed's demeanour was of complete calm. The conversation may have been taped, but it was nothing to do with him. It must have been done by his security people, he explained. But it was the first phrase on the tape which seemed to be almost as enigmatic as the tape's origin. Mr Al Fayed was heard genially telling Mr Rowland, 'I am talking about your cock, not my cock.'

Surprisingly, Mr Carman did not rise to plead that the afore-mentioned member was contrary to Phipson. Surely Phipson had something to say about the member being introduced without warning. But perhaps it did not come within the category of an exhibit previously unseen by the witness. An alternative explanation is that the entity referred to was a metaphor: Mr Al Fayed's characteristic way of referring to his fortune in relation to Mr

Rowland's. Having already had occasion last week to quote Mr Al Fayed in this general area, I apologise to readers for appearing preoccupied with the subject. As the judge occasionally advised Mr Browne when he thought a line of questioning was exhausted, I shall move on to my next subject.

The choice is varied. Mr Browne produced not just a tape, but a video. It thus became a sort of multi-media cross-examination, lacking only the Internet. It was on this video – of Mr Al Fayed having a meal at Harrods with his arch enemy Mr Rowland during one of their truces – that Mr Al Fayed casually assured Mr Rowland that Mr Hamilton was not only greedy but 'a homosexual, a prostitute'. Asked by Mr Browne if he really believed that, Mr Al Fayed explained, 'It was just a discussion. It was rumours.' Mrs Hamilton, seated next to her husband, looked especially unconvinced by that one.

But before we form any opinion of the progress of Hamilton v. Al Fayed, we must hear Mr Hamilton enduring the same ordeal by cross-examination. The case, as Beachcomber would have put it, continues.

Spectator

Chapter 12

September 2000– April 2001
New Labour riding high; Tories in the doldrums

In 2000, Frank went back to writing the sketch for the Daily Telegraph *until his health began to fail him in the autumn of 2004. He continued to write his Saturday weekly column for the* Daily Telegraph *and fortnightly for the* Spectator *from home until the week before he died in December 2006.*

⇥ **29 September 2000** ⇤
**Nelson Mandela, a Xhosa Duke of Devonshire,
addresses the Labour conference in Brighton**

Nelson Mandela's speech to the Labour conference yesterday was preceded by a video about his life and the anti-apartheid movement. It was accompanied by what a colleague, learned in that school of music, explained was a 1960s hit entitled 'He Ain't Heavy, He's My Brother'.

'The road is long, but I'm gonna be strong,' said the hit. This was a warning to those of us professional observers who suffer from stomach trouble when the Labour Party conference, a gathering which we otherwise enjoy, becomes moved.

We had been dreading this occasion. Not the thought of the behaviour and reputation of the guest, but of his hosts. Mr Mandela to appear at the Labour conference! The very words of the announcement some time ago told me that I was gonna have to be strong.

Mr Prescott introduced Mr Mandela with the words: 'We spent 18 years in Opposition, and we hated it. He spent 27 years in prison.'

It was impossible to imagine a more grotesque and dispropor-tionate comparison. Has Mr Mandela any idea what Mr Prescott went through in those 18 years? Reduced to two Jaguars! Barely knowing where the next media lunch was coming from!

Then Mr Mandela spoke. His voice and diction were little short of beautiful. He was one of the week's few platform speakers to speak in sentences. I was therefore moved beyond words, as opposed to Mr Blair, who so often moves beyond verbs.

The video had shown anti-apartheid speeches delivered by Barbara Castle, Hugh Gaitskell, Harold Wilson and Neil Kinnock. But Mr Mandela's speech did not dwell solely on Labour's contri-bution. He said: 'One of the distinguishing features of the anti-apartheid struggle was the very broad support it enjoyed from most political persuasions in all parts of the world.'

That must include Tories. If Mr Mandela wondered why there were none in the video, it would have had to be explained to him that this would have been contrary to our tribal system, in which Tories and Labour cannot be expected to drink together at the bar of the same club, like a bunch of easy-going, backslapping Xhosas and Zulus.

Mr Mandela, by his grand manner, understood everything else about us. He understood that we like a lord. An old African hand among the Brighton press corps explained that, in Xhosa society, he would be considered an aristocrat.

This made him the first toff to address a Labour conference since the figure once content to be known as Anthony Wedgwood Benn who later shortened himself to Tony Benn – akin to yesterday's guest becoming Nel Mandela.

Perhaps Mr Mandela is the Xhosa equivalent of one of our own chieftains, such as the Duke of Devonshire. If the class warriors at this conference had known that, they would have booed him, taxed him at 99 per cent, and subjected him to the right to roam. Fortunately, there is no logic to the class war.

No one could equal Mr Mandela's contribution, but as a whole it was still a good final day.

Daily Telegraph

⚔ 3 October 2000 ⚔
Michael Ancram serves in that toff regiment,
the Mainstream Guards

Michael Ancram, Chairman of the Tory Party (1998–2001),
addressed the last Tory conference before the 2001 election.

'And now,' said the voice announcing various arrivals on the huge platform, 'our Conservative MPs!' So it is a smear that the Conservative Party does not care about minorities.

In single file, the wretched creatures made their way forward. The country will wonder how so many of them got here. Surely in May 1997 the rules keeping Tories out were tightened up. Yet more than 150 of them had still managed to get in.

I do not wish to appear populist, still less opportunist, but plenty of these so-called asylum seekers looked highly bogus. Some were surely economic migrants. They wanted to become Tory MPs to eke out with consultancies their basic living from subsistence merchant banking.

Being something of a liberal in these matters, I am in favour of letting them stay. But the announcer also called to the platform a vast number of prospective parliamentary candidates seeking entry to Parliament. Many of these people have little connection with Britain. Some have scant command of English. If previous Conservative politicians are any guide, a proportion will turn to crime.

'Finally, our leader, William Hague,' said the announcer. Here was a man with a well-founded fear of persecution in his own country. Mr Hague, with a radiant Ffion, appeared to general acclaim.

The question remains, is this conference – with its tolerance of Conservatives – truly representative of the British people? Anecdotal evidence suggests that the country as a whole still thinks that there are too many Tories over here. Most people refuse their pleas for money. It only encourages them, they say.

Turning from social issues, what are the other themes of the week here in Bournemouth? Well, some of the most famous people in the party, such as Michael Heseltine and Kenneth Clarke, are obviously worried about the outcome of the next general election. They fear that Mr Hague might do well at it.

Inside the hall, the mood was jolly and cautiously confident. All believed that the country had seen through Mr Blair. But, on the fringe, the leader who aroused most opposition was Mr Hague. Word had it that Mr Heseltine was no longer giving money to the Conservative Party, but was diverting it to a body called Conservative Mainstream, a meeting of which he would address in Bournemouth. Mr Clarke would address an equally sinister-sounding body called the Conservative Group for Europe.

Michael Ancram, the Party Chairman, in his speech opening the conference, sought to deal with Mr Heseltine. Being a traditional sort of Tory, he did it in the traditional Tory way: by suggesting that there was no difference between them.

Tories, according to Mr Ancram, were 'far from the shores of extremism' in which their opponents had sought to place them. 'We are the party of the mainstream sharing the values of the mainstream majority in this country,' he said. He went on to use the word 'mainstream' four more times. By the time he had done with Mr Heseltine, the party was meant to be left wondering what Mr Heseltine was complaining about. To hear Mr Ancram tell it, he and Mr Heseltine had long served together amicably in that toff regiment, the Mainstream Guards.

But those of their brother officers who listened to Mr Ancram yesterday knew that 'Hezza', as he was known, was regarded in the officers' mess, not least by Capt. Ancram, as not quite a gentleman.

Hair too long. Furniture too new. Various troubles involving a mace, helicopters and a noisy blonde from Grantham. Now the fella has the nerve to go around boasting about 'my service in the Mainstreams'. Fact is he was damned lucky to escape court martial.

Daily Telegraph

⤝ 24 October 2000 ⤞
A triumphant day for Speaker Martin, a Glasgow boy

MPs last night elected as their new Speaker, in succession to Betty Boothroyd, a Member who first went to work, they were told, 'in an old boiler suit and a pair of boots'.

Hearing only that about the Chair's new occupant, the uninitiated might well ask: 'Why, nowadays, does the Speaker always have to be a woman?'

New Labour discourages the belief that it is still the party of men who go to work in old boiler suits and boots.

It is assumed, in our increasingly middle-class politics, that the only Labour MPs who have ever worn boiler suits and boots are women – preferably for dinner parties, and for early evening drinks, but also for work.

Why could not the House elect as Speaker a man who first went to work in black silk tights and a full-bottom wig, thus showing that he had trained for the job from an early age?

But the boiler-suited and booted one was indeed a man: Michael Martin, aged 55 and Glasgow born.

But perhaps, as in the film *Billy Elliot*, someone as rough as Billy's father would have caught wee Martin wearing black tights and shouting 'Order, order!' when it was assumed that he was at his boxing lessons. The little boy would have been brutally informed: 'We're no havin' a lad of oors end up Speaker of the House a' Commons. That's for gurrrls.'

But Martin must have persisted. He eventually won his family round, though they might still have thought him a wee bit odd. And last night he landed the starring role at Westminster: the Speaker-ship, the Swan Lake of politics!

Many in the audience wept at the end. I urge you to see it.

Mr Martin savoured his triumph after the longest and most contested Speakership election for hundreds of years.

The boiler suit and boots were therefore mentioned – by Mr Martin's proposer, Peter Snape (Lab. West Bromwich East) – for a special purpose: to win residual Old Labour votes and the votes of the guilty middle classes by differentiating Mr Martin from his strongest opponent, Sir George Young, Tory, sixth baronet and Old Etonian.

Thus Mr Snape mentioned that Mr Martin was brought up in a tenement and that his seafaring father had been torpedoed three times during the war.

Mr Martin, in his speech seeking the post, emphasised what an honour it was that 'someone from the poverty of Glasgow can stand before you seeking the great office of Speaker'.

He added 'My origin should be no reason for me being elected. Nor should my origin be a reason to debar me.'

This posed a problem for Sir George. Perhaps he should have romanticised his own origins: 'My house at Eton was torpedoed three times during the war.'

He might have won, since the House was in sentimental mood. But he made a rather patrician speech about the nature of the Speakership. Come the vote, he was therefore torpedoed during the class war. The election went on for hours because MPs, out of irritation at what they think is the Government's 'manipulative' way, contrived that candidates be proposed, seconded and voted on, who had no chance. By tradition, the election was presided over by the Father of the House, Sir Edward Heath. But judging by the many complaints about the voting procedure, not least from Tony Benn, the Father did not seem to have educated his family in how to understand a contested Speakership election. But it is easy to blame the parents. This Father was torpedoed more than three times by Mrs Thatcher.

Daily Telegraph

I always expected Frank's writing to be refreshingly oblique and accurate so it was no surprise that he caught my feelings exactly on the day that I was elected Speaker. I was thinking of my family, my teachers, my apprenticeships and the journey that has brought me to the Speaker's Chair. Frank projected that kindly and with the sparkling link to that just-released film Billy Elliot. *And he had put me in the starring role! But in the next of his sketches that included me, the title was: 'Anti-Speaker Riots' or some such.*

Unlike young Billy I had come back to earth with such a bump.

Speaker Martin (2000–2009)

◄ 25 January 2001 ►

Blair, in a historic precedent, sacks his minister, Peter Mandleson, a second time

Peter Mandelson, Secretary of State for Northern Ireland (1999–2001), resigned after helping the Hinduja brothers, who later became sponsors of the Millennium Dome, acquire British citizenship. He was exonerated of any wrongdoing by the Hammond Report.

Mr Mandelson insisted on coming to the Commons to answer Northern Ireland questions, as planned before his resignation. Knowing him, it was at first assumed that he intended to become the first minister in history to resign while retaining his job.

He rose to a surprising cheer from the party to whose destruction he had dedicated his career (Labour). It would not have cheered had there been any danger of his remaining in office.

In Labour's view, by resigning he had for once done the right thing, as opposed to his more usual extreme right thing. What Labour backbenchers tend to regard as the extreme right thing was what won so many of them their seats: sanity. But they do not like to be reminded of that. Mr Mandelson's presence reminds them of it all the time. In their ideal world, they would have Mandelsonism without the Mandelson. Unlike most ideal worlds, yesterday it became reality.

The Labour cheer came when Mr Mandelson rose to answer the first question, a routine query from Mr Julian Brazier (Con. Canterbury) asking him to comment on the future of the Royal Ulster Constabulary. Mr Mandelson added, 'on a personal basis', some praise of the RUC.

For the moment the House as a whole proceeded on the assumption that this was a sad occasion. Resigning from the Cabinet is the only way to find out what one's obsequies would be like, without having to endure the unpleasantness and inconvenience of dying. Every now and then during this extraordinary Ulster Question Time a Labour backbencher would pay tribute to Mr Mandelson.

He represents a very different party from them: the London Dinner Party. He is a stalwart of a typical inner-city branch (Mayfair). His idea of a night out is a few drinks and a bowl of caviar with fellow party members at the Hindujas. Some say that he still has a future in the Dinner Party. He will continue to campaign for it. Yesterday Labour affected cross-party sympathy for him. For his sense of his own worth, Mr Mandelson should resign more often. Actually, he does.

It being Wednesday, the Prime Minister was due to answer questions. One by one, the senior Members of the Cabinet began to arrive on the Government front bench. It must be said that most of them seemed to take Mr Mandelson's misfortune extremely well. There was, for example, Mr Gordon Brown. As joint heads of Labour's election campaign, he and Mr Mandelson had looked forward to working against each other. Now it was not to be.

When Mr Brown reached the front bench, there was a large space next to Mr Mandelson, and a small one next to the Home Secretary. Naturally, Mr Brown wedged himself alongside the Home Secretary. As Ulster questions proceeded, Andrew Mackay, Shadow Northern Ireland Secretary, rose to say that Mr Mandelson's resignation was the 'right decision', and 'the only decision in the circumstances' – an unpartisan intervention. Most Tories were shocked and disappointed at him for misjudging their mood; for so signally failing to lower himself to the occasion.

William Hague put that right. After Tony Blair had announced the circumstances of Mr Mandelson's departure, Mr Hague raged effectively against Mr Blair's having created the historic precedent of being 'forced to sack the same minister for the same offence twice in 25 months'; and against Mr Blair's 'monumental error of judgement' for his 'career-long dependence' on Mr Mandelson. At last someone had spoken for Labour.

Daily Telegraph

⊰ **30 March 2001** ⊱

The clash of two speakers, past and present,
and the five tests for the euro

Bored by being asked if there should be a May poll, I reply: certainly. We traditionalists are all for Maypoles. A fine old

English custom. It is treasonable for the multi-culturalists and the politically-correct brigade to smear Maypoles as xenophobic. If Labour gets back, Maypoles will be abolished. As William Hague might put it, let me take you to a foreign village green. No Maypoles. Morris dancers banned as racist. Bogus asylum seekers doing Albanian folk dances. But as the Commons discussed Treasury matters yesterday, Mr Blair was across at Number 10, dancing round the May poll. As far as the House was concerned, the May poll was already on. Michael Portillo, Shadow Chancellor, asked Gordon Brown, Chancellor, what the position now was on the five tests for British membership of the Euro. The Chancellor replied that the position was unchanged. Owen Paterson (Con. Shropshire North) wanted to know what today's figures were on the five tests. Not wishing to answer that question, Mr Brown embarked on a sponsored walk around the subject. Mr Paterson shouted an interruption: 'What are the figures?' Mr Brown told him: 'I'm not going to start a running commentary on the issue.'

Some of us thought of another question about the five tests: what are the five tests? Who, apart from Mr Brown, can ever remember them; certainly not Mr Blair?

The Five Tests. A good title for Sherlock Holmes or Agatha Christie; only the mysterious, brooding Chancellor knew the whereabouts of the legendary Five Tests. To discover them, some men had been prepared to risk death by slow boredom. But what were they? I would be grateful if readers do not tell me. That would be to give away the ending. Mercifully, David Taylor (Lab. Leicestershire North West) changed the subject. He urged Mr Brown to disregard Mr Portillo and the Tories because of 'the disastrous Tory experiment with the ERM which costs thousands of jobs'.

Mr Taylor did not mention that Mr Brown, as Labour front bench Treasury spokesman in opposition, had urged the Tories to join the ERM. Among the conventionally-minded, joining the ERM was a great cause of the period – uniting Tory wets and New Labour – just as joining the single currency is now. These days, Mr Brown very occasionally hints that the only thing wrong with joining the ERM was that the exchange rate for the pound was too high. But he never said that at the time. Perhaps aware that some of us remember all that, Mr Brown chose his words carefully in replying to Mr Taylor. For joining the ERM, the Tories 'must accept, as the government, full responsibility', he said, which was true of those who took us in, but also true of those who shouted us in. Mr Portillo, understandably, saw no point in dwelling on the Tories' time in the ERM. He turned to the wording of any future Labour government's referendum on the single currency. Mr Brown replied that he was only too pleased for the single currency to become an election issue because Labour's policy on it, unlike the Tories', was not one of 'dogma'. But he would not offer the wording.

Suddenly, the Speaker, Mr Michael Martin, shouted at the Tory backbenches: 'The Hon Gentleman has used an unparliamentary expression. He should withdraw it.'

None of us in our part of the gallery had heard anything unparliamentary. Then Mr John Bercow (Con. Buckingham) rose and announced with massive irony: 'O, readily, Mr Speaker, I withdraw.' The Speaker seems to dislike Mr Bercow. A Hansard staff member, who heard it, later told us that Mr Bercow had shouted that Mr Brown was a 'conman'. So the Speaker had questioned Mr Bercow's authority again. Mr Martin does not seem to understand that Parliament's Bercows embody centuries of tradition. Without them, Parliament could not function. Almost anyone can be a Speaker. Few can be a Bercow. Conman unparliamentary, indeed! Mr Bercow let him off this time, but Mr Speaker should not try it on again.

Daily Telegraph

Chapter 13

May–July 2001
The build-up to the general election on 7 June and the Tory leadership election

⚔ 16 May 2001 ⚔

Oliver Letwin, Shadow Chief Secretary to the Treasury, goes to ground and Charles Kennedy canvasses cockneys

Charles Kennedy, Liberal Democrat Leader, yesterday presented his manifesto promising to put our taxes up. Or, as he would prefer it, promising to improve health and education.

I shall return in a moment to that heroic figure; Mr Kennedy, that is, not his tax increase. For the Liberal Democrats' promise of higher taxation, traditionally the most festive occasion of the campaign, was overshadowed by the disappearance of Oliver Letwin, Tory Treasury spokesman.

Some of us thought that all parties should suspend campaigning until Mr Letwin was found. But others believed that the campaign should continue as if he were still participating in it. They said that Mr Letwin would have liked it that way.

Mr Letwin, 45, disappeared after a domestic argument. William Hague's policy is that the Tories should cut taxes by only 8 billion pounds a year by 2003. But the *Financial Times* this week quoted an anonymous Tory spokesman as saying the cut would be 20 billion pounds a year by 2006. Labour officialdom moved among us spreading word that the anonymous spokesman was Mr Letwin.

Mr Letwin yesterday became unavailable for interviews. Nor was he to be found on the hustings. Both are unique for a frontbencher during a general election. Mr Hague and his election team were said to be furious with him. As they saw it, voters would think that the popular 20 billion pounds tax cut would only be made possible by unpopular cuts in what was to be spent on health, education, etc.

Gordon Brown, Chancellor, at Labour's early morning press conference skilfully made trouble for all Tories concerned. He quoted Mr Hague, after the Letwin matter arose, as restating the 8 billion pounds, and Mr Portillo, in guarded comments the previous day, as restating more or less the 20 billion pounds. Mr Brown then announced that Mr Letwin had gone to ground. The Chancellor sat back triumphant. He had created a Tory split.

The search was on for Mr Letwin. We at first assumed that he had fled to Dorset where he has a constituency. But that was too obvious. Perhaps he was hiding in a party election broadcast. There he would know that he was not being watched. Whatever the explanation, Mr Letwin was gone. Perhaps the butler did it. Shaun Woodward's, of course. There is no other famous living butler. The possibility is raised here only because it seems readers cannot hear enough about Mr Woodward's butler, and it was the only way he could be worked in today.

Back to Mr Kennedy: after announcing his manifesto, he plunged into a south London street market. With his entourage, several camera crews, and Tories harassing him with 'Save the Pound' banners, he brought amiable chaos to the narrow thoroughfare.

'It's that ginger bloke,' one woman customer told another. 'You know, the Liberal wassisname.' Name recognition having been established, another woman observed: 'It's all bullshit innit?' Her friend replied: 'Yeah, but it's nice to know the crap they're talkin' abaht.' Cockneys have a thirst for knowledge.

A third woman explained to a fourth that the occasion was to do with 'the Europound'. A male stallholder, a Tory, told some of us reporters that Mr Hague looked as if he would start a war, and that the one he preferred was 'that Nigel Portillo'. Voters are much more interested in politics than we sometimes think.

Once Mr Kennedy spoke to one of them, they naturally liked him. After promising a single currency referendum to a Eurosceptic fruit stall proprietor, he bought a bunch of bananas. A photographer cried: 'Let them dangle, Mr Kennedy.' Mr Kennedy: 'I beg your pardon. What an improper suggestion.' As these cockneys would have told their spouses last night: 'E was a right saucy bugger, ole ginger wassisname.'

Daily Telegraph

This was the first major visit of my first election campaign as leader and was a very enjoyable afternoon aside from the multiple cases of mistaken identity! I've always liked East Street Market and we went there quite a lot over the campaign. The people were always very friendly and it was good to see Frank again taking note of any 'double entendres' I might come out with. I had a lot of amusing moments that day culminating with the bananas; clearly the stress was getting to me!

Charles Kennedy MP

⊰ 6 June 2001 ⊱
Boris Johnson and Michael Heseltine share a platform
in the build-up to the election

Boris Johnson, editor of the Spectator *and the Tommy Cooper of politics, stood for Michael Heseltine's seat, Henley-on-Thames.*

I followed William Hague to Oxford West and Abingdon yesterday. The previous night I was in nearby Henley-on-Thames town hall; filled by 400 local people, huge for this campaign. Michael (now Lord) Heseltine, the outgoing MP, shared a platform with the (we must assume) incoming MP, Boris Johnson.

It must have been nerve-racking to have to share a platform with a charismatic orator both famous and notorious. Nonetheless, Lord Heseltine performed rather well. He lacked Mr Johnson's gravitas. He did not seem to know much about Tory policy. At 68, he still has much to learn.

Lord Heseltine's speech was somewhat party political: about how disappointing Mr Blair had proved. As he talked on, a woman muttered: 'We've come to hear Boris, not him.' Mr Johnson's was the speech of a statesman. He dealt with this campaign's issues in a way the audience understood. He ignored them. He also made them laugh. Except, that is, Lord Heseltine. Lord Heseltine had hoped to be succeeded by someone who shared his views on Europe, but of course his local association, like Conservative associations every-where, did not share his views on Europe, nor his views on Lady Thatcher, whom all local Conservative associations worship.

So, with many of them doubtless anxious to annoy Lord Heseltine, they gave the candidacy to Mr Johnson. One would have thought that the idea of his being succeeded by Mr Johnson, and then having to share a platform with him, would itself have convulsed him with laughter, but apparently not. Mr Johnson went through almost his entire repertoire. The Boris Johnson show, already well-loved by this newspaper's readers, is shortly opening in Parliament. Henley town hall was the out-of-Westminster tryout. But it needs hardly anything done to it, and is ready for the West End.

The essence of the act is that Mr Johnson does not really know how to do it, but that the audience has come to see him, not his tricks. He is the Tommy Cooper of politics. The secret of the Tommy Coopers and Boris Johnsons is timing. Even when he is unintentionally funny, Mr Johnson quickly retrieves the situation by becoming intentionally so. Thus, at Henley, he praised his children's Islington headmaster even though 'he has an earring in his ear'. He added: 'In his ear, as you would expect.' We laughed, except Lord Heseltine. One could almost see him asking himself: why was that funny? I wanted to rush on to the platform and explain it. Don't you see, Lord Heseltine, Boris realised it was superfluous to say the teacher wore an earring in his ear.

Lord Heseltine would just have said something like: 'But the teacher could have worn it in his nose.' Best to leave some things unexplained. The only time Lord Heseltine came close to smiling was when Mr Johnson described himself as 'a passionate European'. So at least he went home happier than when he arrived.

Daily Telegraph

Labour won another landslide over the Conservative Party. After this
crushing defeat, William Hague resigned and a leadership election followed.

≼ 29 June 2001 ≽
Iain Duncan Smith throws his hat in the ring whilst
David Cameron quietly makes his maiden speech

Iain Duncan Smith yesterday reached the moment in a
Conservative leadership campaign when he had to offer us jaded
reporters something that would wake us up. That is, breakfast.

Mr Portillo's was held in one of those St James's restaurants that
are always opening and closing. The menu was modishly healthy.
The bacon sandwiches were so small they needed a search party. The
occasion may have made Mr Portillo look too many calories short of
a fry up.

The Duncan Smith campaign also held its breakfast in the St James's
area, but in one of those functional hotels with rooms hired out for
conferences. Mr Duncan Smith's backers undoubtedly thought that
the Portillo camp was vulnerable on the bacon sandwich issue. The
Duncan Smith bacon sandwiches were big and tasty. They were
inclusive. They included lots of lovely fat. As we awaited the candidate's
arrival, we of the press and some of the MPs supporting Mr Duncan
Smith, contentedly talked at one another with our mouths full.

I asked an MP what he thought of a report in one paper about
Kenneth Clarke finding it unexpectedly hard to win enough votes to
come second in the parliamentary ballot – thus preventing him from
being voted on by the party rank and file in the country. 'You've
gotta remember,' chomped the MP, 'that we're all lying.'

This drew from me the obvious reply: 'When you say you're all
lying, how do I know you're telling me the truth?' Since I tend to
laugh uproariously at my own remarks, the MP was by now
spattered with my bacon sandwich. Mr Duncan Smith, a former
professional soldier, arrived and briskly entered into the spirit of
things by mockingly attaching much importance to the bacon

sandwiches: 'Good enough? I put one of my best men in charge of them. Sorry there's no brown sauce, though.'

Mr Duncan Smith launched into a statement on 'Renewing Public Service and the Welfare Society'. I have the controversial, perhaps eccentric, view that this leadership election has rather a strong field. Any of the candidates would be better for country and party than, for example, the winner of the first Tory leadership election, in 1965 (Sir Edward Heath). Mr Duncan Smith thought that the NHS's deficiencies were caused by its being a state monopoly. But private profit was not the only alternative, he said. He praised voluntary work. For a Tory to do so is less of a platitude than it sounds, for Labour can always seize on it as meaning that Tories want to consign the sick and poor to charity. But, as Mr Duncan Smith put it, 'the Conservative Party has historically been the backbone of voluntarism. If a local problem needs fixing, Tories were the kind of people who got up a committee to sort it out.' He mentioned hospices as an example of voluntarism: 'Does anyone think that hospices would be better off run by a state monopoly?'

As he becomes better known, the country will see in Mr Duncan Smith an officer and gentleman. Nonetheless, he should still be considered for Leader of the Tory Party.

In yesterday's column, I mentioned the dilemma which David Cameron, newly-elected Tory MP for Witney, would face when he made his maiden speech. Maiden speakers have to praise their predecessor in the seat, but Mr Cameron's was Shaun Woodward, now Labour MP for St Helen's South and said to be the most disliked MP on either side of the House.

Mr Cameron duly made his maiden speech yesterday. He mentioned how distinguished all the Tory MPs for Witney had been since the war, culminating in Douglas (now Lord) Hurd. 'Which brings me neatly to the Honourable Member for St Helen's South . . . he remains a constituent, and a most significant local employer, not least in the area of domestic service . . . We are in fact quite close neighbours and on a clear day, from the hill behind my cottage, I can almost see some of the glittering spires of his great house.'

Mr Woodward was not in the Chamber, which was sad for him because he missed a good speech.

Daily Telegraph

⊰ 18 July 2001 ⊱
The Tory leadership election. Michael Portillo
quits front line politics.

There were now three candidates in the final parliamentary ballot. Kenneth Clarke and Iain Duncan Smith filled the first two slots and then went on to the ballot of the grass roots membership.

All day long, all we were told, in the corridor outside the voting room, by the spinners for all three campaigns, was that 'it's tight, very tight'. On and on they went about the tightness. 'It doesn't get much tighter than this . . . tight, that's what it is.'

We cried out for further information. But tightness was all we got. A Tory of above-average self-importance – one of those who refused to tell us who they voted for – moved down towards the room. One longed to tell him: 'You're tight – very tight.' Tight was how you had to describe it if you wanted to appear in the know. By the end of the day, 'very tight' was what I would have replied had a Tory asked me what I thought of his new trousers.

In the absence of any more exciting information, we took an interest in any information. Andrew Murrison (Westbury) arrived to vote. 'He was a ship's surgeon,' a colleague informed me. 'Now he's a sinking ship's surgeon,' I replied. My colleague was kind enough to laugh. We were all desperate.

A Labour MP appeared with some constituents from the north whom he was showing around the building. 'The Tories are electing their leader in there,' he told them. The northerners showed a complete lack of interest. Or they had been told that there are some things they get up to in London that respectable folk have nowt to do with. They hurried on.

Some of us assumed that all that talk of tightness was a cunning tactic by all three camps. As it turned out, they just had not known.

The result staggered everyone. It was a defeat for Mr Portillo. Worse. It was a defeat for us experts. No one predicted that Mr Clarke would come first.

Suddenly, at 5.23pm, the voice of Sir Michael Spicer, Chairman of the 1922 Committee, was relayed into the corridor, bearing the figures that revived Mr Clarke's career at the age of 61, and ended Mr Portillo's at 48. Mercifully, we experts, at whatever age, remained in office. Someone has to explain what politics is about to people who do not know.

We squeezed out of the corridor in the direction of College Green: a patch of ground just opposite the House where the television people interview those whom politics raises up and casts down. Rain fell. Unlike at Wimbledon, the sport continued. From under an umbrella barely adequate to protect it the vast form of Nicholas Soames, a genuinely sad-seeming Member for Mid Sussex – sad because he was a Portillista – was already assuring some channel or other that the result 'made flesh the polarisation that exists in the party'.

A serpent comprising cameras, photographers and microphones made its way on to the green. In its belly was concealed Mr Duncan Smith. The serpent's mouth disgorged him on to Sky News. He beamed, and was gentlemanly about himself, Mr Clarke, and the vanquished Mr Portillo. Suddenly, in mid-interview, an even bigger beast slinked on to the green. It spewed forth Mr Clarke on to ITN. He was wearing a Barbour. Good for the rural activists' vote. What a campaigner this man is. He began being blokey into a microphone. Many of us assumed that, when he should have been campaigning, he was selling cigarettes to vulnerable people who have few other pleasures in their lives (the Tories). But all along he had been steadily gaining votes, spelling disaster for Mr Portillo, and perhaps if he wins in September, for the Conservative Party. As Mr Soames would put it, he could be the split made flesh.

Then, someone at a rival microphone could be heard telling the world that Mr Portillo had 'quit front line politics'. That made him sound rather unmartial. But his enemies always said he had no stomach for the front line. His strength was back line politics.

Now, more or less, he was no longer in politics at all. Most of us suddenly decided that life had been cruel to him over the last week. Perhaps it was that mythical Thatcher support that finished him.

Daily Telegraph

Chapter 14

October 2001–
December 2002

September 11 and the
bombing of the Taliban

On the fateful day of 11 September, Parliament was in recess. It wasn't until the Labour Party conference in early October that Frank alluded to it. But first he had to put John Edmonds, head of the massive GMB trade union, in his place.

⊰ **3 October 2001** ⊱

'The kaleidoscope [of history] has been shaken. The pieces are in flux. Soon they will settle again . . . let us reorder the world,' proclaims Blair.

Never mind bin Laden, the real enemy is John Edmonds. Mr Edmonds and his followers had planned a 'week of rage' in Brighton.

Tony Blair made clear yesterday that he has no quarrel with the Labour Party as such. The only people the Prime Minister wants to destroy are those harbouring John Edmonds.

For readers under the impression that Mr Blair's long-term worry this week was Osama bin Laden, it should be explained that Mr Edmonds is the fanatical public service workers' leader assumed to be somewhere in Brighton.

Though educated in the West, Mr Edmonds is believed to have become enraged by Mr Blair's plan to allow private enterprise to operate in such holy places as the National Health Service. Mr Edmonds and his followers had planned a 'week of rage' in Brighton. They were forced to abort their mission because of the events of September 11. But they are still out there somewhere.

So, though most of Mr Blair's speech yesterday was about terrorism and the Taliban, the Prime Minister included a passage about the threat to the Western way of life posed by Mr Edmonds.

The passage began with the words: 'This party believes in public services; believes in the ethos of public service; and believes in the dedication the vast majority of public servants show.'

But this would not have deceived the fundamentalists. A few breaths later, Mr Blair declared: 'There has to be choice for the user of public services and the ability, where provision of the service fails, to have an alternative provider.' There had to be reform. Furthermore, 'part of that reform programme is partnership with the private or voluntary sector'.

This strike against Mr Edmonds and his forces was daringly carried out in the middle of a speech most of the attention of whose listeners would have been concentrated on the uncontroversial subject of the Taliban and bin Laden.

Admittedly, the way he dealt with the Taliban and bin Laden ensured that the speech was widely agreed to be the best of Mr Blair's career. It seemed to be admired by nearly everyone in the hall, except, of course, Mr Edmonds.

Mr Blair began with moving words about his visit to a stricken New York. He assured us that 'bin Laden and his people organised this atrocity'; denounced what the Taliban had done to Afghanistan; issued a warning to that regime to surrender bin Laden; and made clear what would happen if that regime did not.

'The action we will take will be proportionate; targeted; we will do all we humanly can to avoid civilian casualties. But understand what we are dealing with . . .'

He also became the first person at a Labour Party conference ever to shout pro-American slogans.

But later the speech steadily got out of hand. He speculated about what 'the power of the international community' could do 'together, if it chose to'.

It could, for instance, 'sort out the blight that is the continuing conflict in the Democratic Republic of the Congo'.

He then became delirious, as some explorers do when they go too far up country in the Congo.

The impeccably liberal words, slogans and causes tumbled out: '. . . provide more aid . . . write off debt . . . We could defeat climate change if we chose to. Kyoto is right . . . And if we wanted to, we could breathe new life into the Middle East peace process and we must.'

What about breathing new life into the Rochdale peace process? Or is that too boringly near home? But I carp. He is still, after all, a Labour Prime Minister.

Labour Prime Ministers are still supposed to aspire to reordering the world around us. In fact, Mr Blair did. After September 11, 'the kaleidoscope has been shaken. The pieces are in flux. Soon they will settle again. Before they do, let us reorder the world around us.' Mr Edmonds has been warned.

Daily Telegraph

⊰ 9 October 2001 ⊱
The three parties are in agreement about bombing the Taliban

The Commons was in broad agreement. Traditionally, this is cause for alarm. Many a time in our history a government has proceeded to disaster while supported by all persons of goodwill on both sides of the Chamber.

But for the moment, Tony Blair was having the benefit of any doubts. Not that there were many. Iain Duncan Smith, for the Conservatives, agreed that we had to bomb. So, too, did even Charles Kennedy for the Liberal Democrats.

Still, a very faint air of potential rebellion hung over some parts of the Labour back benches. No one here said anything openly hostile towards the course on which Mr Blair has embarked. But one erring missile, hitting a hospital or an orphanage, would change that. If that happens, there would be no more stomach in the Labour Party for this war. And as history teaches, brutal anti-Western regimes have a habit of placing their military installations near hospitals and orphanages.

But for the time being any Labour dissidents, like the rest of the House, suffered from a sheer lack of information as to what was happening on the ground, at Kabul, Kandahar and elsewhere. If the Taliban understood the black Western arts of public relations, they would be inviting in Western television teams and presenting them with Western atrocities against civilians, real or invented.

The House was packed. War had rescued dozens of Tories from the rigours of Blackpool. Mr Blair was so much better than in Brighton last week. This was because he was confined to something specific and something that had actually happened: the Anglo-American attack on Afghanistan.

'Mr Speaker, thank you for agreeing to the third recall of Parliament since September 11. At 5.30pm British time yesterday a series of air and cruise missile attacks began on the terrorist camps of Osama bin Laden and the military installations of the Taliban regime. These were carried out by American and British armed forces with the support of other allies. There were 30 targets . . .' And so on. His manner was that of an outstanding young staff officer reporting to the top brass. Except, of course, he is the top brass.

The Labour Party, even when the ruling party in time of war, still remained the Labour Party deep down. Thus there was not a murmur of a Labour cheer when Mr Blair praised President Bush's 'statesmanship'. Labour, even New Labour, does not cheer Republican presidents.

Mr Duncan Smith, replying, was impressive too. Slightly weightier in manner: a commander in the field rather than a staff officer. Except of course he has no field to command: just a diminished force cut off at Blackpool. A few nuances reminded us that, non-partisan though he was, Mr Duncan Smith was the Tory. Thus he said that 'our first thoughts today are with our Armed forces' – as a Tory should.

Labour speakers, in turn, said what Labour speakers should say. Thus Ann Clwyd (Lab. Cynon Valley) said that the Taliban 'humiliated and degraded women'.

Nicholas Soames (Con. Mid Sussex) seemed to urge on Mr Blair that Afghanistan's Northern Alliance be encouraged to be important in the future government of Afghanistan. Mr Blair was understandably cautious about that. We have encouraged Afghanistan factions before with unhappy results, which was why we were now attacking the Taliban.

Tam Dalyell (Lab. Linlithgow) and the left-wing lawyer Bob Marshall-Andrews (Lab. Medway) – who seemed to be two potential opponents of this war – sat next to one another, brooding. But both their questions were confined to legalistic points, the gist of which was that it would be better if the United Nations was in charge of this situation.

The situation on the Labour backbenches, then, resembled that in Pakistan: potential radical dissent watched warily by the nervous authorities.

Daily Telegraph

⊰ 25 October 2001 ⊱
Tolerance that dare not speak its name: the Civil Partnership Bill

Whilst there were momentous global events dominating the news, the highly controversial Civil Partnership Bill got an airing. After his election as Tory Party Leader, Iain Duncan Smith appropriated some of the modernising ideas of Michael Portillo but there was much ambivalence over this Bill.

Jane Griffiths (Lab. Reading East) yesterday sought leave to bring in a Bill, one of the provisions of which would be to legitimise 'gay and lesbian partnerships' in law. Most homophobic Tory MPs – already terrorised by the new regime of tolerance imposed by anyone contesting, or winning, the party leadership – fled the Chamber.

They are the Conservative Party's oppressed majority. They felt safe only when they could talk about the more innocuous subjects that came up in yesterday's proceedings: Northern Ireland, Afghanistan and terrorism's threat to Western civilisation.

Miss Griffiths introduced her Bill under the 10-minute rule: a procedural device that allows a backbencher to speak for 10 minutes on the need for a change in the law on more or less any matter. This she ably did.

But one other backbencher is allowed to put the case against the proposed measure. Here was a chance for a traditionalist Conservative who thought marriage should be restricted to two heterosexuals. As it happened, the opposing speech – urging heterosexual marriage as the only form of legalised partnership – was made by a Labour backbencher and Anglican Churchman, Stuart Bell (Middlesbrough). No Tory, it seemed, would dare.

Miss Griffiths's proposed measure was described on the order paper as the 'Relationships (Civil Registration) Bill'. It sought 'leave to bring in a Bill to provide for civil registration of a relationship between two people who are cohabiting, and for such registration to afford certain legal rights . . .' No mention of 'gays and lesbians'; but this did not mean that Tory homophobes were safe. The shrewder of them had noticed the phrase 'two people'. Not 'a man and a woman'.

In the Tory Party, that could mean only one thing: the two people could be two people of the same kind. By which they did not mean two Conservatives. From the traditionalist point of view, it could have been worse. Miss Griffiths could have wanted civil registration of a relationship between three people who were cohabitating, or an even bigger number of cohabitees: a sort of permanent orgy. But that is for the future.

In the past, Tory backbenchers would have competed to win the right to speak for 10 minutes in defence of marriage as the foundation of society. But tolerance of 'minority lifestyles' has descended on the Party in the unlikely form of Iain Duncan Smith.

As Miss Griffiths spoke the Opposition front bench was all but deserted. A Shadow Cabinet meeting had apparently decided that no frontbencher should have anything to do with the measure, for or against, especially against. It was a posthumous triumph for Michael Portillo's leadership campaign.

Miss Griffiths began by putting the case for civil registration of heterosexual partnerships. Actually, we already have such a system: marriage. But for some reason the progressive mind disapproves of the notion that marriage should be the standard name for heterosexual cohabitation.

She did not explain what the difference would be between a civil-registered heterosexual partnership and a marriage. But it is not for the rest of us to try to fathom the progressive mind in these most delicate of matters. It is hard enough trying to understand what they would do about bin Laden.

But, before long, she turned to the gays and lesbians. Not literally, of course, though there were indeed one or two gays and lesbians on the Labour backbenches around her. It was to the subject of gays and lesbians to which she turned.

Here she made a point at which the few Tories who were present remained silent: it was often complained that homosexuals were promiscuous, but her Bill would make their relationships more stable. Still, at another stage, Ann Widdecombe (Con. Maidstone) shouted a vigorous: 'No!' One was wondering what became of her?

In the division, in which no Conservative Shadow Cabinet Member voted, Miss Griffiths had a majority of 120. Just over 50 Tories emerged from hiding to vote against – but not to speak against.

Daily Telegraph

◃ 21 March 2002 ▹
Debate on Iraq and on sending more troops to Afghanistan.
PM and Foreign Secretary absent.

Conservative forces were yesterday deployed on the sort of ill-will mission for which many of them have been superbly trained.

They had reason to believe that much of the Labour Party was opposed to Mr Blair on Iraq. Then, on Monday, it was announced that we were sending more troops to Afghanistan.

Tory intelligence – not intended as a contradiction in terms – reconnoitred the Labour back benches. The party's orders were to bring instability to that normally placid region. On Tuesday, the Tories had persuaded the Speaker to order an emergency debate, for yesterday, on the extra troops.

The hope was that the debate would draw attention to the Labour back bench revolt on Iraq. The theory is that back bench revolts make voters think that the party concerned is split, and that voters do not carry on voting for split parties. There is not much evidence for that. The evidence is that voters do not vote for split governments: a different matter, as John Major discovered.

But the debate, intended to emphasise a split on Iraq, was actually about Afghanistan. Tories with a knowledge of geography knew that Afghanistan and Iraq were two completely different countries. It would therefore be out of order to raise Iraq. But they hoped that geography was not the Chair's special subject. The debate got under way with the good prospect of much tribal unrest on the Labour benches against the Government.

It being a debate which the Opposition had instigated, Bernard Jenkin, Shadow Defence Secretary, opened it. He, and the Tory front bench, do not disagree with the Government about Afghanistan. He had to confine himself to statesmanlike generalities, plus points of detail, until the Labour back bench speeches made trouble for Mr Blair. His mission, then, was to be as dull as possible.

Thus he found himself asking: 'What lessons can we learn from Tora Bora and Anaconda?' For a Conservative carrying out such an operation, the danger is that he pronounces 'Tora Bora' as 'Tory Borer'. He must be a Tory Borer, but he must not admit it. Mr Jenkin carried out that task admirably.

He also discharged, successfully, one other aspect of his mission. A secondary reason for the Tories wanting the debate was to emphasise their constant theme that Mr Blair and the Cabinet do not care about Parliament. They suspected that Mr Blair and the Foreign Secretary would disdain to be present. Iain Duncan Smith, Michael Ancram (Shadow Foreign Secretary) and Michael Howard (Shadow Chancellor) were of course there.

'It is regrettable that the Prime Minister and the Foreign Secretary are not here,' said Mr Jenkin. Mr Duncan Smith and Mr Ancram pointed across at the Government front bench. If they knew that the Prime Minister and the Foreign Secretary were not there, why were they pointing? I do not know the answer. I simply know that, when someone mentions that a Member is not present, other Members nearly always point at the non-present Member. Perhaps, when a Member is absent from home for no good reason, Members' spouses point at the vacant armchair in front of the television. People connected with politics are not as others.

The Minister who was indeed present was Geoff Hoon, Defence Secretary. He is the sort of loyal, dedicated soldier who in war films is eliminated fairly early on. The actor playing him gets the Oscar for best supporting role. Mr Hoon explained the Afghanistan deployment with his usual efficiency.

Eventually, Malcolm Savidge (Lab. Aberdeen North) and Alex Salmond (Scot Nat. Banff and Buchan) successively interrupted him to raise Iraq. Mr Hoon was evasive.

On the Opposition front bench, the smiles of the Conservative General Staff suggested that the op was going to plan. But one of the wigged clerks who sit in front of the Chair – and are the only people who understand the place – turned and spoke to Sylvia Heal, the Deputy Speaker presiding over the debate. She rose and told the House that this was a debate on Afghanistan, not Iraq.

When we bomb Iraq, the Tories – like the bombers – must get the right country.

Daily Telegraph

⚜ 11 April 2002 ⚜
IDS urges Blair to support American action against Iraq nine months before the war

The Commons returned from the Easter recess yesterday amid a renewed uprising by leftish Labour backbenchers over the Middle East. Mr Blair bombarded them with reassurances. The fact is that the backbenchers will never make peace until they can govern a country of their own (Britain).

Mr Blair could never give in to that demand. He and his followers in the Blairite movement will never consent to be ruled by their own party.

Initially, when Mr Blair arrived for his first Prime Minister's Questions for three weeks, the Prime Minister was supported by collaborationist elements on the Labour benches.

Peter Bradley (Lab. The Wrekin) asked him if he was aware that this was 'a momentous day' for many parents including Mr and Mrs Bradley because 'my wife took our two children to school for the first time'.

The less momentous point he went on to make seemed to be that this Government was spending more than the Tories on education.

Mr Blair, these days, expects more destructive criticism than that from his own party. He seemed at first unprepared for Mr Bradley's weapon of mass construction. He paused, but then confirmed that the Government favoured 'investment in public services for all'.

On Iraq, Iain Duncan Smith also decided to be constructive. His way of being so was to support Mr Blair's presumed support for an American attack on Saddam Hussein. That also had the merit, from Mr Duncan Smith's point of view, and given the tense situation on the Labour benches, of being the most destructive thing he could do to Mr Blair at the moment.

Mr Duncan Smith told Mr Blair that Saddam would soon have weapons which could hit Western Europe. Would Mr Blair, he added, confirm reports from the meeting in Texas that he would support military action against Iraq?

Mr Blair replied that the time for that was not yet. The Labour benches did not seem to see that as reassuring. Mr Blair added that Iraq's weapons of mass destruction must be 'dealt with'. He did not say how.

Mr Duncan Smith now became a disruptive outside influence, seeking to stir up trouble in the Labour Party. Saddam pursues a similar strategy towards Palestine.

The Conservative Leader rose a second time to say that Saddam was a sponsor of terrorism. Was 'getting rid' of Saddam the policy of the Government? Mr Blair replied that the method of removing Saddam was 'open to consultation'. This probably did not mean open to consultation with the Labour Party. Doggedly, Mr Duncan Smith continued to do his worst for Mr Blair. He rose a third time implicitly to approve of Mr Blair's describing as 'naive' those who opposed his Iraq policy.

Why did people disagree with that policy? he mused innocently.

Mr Blair replied that he could not comment on other people's motives. It was clear that he was aware of what Mr Duncan Smith was up to. 'I'm sure he's trying to be helpful,' he said, smilingly.

Goaded by all this, one of the dispossessed, Peter Kilfoyle (Lab. Liverpool Walton) launched an attack. He quoted the Prime Minister as saying that opponents of his Middle East policy were 'utterly naive'.

He went on: 'Is it naive to beware of the bellicosity of elements within the American administration based on ideology or is it naive to believe in the centrality of the UN in resolving the problems of the Middle East?'

Mr Blair undoubtedly thinks it naive to believe the latter. But he chose not to say so with the Labour Party listening. He confined himself to saying that he used 'naive' only about those who said weapons of mass destruction were not an issue.

Charles Kennedy, Liberal Democrat Leader, asked a lengthy question which covered the entire Middle East and Islamic world. Doubtless he was, as usual, well-informed. Unfortunately, all we could remember was that he at first described the Royal Anglian Regiment – now in Afghanistan – as the 'Royal Anglican Regiment'.

As far as we know, the Prime Minister has no plans to send in the Royal Anglicans – 'Carey's Own' or the Old Chasubles. The situation in Afghanistan is not that bad.

Daily Telegraph

Affairs nearer home

⊰ 3 July 2002 ⊱

Gordon Brown and the Robert Maxwell pension swindle

This pensions row is beginning to make Robert Maxwell look like the Gordon Brown of his day. Perhaps that is an exaggeration. Maxwell pillaged only one pension fund.

Pensions are the Tories' new cause. Recent events have caused much of the population to be terrified as to how to provide for themselves in later life. Yesterday was one of those days when the Opposition chooses the subject of debate, so the Tories chose pensions.

David Willetts, Shadow Work and Pensions Secretary, quoted from Mr Brown's first Budget speech, in 1997. Mr Brown had said that the private pension funds were in 'substantial surplus'. He would therefore tax them. But now the funds were not anywhere near as in surplus as they had been before Mr Brown struck at them.

The two sides of the House disagreed as to why. Labour claimed it was because of stock market vagaries beyond the Government's control, and because of various complicated reasons conveniently related to the 18 years of Conservative Government. The Tories insisted it was because of Mr Brown's taxation. Before our eyes, they created this Mr Brown as a terrifying, epic swindler. It made him so exciting.

There was, however, one difference between Mr Brown and his by now rather small-time predecessor, Maxwell. Mr Brown was still alive. Or at least, we assumed he was. He was not in the House. Perhaps, like Maxwell, he had become unable to face the public humiliation, at the hands of his enemies, which the unmasking of his fraud would bring. Long had he aroused the envy of those lesser men – Tony Blair, Peter Mandelson, Charles Clarke. How they would rejoice at his fall!

Not that he would have admitted the fraud even to himself. He had only taken the money out of the pensions funds in order to tide him over a difficult period between now and his becoming Prime Minister. He had needed the money to pay for his higher spending on the NHS – his method of buying votes in the next Labour leadership election. But he was not to know that the stock market would go down and make everyone's pension less valuable than it had been. He was only the Chancellor of the Exchequer.

Andrew Smith, the new Work and Pensions Secretary, was yesterday left to pick up the pieces. He had no news of Mr Brown's whereabouts.

Mr Smith depicted the Tories as the ones whom pensioners should fear: 'Their vision is to privatise the basic state pension . . . We believe in partnership.'

This satisfied the Labour benches well enough. For a wider audience, Mr Smith had a public relations difficulty. He had been a member of the Brown organisation. Until a few weeks ago, he worked at the Treasury – the London address from which the Tories claim the fraud was organised. How much did Mr Smith know? Is Smith his real name? All sorts of worrying people sign themselves 'Mr Smith'.

When the Secretary of State insisted that pensioners did better under Labour, Tory backbenchers cried: 'Robert Maxwell, Robert Maxwell.' (He was a Labour supporter – indeed, once a Labour MP.) Those Tories clearly looked forward to the day when future Labour Pensions Ministers, faced with a similar depletion of the funds, could be heckled with the cry of: 'Gordon Brown, Gordon Brown.'

Douglas Hogg (Con. Sleaford) asked Mr Smith an impressive, technical question which was above my head, and more importantly, above Mr Smith's. Yet earlier, during Question Time, Michael Fabricant (Con. Lichfield) had tried to reach his usual seat, and found his way impeded by a slumped Mr Hogg – apparently asleep.

Rather than disturb him, Mr Fabricant, a considerate person, walked four rows up the aisle, one row across the back of the Chamber, four rows back again, and sat down next to Mr Hogg on the other side. Sat down rather too heavily, though, for Mr Hogg suddenly awoke. He left the Chamber. Presumably an early riser, he perhaps thought it time to get up and go to work.

He returned refreshed for the pensions debate. The quality of his later question to Mr Smith attested to the importance of our politicians' avoiding late afternoons.

Daily Telegraph

⊰ 19 November 2002 ⊱
Brown collects Shadow Chancellors' autographs.
An early question from David Cameron.

*For a period before he became Prime Minister, Gordon Brown was
hailed by many as the greatest post war Chancellor. He seemed to
carry all before him while Tory Shadow Chancellors came and went
with alarming regularity.*

MPs on all sides yesterday went through the motions – during
questions to the Culture, Media and Sport Department – of
encouraging new British films. But later, the resumed Queen's
Speech debate showed that what really excites MPs are old British
chancellors.

Kenneth Clarke (Con. Rushcliffe) made a personal appearance.
The British chancellor industry doesn't make them like him any
more. That is, ones who keep to Tory spending plans. Gordon
Brown is the last.

Not that the Tories can admit that. Or when they admit it, they
have to go on to say that it won't last.

Michael Howard, the Shadow Chancellor, does that better than
any of his predecessors since his party went into opposition, which
makes him the greatest living Shadow Chancellor. (Conservative
politicians must these days be content with such accolades as are
available to them.) Mr Howard said he was not interested in history.
What distressed him were the troubles that, he claimed, threatened
the economy.

Mr Brown, however, was very interested in history. He relished
the appearance of a star from the old days in Mr Clarke. Mr Brown
had just said that unemployment in the private sector had fallen. Mr
Clarke rose from the back benches to say that, on the contrary, in the
third quarter of this year, unemployment in the private sector rose.

Mr Brown denied it. He then demonstrated what appeared to us
laymen to be a comprehensive knowledge of all Mr Clarke's
pronouncements since the latter ceased to be Chancellor, many of
them consisting of Mr Clarke forecasting recession. Just after the

1997 election, Mr Clarke was briefly Shadow Chancellor before what he doubtless saw as the Hague Terror drove him into exile or at least into cigarette salesmanship. But Mr Brown could remember who all the subsequent Shadow Chancellors were. Here was proof that politicians are not really interested in new films or indeed old films. Mr Brown went on to display an interest in, and knowledge of, not just old Chancellors, but old Shadow Chancellors.

What sort of a sad case is it who has such interests? Does he keep a Shadow Chancellors' scrapbook? Do he and his fellow Shadow Chancellor fans spend their time swapping Francis Maude's autograph for Peter Lilley's? Perhaps Gordon was always an unusual boy.

Mr Brown pointed out that there had been five Shadow Chancellors since Labour returned to power; itself a piece of information that no boy with healthy, normal interests should know. All of these Shadow Chancellors forecast recession. 'It was not the recessions that came,' he added. 'it was the Shadow Chancellors who went.'

David Cameron (Con. Witney), elected last year, intervened in Mr Brown's speech to put a suitably weighty point. Mr Brown brushed it aside by saying that he was not going to take any lectures from 'a person who was a former adviser to Lord Lamont'.

So Mr Brown collects special advisers to Chancellors too. As the young say, a real saddo! Mr Brown went on to show a detailed knowledge of almost everything that the present Shadow Chancellor did when he was in office. Crime doubled when Mr Howard was Home Secretary, he claimed. As Employment Secretary, he did bad things about pensions. At environment, he was for the poll tax. Through all this, Mr Howard smiled. Labour backbenchers cheered. Nearly everyone, then, was happy.

So it had been a feat to induce MPs to mention the, to them, less glamorous subject of films. To MPs who urged that he help to encourage British film skills, Kim Howells, the relevant minister, said we should acknowledge all the industry's skills, as they do in America, where the 'person who does the seventh rewrite turns it into a great film' – presumably because the first six rewrites were literate.

Mr Howells also had to answer MPs' demands to revive the tourist industry in British seaside resorts. He promised an 'overall benchmarking standard'.

A thrilling ride on an overall benchmarking standard would certainly attract tourists.

Daily Telegraph

◄ 22 November 2002 ►

Blair is named the *Spectator*'s Parliamentarian of the Year, much to the surprise of the judges!

Tony Blair was named Parliamentarian of the Year yesterday by the *Spectator*, a magazine of right-wing repute which is edited by a Conservative MP, Boris Johnson (Henley). It could have been worse for Mr Blair. It could have been a left-wing magazine.

Nonetheless the Prime Minister's career is expected to recover. Whether Boris Johnson's will is another matter.

The award seems to have caused some offence in Mr Johnson's party. Doubtless he would wish it to be known that he was powerless to prevent it going to the Prime Minister. Doubtless he would also wish the Prime Minister to know that he was strongly in favour of it going to him. Mr Johnson, like all of us, simply does not know how long Mr Blair will remain in office.

Mr Johnson was merely the chairman of the awards committee. He therefore could not have known what was going on. As with all men of action, meetings are not his strength. The committee consists of parliamentary journalists of impeccable objectivity, plus me. As with Cabinet decisions, responsibility is collective. We agreed to blame one another.

The award was handed out yesterday at a function in a London hotel. Every autumn, some weeks before this ceremony, we judges decide the awards – of which Parliamentarian of the Year is but one, though the most important – during a long lunch. Such is the lunch's length and conviviality that, a few weeks later, we are always pleasantly surprised to discover who we gave the awards to.

So it is possible that we never gave one to Mr Blair at all and that the whole thing was arranged, as most things are, by 10 Downing Street. I thought I had better explain all that in order to reassure Mr Gordon Brown. On hearing of the award, he was last night being comforted by friends. Yesterday's function was attended by MPs invited for all manner of reasons except merit. Admittedly, some of them deserved to be there. It is impossible to prevent such characters slipping through.

The proceedings began with a toastmaster asking us all to turn off our pagers and mobile telephones. This meant that for the rest of the occasion certain New Labour MPs who had managed to get themselves invited had no opinions. The Speaker, Michael Martin, handed out the awards. Mr Johnson announced them in turn. Each announcement is always a thrilling moment for us judges. We discovered, for example, that we had made Gerald Kaufman (Lab. Gorton) Survivor of the Year. What had he survived? For a start, he had survived the year. He is already in his seventies.

He also survived being one of Harold Wilson's Downing Street staff in the 1960s, as well as the leaderships of Michael Foot and Neil Kinnock. He thus symbolises hope for many young MPs; Tories, that is. The next time their party is in power, they too could make excellent back bench speeches in its support at the age of 72.

The other awards were equally deserved, whoever made them. That for 'minister to watch' went to Yvette Cooper, of the Lord Chancellor's office. She is married to Gordon Brown's chief economic adviser Ed Balls. It is possible that this award was made in order to see whether Mr Johnson would resist a distressing play on words about her possessing the properties indicated by her husband's surname. Mr Johnson did not resist it. Or, to do him justice, he embarked on the joke, announced it a bad one, and swiftly abandoned it. It is important that a rising politician knows when to retreat.

Finally, came the moment that Mr Johnson is even now probably explaining away as the work of some other Johnson. He announced that the Parliamentarian of the Year was indeed Mr Blair. Boris took the announcement very well.

Being at the NATO summit in Prague, the Prime Minister could not be with us. But he appeared on a video, holding the award – a silver salver – in front of his lower abdomen, as if Mr Mandelson, or whoever was responsible for laying out his trousers that morning, had neglected his duties. Under the circumstances, he managed to accept the honour with grace and dignity.

Daily Telegraph

I am afraid that Frank has accurately recorded a shameful episode in which the Spectator *judges decided that Tony Blair should be made Parliamentarian of the Year. This was tricky for me, since I was then a Tory MP as well as editor of the magazine and in desperation I tried (jokingly) to blame Frank. All I can say in my defence is that we had all drunk a lot and that it was before the Iraq War.*

Boris Johnson

⊰ 27 November 2002 ⊱
Prescott reverts to code for security reasons.
Cryptologists are working on it.

Andy Gilchrist, Fire Brigades Union General Secretary, yesterday sat in the Gallery, leaning forward and listening intently to John Prescott's latest report to the House on the firemen's dispute – occasionally taking notes. Mr Gilchrist at first seemed to understand what Mr Prescott was saying.

This raised fears that FBU codebreakers may have cracked the code in which Mr Prescott's statements to the Commons are transmitted. The cryptologists working under the Deputy Prime Minister have long boasted that the code was unbreakable. Certainly, it has always posed quite a challenge in the place where I usually listen to Mr Prescott's speeches (Bletchley).

There, his remarks are studied by cipher experts who are often crossword enthusiasts and mathematicians who have volunteered for the task. But under the Official Secrets Act I am not allowed to say any more about my work. Mr Prescott initially read out a statement on the latest situation in the dispute. This was transmitted *en claire*. But when replying without a text to questions from his Opposition shadow, David Davis, and others on both sides of the Chamber, Mr Prescott, for security reasons, reverted to code.

At one stage, apparently seeking to explain the situation concerning strikers' attitudes to serious emergencies, it came out as: 'As for the question about whether the TUC have an agree with its members on the 1979 agreement, that is a matter for the TUC. It's their agreement. But it was a matter for me to have an agreement, as I informed the House, to seek to find an agreement – which I failed on the first occasion – dealing with those really exceptional intro, er, in conflicts. Well, on those difficult interests where we find there's a train crash or an explosion in our transport system.'

After a while, Mr Gilchrist stopped taking notes. His brow furrowed and he began to look baffled. He was beaten. The code was unbroken. Later, Mr Prescott referred to 'Mr Gilcrust'. This was too obvious a code name for Mr Gilchrist. It sounded more like the code name for a British agent deep within the Fire Brigades Union; all in all, a black day for the FBU counter-espionage operation.

Mr Davis asked about, among other things, confusion at Newcastle upon Tyne. There, according to the *Newcastle Journal*, as quoted by Mr Davis, the Army had been allowed to use modern appliances, then that decision had been reversed, then it had been reversed again. Mr Prescott replied that he had looked into that. There had indeed been 'some dispute about whether they should have red goddesses'.

Red fire engines are of course not referred to as 'red goddesses'. Was 'red goddesses' therefore code for 'green goddesses'? I am not at liberty to say.

Mr Davis asked Mr Prescott a mass of other questions all intended to show that the Government's response to the strike was chaotic. He ended by saying that there was only one person sleeping peacefully, and that was the Deputy Prime Minister. This was on the face of it an odd remark on Mr Davis's part.

It appeared to be a reference to the firemen's employers' attempts to extract a large sum of taxpayers' money from Mr Prescott last week late at night. But Mr Prescott, the following morning, had said he had indeed got out of bed.

Later, it dawned on some of us that Mr Davis was retaliating for something Mr Prescott had said a few weeks ago. It was during Mr

Duncan Smith's leadership troubles. Mr Prescott had said that Mr Duncan Smith could 'sleep peacefully' after what the Deputy Prime Minister thought was a pedestrian Dispatch Box performance by Mr Davis, sometimes thought of as an alternative leader. If that explains Mr Davis's remark yesterday, it is reassuring that this firemen's dispute is not so grave as to interfere with the rancours of party politics.

Mr Prescott described the remark as 'a typically cheap contribution'. So, when he wants to be, Mr Prescott can be as clear as anyone. Above all, he is clear about not giving in to – as he would put it – these green goddesses.

Daily Telegraph

⊰ 4 December 2002 ⊱
Labour huntsmen are on Nicholas Soames' scent

It remained as inexplicable as ever; this obsession with the pursuit of wild mammals – justified by the claim that they are dangerous pests. Yet in what way are rural Conservative backbenchers pests?

Labour backbenchers hunt them on the grounds that they are toffs. Actually, anybody who knows anything about the ecology of the Conservative Party knows that there are hardly any toffs left in it. They are now in the restaurant business or interior design.

Alun Michael, the Rural Affairs Minister, had announced a Bill to ensure that hunting of foxes with hounds would in future only be allowed according to whether a particular hunt was marked by 'cruelty', in which case it would be illegal, or 'utility', in which case it would be legal. A hunt would possess this elusive and mysterious quality of 'utility' if the foxes concerned were a serious threat to livestock, crops, other property or 'biological diversity'.

Mr Michael said that utility and cruelty were the 'golden thread' which ran through his policy – a phrase he used three times to mounting Conservative groans.

Mention of cruelty inflamed Labour backbenchers. With a few idealistic exceptions, what attracts them to hunting is cruelty. They are the sort of people who get a thrill out of being cruel to Conservatives.

It was indeed a thrilling sight yesterday – watching them set out in pursuit of Nicholas Soames (Con. Mid Sussex). The magnificent creature rose from the back benches. The Labour huntsmen were instantly on to his scent – probably an expensive eau de cologne from Trumper's, the grand Mayfair barber. Before he could even speak, they were imitating hunting horns. In the direction of Mr Michael, the beast gave out of a cry of 'Hunting will fight, and hunting will be right'. This made the Labour pack even more crazed.

Of course Mr Soames cannot be justified on grounds of utility. But Labour backbenchers defend hunting him on the grounds that it is part of their way of life going back centuries. They say it is the only way of keeping down the toff population. They claim that Mr Soames is not a sentient being and therefore cannot feel pain. Prod him after lunch and he will just fall asleep. To me he represents biological diversity.

By becoming passionate and indignant, Douglas Hogg (Con. Sleaford and North Hykeham), son of that fine gentleman Quintin Hogg, gave them further sport. 'It is the business of this House to protect minorities and not to trample on the rights of minorities. In a free society the golden thread should be the liberty of the individual, not the tyranny of the Government.'

Mr Hogg shouted the last phrase. He became increasingly red in face and neck. Mr Michael replied that Mr Hogg needed a doctor. Furthermore, Mr Hogg was 'absurd'. Thank heavens Mr Michael had seen the point of Mr Hogg.

Mr Michael treats with complete impartiality both Conservatives and Labour. The Tories thought that he was outlawing too much hunting, Labour not enough. Labour worried about this talk of 'utility'. Who would decide which hunts were cruel and which had utility? Someone whom Mr Michael described as 'an independent registrar'.

There would be a right of appeal against this functionary's decision. It would be heard by 'a national body with a president at its head appointed by the Lord Chancellor'.

Mr Michael had decided, then, that what our countryside needs is a breath of fresh Whitehall. What Labour backbenchers well know is that the Prime Minister has no enthusiasm for a complete ban. Mr Blair's sport is hunting votes.

Finally, Boris Johnson (Con. Henley) yesterday went on the back benches. Is there any appearance that this publicity-crazed celebrity will not turn down?

His constituents expect him to go on television, not on the back benches. They must be fed up with him clowning around with a load of politicians.

Presumably, he was there yesterday because he needs the money. He will never be taken seriously in television entertainment if he is constantly in Parliament.

Daily Telegraph

Chapter 15

January–June 2003
The Iraq War

We went to war. Saddam was toppled and President Bush made his 'Mission Accomplished' speech. Robin Cook resigned from the cabinet and millions took to the streets of London to demonstrate.

⇥ **14 January 2003** ⇤
'As British Prime Minister I have access to intelligence information,' declares Blair

Clare Short, Secretary of State for International Development, held an unclear position over Iraq but eventually resigned.

Clare Short and the Cabinet were still no nearer last night to disarming Tony Blair. Quite the opposite; more than ever, he continued to defy the world.

He gave a press conference at which he made it clear that he intended to go to war. He sought once again to rally his people for the struggle.

Theoretically, the press conference was held to enable the Prime Minister to answer questions about domestic policy as well as foreign.

He began by reading a statement in which he said that on public services, the euro, taxation and so on, as well as Iraq, 'we shall do what is right'. But it was unclear what he had at his disposal on those other matters.

On education, for example, it does look as if, to judge by the latest figures on numeracy among state school pupils, he has no weapons of mass instruction. Judging by recent events, he also seems unable to disarm Aston, Birmingham. Partly for that reason, he preferred the easier course of disarming Baghdad, Iraq. Both at home and abroad, 'a difficult period lies ahead'.

Lies ahead? His harsher critics certainly think there will be lies ahead. They are for ever accusing him of telling lies. But he appeared more than ever convinced of his own trustworthiness. 'Wait a couple of weeks,' he told several questioners on whether Saddam possesses those especially frightening weapons. 'As British Prime Minister, I have access to intelligence information.'

He knew that some people were sceptical about the intelligence services. 'But I think they do a good job. I don't think they would be advising me wrongly.'

Many leaders, in many climes, have adopted this course with their people: trust me; I know things that at the moment I cannot tell you about. Let us hope that Mr Blair is one of the rare ones who deserve that trust.

If the UN inspectors declined to say that Saddam still had the weapons in question, and no new UN resolution authorising the use of force was forthcoming, and the United States still went to war, would Britain still go to war too?

That was the only question worth asking Mr Blair and the only one in which the country could possibly be interested. As with so many equally massive questions down the ages, the Prime Minister of the day avoided answering it.

To successive attempts to manoeuvre him into doing so, he used a formula to the effect that 'if' Saddam was found to be in breach of the UN, he would be disarmed.

But what if the inspectors said they could not find those weapons? Would Saddam still be 'in breach'? Mr Blair repeatedly told the press that Saddam's autumn 'dossier' – on what weapons he had – was a pack of lies. Therefore, he must be in breach already. Why do not Mr Blair and Mr Bush attack him without delay?

The answer to that was a combination of opinion in the polls and opinion in the Labour Party. Mr Blair has a history of defying the latter.

Defying both, however, is something he does not want to do until he has to. Yesterday he clung to the hope that, when the time comes, perhaps after he has shared some of his intelligence information with us, the voters will support him.

Then he will only have to take on his traditional enemies, Saddam and Labour.

An ITN man asked him what he would say to the mother of a soldier just sent off on the *Ark Royal*, bearing in mind what the reporter said was the 'overwhelming' scepticism about this war in the latest opinion polls.

Mr Blair paused, furrowed his brow, looked moved and turned all his sincerity on that poor woman. Having just seen her son sent to a war which her country did not support, was she to be spared nothing?

Daily Telegraph

⊰ 14 February 2003 ⊱
John Reid, Chairman of the Labour Party (2002–2003) or
'Minister with Special Responsibility for Panic',
deploys tanks at Heathrow

MPs yesterday pondered the deployment, in relation to the terrorist threat, of John Reid. Deploying tanks is one thing. We Britons can take that in our stride. But the Government's deployment of Mr Reid in our cities has aroused perhaps unwarranted fears among the public.

Mr Reid has the nominal title of Labour Party Chairman. But he is really Minister with Special Responsibility for Panic. When things look worrying for the Prime Minister, his function under the constitution is to go on the *Today* programme and say that Mr Blair has the situation under control, and if Mr Blair has not, that the media and the Tories have made the situation up. All agree that he is good at it.

On Wednesday, the Government decided to deploy Mr Reid in support of tanks and troops at Heathrow. He told reporters that the military presence was to do with 'a threat of the nature that massacred thousands of people in New York'. It was his way of reassuring us. Amid the resultant hysteria, Mr Reid said later in the day that his remarks had been 'misinterpreted' – the word which politicians use when they have said something they regret, as a synonym for 'quoted'.

Yesterday the Conservatives sought to make suitable trouble out of all this. Their difficulty was that the Shadow Home Secretary, Oliver Letwin, is not a suitable troublemaker. He has made his name by being written up in the liberal prints as the Tory Party's opponents' preferred Tory. That is, a Tory who bears no relation to Tory Party members and Tory voters actual or potential.

For the sake of his future in the Tory Party, he needs some non-Tory enemies. Yesterday he may have managed to acquire some. For David Blunkett, the Home Secretary, and much of the Labour Party became irritated with him. 'Uriah Heep,' someone shouted.

The Speaker had granted an urgent question from Mr Letwin to Mr Blunkett about the security deployment at Heathrow and elsewhere. Mr Blunkett gave the operational details without mentioning Mr Reid. The Home Secretary said it was important to 'avoid frightening people unnecessarily'. Various Tories scoffed. 'John Reid, John Reid,' they muttered, confident that the very name frightens everyone by now, except of course al-Qa'eda.

Mr Letwin complained to Mr Blunkett about 'confusing and conflicting signals given by other ministers on the airways' – by which he meant Dr Reid.

A Labour voice shouted 'scaremongering'. The word seemed odd when directed at Mr Letwin rather than Mr Reid, with his talk of a British September 11.

Mr Letwin also called for a minister to co-ordinate all nine Whitehall departments dealing with security; there being a similar functionary in the United States. This further irritated Mr Blunkett who is under the impression that he is himself that minister.

Replying to Mr Letwin, Mr Blunkett adhered to the Government's line of the previous 24 hours that Mr Reid's remarks had been 'entirely misquoted'. John Smith (Lab. Vale of Glamorgan) told an appreciative Mr Blunkett that Mr Letwin's use of an urgent question to spread such concern had been 'the height of irresponsibility'. This was to treat the emollient Shadow Home Secretary as if he were, say, Lord Tebbit, and thus further improving his standing among staunch Tories.

Francis Maude (Con. Horsham) intervened to say that Mr Letwin was 'the least partisan of politicians'. So Mr Letwin's career is not safe yet.

Boris Johnson (Con. Henley) was in the Chamber throughout, and indeed for some two hours; unsuccessfully attempting, at one stage, to ask a question. On Tuesday he had succeeded in asking one about a hospital in his constituency.

His assiduity could be explained by his constituency Conservative association's AGM being imminent, and his need to do something about weeks of campaigning among certain journalists suggesting that he was not in the Chamber often enough. I shall not name the culprits.

This security alert to deal with a possible threat to Mr Johnson's parliamentary career should not cause panic among the public. There is no corresponding threat to his media career.

Daily Telegraph

⊰ 19 March 2003 ⊱
Blair adopts his tremulous 'Diana's funeral' voice
and wins the vote to go to war

Five minutes before the figures were announced, Hilary Armstrong, the Chief Whip, walked in and stood in front of the Prime Minister, seated on the front bench. She told him the voting. Mr Blair smiled. A colleague in the gallery, who has a certain lip-reading skill, assured me that he replied with something like: 'So we're OK, then?'

The number of rebels was up on last month. But Mr Blair had won without having to rely on Conservative votes. So the debate ended for him with relative success. We shall now see whether the war does too.

Mr Blair had opened the big debate by deploying his tremulous,

'Diana's funeral' voice. Those MPs, mainly Conservatives, who were not in touch with their feminine side, stirred with embarrassment. I mean, the Conservative women.

But even some Conservative men seemed to be embarrassed too: '. . . this is a tough choice . . . I believe we must hold firm . . . the main parties divided.'

Several Liberal Democrats shouted: 'Not us.' Mr Blair muttered the Liberal Democrat name, and in a louder voice added: 'Unified as ever in opportunism and error.'

A huge cheer went up, not least from the Tories. Something approaching contempt for the Liberal Democrats was to be a theme of Conservatives and loyalist Labour throughout the debate.

From that moment, Mr Blair's voice became less ecclesiastical – firmer, more convincing. The speech gathered speed, and success.

A House with every seat full, and the gangways jammed with sitting Members, had awaited Mr Blair's arrival. He sat down between John Prescott and Jack Straw. Further down the front bench, next to David Blunkett, was Clare Short. She had decided to carry on drawing her Cabinet salary in order to carry on helping the world's poor.

Robin Cook sat in a seat as far from the front bench as it was possible to be. From the gallery, he was a blurred, Gothic gargoyle.

Mr Blair's speech was remarkable not for what he said, since he said nothing new, but for the eloquent way he said it. There were none of those verbless sentences.

He dealt effortlessly with the interventions of anti-war MPs. The only intervention he refused to take was that of Glenda Jackson (Lab. Hampstead), but that was because she sought to intervene in mid-peroration. To watch her rising majestically, and him courteously but firmly waving her down, was to be in the audience for two of our greatest living actors.

Iain Duncan Smith's speech made just as many good points, but he lacked – or perhaps scorned – Mr Blair's theatre arts.

Charles Kennedy's speech was much shredded by Labour and Tory interruptions. He accused the Tories of having sold Saddam anthrax. Peter Lilley, a relevant minister at around that period, became indignant and constantly tried to intervene. Mr Kennedy refused, but still took several Labour interventions. Tories shouted for him to give way to Mr Lilley. Michael Fabricant (Con. Lichfield) cried: 'It's a disgrace.'

Mr Kennedy, irrespective of his anti-war arguments, seemed diminished.

Daily Telegraph

⊰ 21 March 2003 ⊱

Hans Blix has found nothing and George Galloway is in full flood

Hans Blix (Swedish diplomat, Chairman of UN Weapons Inspection Commission) did not find weapons of mass destruction. The Chief Whip, Hilary Armstrong, whips George Galloway MP in vain.

Outside, in Parliament Square, the protesters were more numerous and louder than before. Inside, in the Chamber, they were fewer and quieter. Our forces were, or were about to be, in action. This imposed, on most opponents of the war, a certain restraint.

There is a belief among politicians – perhaps a myth – that, even if they oppose a war, they should not be noisy about it when the country's troops are fighting it.

The irreverent thought occurred: perhaps Labour would be organising the uproar at this moment if the party were in opposition and this were a Tory war. Mr Blair, as Opposition Leader, might even be joining in the noise, or at least acquiescing in it. The thought occurred only for it to be banished as unworthy.

For only a few Labour opponents of the war did life go on as normal yesterday. The most effective was George Galloway (Lab. Glasgow Kelvin).

Geoff Hoon, the Defence Secretary, arrived at the Dispatch Box to report on the situation. Questioning of Mr Hoon, even from Labour and Liberal Democrat anti-warriors, was decorous. Below the gangway, Mr Galloway listened with a contemptuous look.

Loyal Tom Levitt (Lab. High Peak) told Mr Hoon what a good

thing it was that 30 countries were participating in the coalition against Iraq. Some of us searched our memories for the names of those, apart from Britain, the United States and Australia, who were contributing actual soldiers.

Mr Galloway, the same thought having perhaps occurred to him, smiled and shook his head at Mr Levitt's words. Eventually, he was called to ask his own question.

In his statement, Mr Hoon had said that, the previous day, Hans Blix had said he was disappointed that three and a half months of inspections had not brought clear Iraqi assurances that they had no weapons of mass destruction. Was it not 'the ultimate spin doctoring', Mr Galloway roared, for Mr Hoon to pray in aid of Mr Blix?

From her corner seat on the front bench, Hilary Armstrong, the Government Chief Whip, turned her head rightwards towards Mr Galloway, and muttered something at him.

Mr Galloway interrupted himself. 'The Chief Whip's heckling me,' he said. 'Let me say, this is a free Parliament and I'll be heard in it.'

Plenty of Tories, not opponents of the war, joined with the Labour anti-warriors in cheering him for that. Any enemy of a Government Chief Whip, still more of Government spinning, is temporarily the Tories' friend.

Mr Galloway resumed: 'Dr Blix has denounced the action which the minister has just been boasting about this morning, as have an overwhelming number of world leaders, including some of our closest friends, partners and allies.' He went on to refer to the opinion of what he claimed was the overwhelming opposition to the war of international legal experts. Or, as he put it, in what must be taken as an irreverent reference to the law officers of the Crown, unpurchased international legal experts.

What assurances could Mr Hoon give British forces that they would not face prosecution in the International Criminal Court for the actions Mr Hoon had ordered them to carry out? Mr Galloway did not say who would arrest them.

Happily, this sketch must judge politicians as parliamentarians, not as logicians. It is not what they say, but the way they say it; and it is an added point in their favour if what they say is unpopular with higher authority.

Mr Galloway yesterday remained a tremendous parliamentarian. Also, his point about Mr Hoon's use of Mr Blix amounted to a direct hit.

Mr Hoon did not have much of an answer. Elsewhere he was his usual, safe staff officer self. But events had only just begun to unfold. With many others, he will be judged later.

Daily Telegraph

I think I only ever met Frank once, and then briefly, though I felt I knew him well. The few times he wrote about me indicated that he rather liked me (or at least my parliamentary style) and I was always very proud of that.

His sketch of 21 March 2003 features Frank's normal acute observation of character – 'loyal Tom Levitt (Lab. High Peak)' could otherwise have been expressed by a less elegant writer as 'toady Tom'. Geoff Hoon as 'safe staff officer' sums up exactly the apolitical quartermaster-type role the Defence Secretary sought to play in the Iraq War. Of course, many British servicemen would still be alive today if Hoon had even been a half-decent quartermaster.

Frank is kind enough in this column to describe my 'direct hit' on the Government, but his final sentence really hits the bull's eye. Writing long before the war turned into a major league disaster that would bring down (indirectly) the Prime Minister and destroy the presidency of George W. Bush, Frank Johnson writes of Mr Hoon, 'With many others, he will be judged later.'

Frank Johnson's suspicions of people and their motives was almost always right; his judgement of their character merciless and hilarious. It is an honour to have caught his eye from time to time.

George Galloway MP

⊰ **26 March 2003** ⊱

Iraqis have not welcomed our forces with open arms. The prospect of street fighting looms. Galloway combusts!

Tony Blair sought to assure us yesterday that all was going to plan, and that there was no cause for alarm. From any head of government in the post-Vietnam, media age that would normally spread panic.

But Mr Blair partially succeeded in spreading some reassurance. Still, for most of the day, there was an air of unease around Westminster and Whitehall. We should put it no stronger than that. It was not panic or despair – just unease.

I spent part of the day moving between Foreign Office Questions, and the television showing Mr Blair's press conference a few hundred yards away in Downing Street. Put at its simplest, the unease was caused by the disappointing of the belief of most politicians on both sides of the House, and of the political class in general, that the Iraqis would not put up much of a fight, and that their streets would welcome our forces.

Mr Blair doubtless feared that disappointment had spread to the British people at large. Mr Blair's purpose, with his press conference, was to convince them that nothing unexpected was going on.

He was soon asked about the absence of the Iraqi welcome. Among other things, he replied: 'We have let Iraq down in the past' – a reference to our encouraging them to rise up against Saddam after his expulsion from Kuwait in 1991, and the American-led coalition's failure to come to their aid when they did. Like all unusually candid replies by politicians, this had the merit of being much more convincing than a routine spin or fib.

Then someone asked the question that was on all our minds. Why were the Iraqis resisting more than we were told they would? Mr Blair replied that there was 'not the same degree of fighting' from Iraq's regular army as from the more fanatical Republican Guard – a brave reply since it could, in a few days' time, be proved wrong.

Thereafter, Mr Blair became more of the politician we knew him to be. What did he think of a 'scenario' which, it seems, involves Anglo-Americans fighting in the streets? 'This scenario is entirely what we expected,' he said. Entirely? It was hard to believe that he had entirely expected that with which our forces were now confronted.

He made a point of refusing to speculate as to how long he thought the war would last. Nobody thought he would. But he reminded us that it had taken only 5 days to reach within 60 miles of Baghdad.

The logic of that – or at least the implication of his tone – was that it would not take long to subdue Baghdad. Wisely, he did not pursue that train of thought to its logical conclusion.

In the Commons, the anti-war faction held its fire except for its incendiary orator, George Galloway (Lab. Glasgow Kelvin). The Foreign Secretary had mused that the Arab leaders' public opposition to the coalition was not the same as what they said privately.

Mr Galloway caught fire: 'Arab leaders will have heard the Foreign Secretary publicly brand them as liars.' He quoted a British military spokesman as saying that they had expected a lot of hands up in Iraq, but that it had not worked out that way.

The 'weapons of forgery, plagiarism, fabrication and lies' that the Government had fed to the world had 'become boomerangs which are now cutting, alas, not the bodies of the donkeys who sent our people into battle, but the lions who are having to stand and fight in defence of the British Government's lies, forgery and deception'.

Some Tories shouted: 'Disgraceful.' But, irrespective of whether one was persuaded by it, that was a magnificent sentence. At first, one thought that Mr Straw's reply, though less eloquent, was convincing. He pointed out that Mr Galloway had used exactly the same 'rhetoric' about the military action in Afghanistan.

But Mr Galloway defied the rules of order to rise in his seat, without the Speaker's bidding, and shouting of the Afghanistan intervention: 'You said it would be over. A year ago, you said it was over.'

The Speaker ordered him down. But he had made his point spectacularly. Whatever the Iraqis do, he will fight for ever.

Daily Telegraph

⊰ **10 April 2003** ⊱

Blair arranges for Baghdad to fall on Brown's Budget Day

Gordon Brown arrived on the front bench and exchanged only the most formal greeting with the Prime Minister. Trust Tony, he must have been thinking, to arrange for Baghdad to fall so as to spoil his Budget Day publicity.

Mr Blair was thinking too. On to Damascus! On to Teheran! On to Brown! Could I overthrow Gordon in a summer reshuffle? It would be a dangerous operation. But Mr Brown enjoys no support among the broad middle classes. Too many of them have been persecuted by the only organised force still loyal to him (the Inland Revenue).

True, he is said to have the support of his own tribe: Old Labour. But they do not count as an organised force, and how many of them would really fight for him if he looked like falling? Especially if Mr Blair hit the ringleaders with the most effective weapon available to him: junior office. A few parliamentary secretaryships for pensions or social services should be enough to make them flee the Brown regime, and go over to Mr Blair.

Certainly, no Chancellor in history could have delivered a Budget on a day of such triumph for his Prime Minister. Budgets are now delivered immediately after Prime Minister's Questions. Yesterday, Mr Blair rose to answer them with every television screen in the Palace of Westminster alive with scenes of Iraqis in the heart of Baghdad exulting in Saddam's fall, and welcoming the Americans as liberators – just as Mr Blair said they would.

Mr Brown had to sit through it. His natural Labour faction had opposed the war. Mr Brown knew that Mr Blair had put himself at risk, especially a week ago when the invasion did not look as if it was going well. All agreed that he would be the beneficiary of the war's failure. Yet here was Iain Duncan Smith yesterday graciously congratulating Mr Blair on his war policy. Mr Brown, and the one-third or so of the Labour benches opposed to the war, endured this as best they could.

Mr Duncan Smith went on to ask Mr Blair whether it was yet known who might be found in Iraq formally to surrender to the coalition forces. Whereupon, David Winnick (Lab. Walsall N), a supporter of the war, produced a masterly heckle which caused both sides of the Chamber to shake with laughter.

'Mister Galloway,' he cried.

Mr Blair smiled, and paused. 'I must resist all temptation at this point,' he said. 'We shall have to wait and see.' George Galloway (Lab. Glasgow Kelvin) was not in the Chamber. Mr Winnick was referring to the war's most oratorically, if not militarily, gifted opponent; though on the military aspect he would undoubtedly argue that the coalition will look less successful in a few months' time.

After what might have seemed to Mr Brown to be an unusually long half hour of Prime Minister's Questions, the Chancellor rose. In his opening sentences, he suddenly became a supporter of the war. He believed the whole House would wish to join him in expressing gratitude and support to our armed forces for the 'zeal, bravery and resilience with which they carry out their duties, and for their outstanding achievements'.

And then: 'I believe we owe a debt of gratitude to the strong leadership in a difficult time of our Prime Minister.' It will be that remark of Mr Brown's, rather than those Iraqis dancing around the dictator's fallen statue, which the world will see as the final proof that the Saddam regime has no hope. Gordon's gone over to Blair, Tariq Aziz would have told Saddam down in the bunker – we're done for now.

The difficult part over, Mr Brown turned to economics. He was so open about all the detail that he must have been hiding something really massive. So it proved. Iain Duncan Smith, when he came to reply, pointed out that the crucial borrowing figures had been in the accompanying Treasury book, not the speech.

Still, no Chancellor has been so gifted at making officialese sound virtuous. 'Today I am reaffirming our symmetrical inflation target based on the current RPIX [Retail Prices Index excluding mortgage interest repayments] measure,' he said. We were meant to be reassured. Never reaffirm a symmetrical inflation target not based on the current RPIX measure, Gordie, laddie, his boyhood neighbours used to tell him.

Daily Telegraph

⊰ 15 April 2003 ⊱
Soames suggests that British police volunteer for duties in Iraq.
'Why are these blokes called the Ba'ath Party, Sarge?'
'Because they're a right shower!'

Nicholas Soames (Con. Mid Sussex) yesterday suggested to the Prime Minister that British police be asked to volunteer for duties in Iraq.

Mr Blair, without committing himself, received the idea with his customary courtesy.

Mr Soames had inspired pleasing thoughts of some Dixon of Basra Green, firm but fair. 'Now, what 'ave we got 'ere? A suicide bomber, eh? I think it's time you gave me that bomb of yours before it can do any 'arm, Sunni boy.'

Doubtless some of our boys on the beat down there will have a firmer grasp of Iraqi culture than others.

'Why are these blokes called the Ba'ath Party, Sarge?'

'Because they're a right shower. And you'd better understand that not many of them are Shi'ites.'

'They could have fooled me, Sarge.'

Before long, Ba'athists would become known in the force as 'spongies' or 'soap suds'.

Then some senior commissioner, anxious for the approbation of the liberal press, would condemn such derogatory language. Several officers would be sacked. It would be just like home.

It was a day of important points being made from the Conservative back benches. Boris Johnson (Con. Henley) asked the Prime Minister for an assurance that no members of the Ba'ath Party would be given asylum in Britain.

Henley is not generally considered to be one of the Ba'ath Party's target seats. Surely Mr Johnson should worry more about the Liberal Democrats. But presumably he had good reason for his concern. Mr Blair reassured him. No Ba'ath Party members would be granted asylum.

The Prime Minister was reporting on the Iraq situation on the last day before the House rose for the Easter recess.

He rose to comparative silence. Few Labour backbenchers cheered him. Among many of them, the war's outcome has been greeted with much more dismay than it has among Conservatives or Iraqis.

Mr Blair reported that the war was nearing the end. But there were 'tough times ahead in building peace'. He was referring to peace in Iraq, rather than peace in the Labour Party. The outlook for the latter was more pessimistic. The vast majority of Iraqis were, he said, 'rejoicing' at Saddam's departure. Labour opponents of the war, however, seemed to have taken it rather badly. Their mood was subdued. They had high hopes that the looting might enable them to say that the Anglo-Americans had made the situation worse. But the latest news before Mr Blair spoke was that the looting was declining. The Labour anti-war faction took this as best they could.

Tam Dalyell (Lab. Linlithgow) asked for an assurance that there were no plans to invade Syria. The Tory benches stirred. 'He's on the next one,' called George Osborne (Con. Tatton). 'He's at it again,' called someone else.

Mr Blair insisted that there were no plans to invade Syria.

He had given the same reply to the same question a few minutes earlier, from Charles Kennedy, the Liberal Democrat Leader whom the Conservatives have so much taken against.

Mr Kennedy had only uttered three words before a Tory shouted: 'Too long!'

After Mr Dalyell, Alex Salmond, for the Scottish National Party, asked the question once more.

Mr Blair contrived not to sound exasperated. He knew that there were these 'conspiracy theories', he said. He conceded that the threat to Syria had been attributed to certain members of the American administration.

But he had been speaking to President Bush nearly every day, he explained. There were no such plans. He did not doubt, however, this conspiracy theory would be 'swiftly replaced by a fresh one'.

Iain Duncan Smith once again congratulated Mr Blair. Mr Blair replied by thanking Mr Duncan Smith for his support. He added that the Government must have presented a 'tempting target for any

'Opposition' at various stages, but Mr Duncan Smith did not take it, and that was 'to his credit'.

The Labour back benches endured this as best they could. Doubtless opportunities will present themselves after the recess to depict the war as having been a disaster. But yesterday they sullenly bided their time; less a pocket, more a turn-up of resistance.

Daily Telegraph

⊰ 19 June 2003 ⊱
Blair tinkers with the constitution and tries to abolish the ancient office of Lord Chancellor

Tony Blair described the Lord Chancellorship yesterday as he never did before he decided to abolish it – at least not in public. What Iain Duncan Smith and the Tories wanted to preserve, he said, was someone 'in a full-bottomed wig, 18th-century breeches and women's tights and sitting on a woolsack'.

He added that if that was the centrepiece of Mr Duncan's Smith's electoral strategy 'then roll on the next election'. He sat down to Labour laughter and cheers.

One wondered if he warned Lord Irvine all those years ago of what he had in store for him. 'Derry, when I come to power, I'm going to give you a job that will involve your wearing women's tights.'

'Thanks, Tony. I'm glad you're broad-minded about my unusual tastes.'

'But there's a downside too, Derry. You'll also have to wear a full-bottomed wig, 18th-century breeches clothes and sit on a woolsack.'

'Now look here, young Blair. What do you think I am – a pervert!'

Nonetheless, Lord Irvine did the job for six years on those terms. Then, last Thursday, Mr Blair's office unexpectedly announced that the office was to be abolished.

It was the first time that socially liberal, live-and-let-live New Labour had done anything to prevent a man wearing women's tights. The permissive society seemed in danger.

The chaos accompanying the reshuffle aroused the Tories. This is not just because the Tories have always included in their ranks plenty of men who wear women's tights.

Admittedly, in the old days, if they were caught, they were thrown out of their clubs and regiments; unless, of course, one could hush it up.

They were also annoyed because they did not think Mr Blair should take it upon himself to abolish Lord Irvine in quite so casual a way.

The reshuffle also caused strange goings on at the Scottish and Welsh Offices. Nothing to do with women's tights or woolsacks; but odd nonetheless. At one point it was announced that the Offices no longer existed.

The Scottish Office removed its plaque. The Welsh Office seemed about to do the same. Then it was announced that both were still in existence but would come under Lord Falconer who would for the time being be sitting on the woolsack in those tights, while at the same time be run by ministers, though both would wear trousers.

Mr Blair had to come before the House yesterday to explain all this. 'Had to' because he had not wanted to.

On Monday, the Tories had complained to Michael Martin, the Speaker, about Mr Blair's not announcing such momentous changes in the House. The Speaker compelled him to come and do so. Mr Martin is not proving to be the creature of the Government that his many hostile critics had said he was when mainly Labour votes elected him to the Chair.

Nicholas Soames (Con. Mid Sussex) thought the manner of the abolition had been 'an affront to the Crown' and demanded that Mr Blair 'desist in dealing with the dignified part of our constitution in a casual and arrogant manner'.

This did not necessarily mean Mr Soames was in favour of men wearing women's tights on woolsacks; merely that the practice should be made illegal only after the Queen has been properly consulted. Mr Blair depicted the constitutional changes in the reshuffle as having been decided with much forethought, when everyone knew that they arose out of Lord Irvine's quarrelling with

David Blunkett. Mr Duncan Smith delivered enough lines to enable him to make that point on the television news that evening.

But in the House a massive wall of Labour barracking, organised by Whips carefully placing themselves around the back benches, made him look rambling and ineffective. But such verbosity, though it may be tactically mistaken, suggests a dogged courage enabling him to keep going on these terrible occasions.

John Redwood (Con. Wokingham) thought that the way out of the 'women's tights' problem was to give the Lord Chancellor a pair of trousers, not abolish him. Mr Redwood is at his best in a tights corner.

Daily Telegraph

⚔ 25 June 2003 ⚔
Is David Blunkett, Home Secretary (2001–2004), the bearded left-winger who gatecrashed Prince William's 21st?

The bearded man who made a statement as Home Secretary to the House yesterday about the security lapse at Prince William's 21st birthday party was really a retired left-wing agitator from Sheffield, it was later revealed.

He was named as David Blunkett, and had been disguising himself as Home Secretary for just over two years. The question was immediately asked – how did he get in?

Preliminary inquiries suggest that he did so by making right-wing remarks about law and order to Tony Blair. This enabled him to gain entry to the Home Office.

Mr Blunkett began by saying that his statement was 'on the serious breach of security at Windsor Castle last Saturday evening'. He had received a 'six-page report' from the Metropolitan Police Commissioner. But this, it seems, was only a 'preliminary report'. There would also be 'a further detailed review'.

Mr Blunkett, then, was anxious to show that he was taking the matter with due seriousness. Doubtless, it is indeed a serious matter. But there was a hint across the House, especially on the Labour benches, that it was also an unserious matter and that we were in danger of taking it too seriously.

The Home Secretary launched into a narrative of the events in question. At 8pm, he said, someone 'appeared at the main entrance of Windsor Castle'. Mr Blunkett said that he did an 'impromptu comic turn'.

Some of us jumped to the conclusion that it was Prince Philip. But apparently it was not. It was, said Mr Blunkett, a certain Aaron Barschak.

But later, this person was able to advance along the north terrace, where 'he was challenged by a contractor. By this time he had changed into fancy dress.'

This raised the issue: why was the contractor wearing fancy dress? But, no, the civil servants who drafted Mr Blunkett's statement had phrased that passage ambiguously. It was Mr Barschak who had changed into fancy dress, not the contractor. At least, this was what we deduced from the context.

But the mention of fancy dress caused the Conservative benches to shout as one: 'The Lord Chancellor!'

Mr Blunkett commented: 'Actually, it's quite serious.' But he did so with a smile, so we did not think that he was being more pompous than the situation warranted.

The Home Secretary pressed on. Mr Barschak 'presented himself as being slightly drunk and said that he was a party guest who was lost'. The contractor escorted him to one of the side entrances to the castle where a police officer was on duty.

Mr Barschak's presenting himself as slightly drunk presumably convinced the police officer that this person was indeed a genuine guest, probably an Etonian or an It girl.

Whatever the reason, Mr Barschak entered the party without further challenge and, Mr Blunkett said, 'was able to get unacceptably close to Prince William'.

The Home Secretary added that, having appeared at the Prince's side, he then made his way to the bar where a member of the staff challenged him. He was handed over to the police, and released on bail.

Replying, Oliver Letwin, the Shadow Home Secretary, said that his party did not want to 'decapitate' Mr Blunkett or anyone else over the incident. That would be just to 'satisfy bloodlust'. But he thought that, in these dangerous times, there should be an extra Cabinet Minister who would be 'a centre of energy' on security policy. Mr Blunkett said he was grateful for there being no bloodlust. But he did not like the idea of that extra minister. He thought that such a functionary would have made no difference on Saturday night.

So, he added, 'it doesn't matter what silly party politics are made of this'. This was Mr Letwin's reward for not making silly party politics.

Andrew Robathan (Con. Blaby), a former Coldstream Guards regular officer, said that he had 'spent a lot of time guarding Windsor Castle'. He suggested that there was a serious potential threat.

The next time it happened, 'some clown in a dress could not just be a gatecrasher'. Equally, he could be a brother Coldstream Guards regular officer, in which case we must assume that the Royal Family would be safe.

Daily Telegraph

I was very entertained by this sketch.

We'd had a major incursion into Windsor Castle – I was answering on behalf of the Metropolitan Police who were responsible. The bizarre attire of the intruder certainly led to mirth within the House of Commons! Frank's interesting reflections bring back slightly more happy memories than I thought they would!

David Blunkett MP

Chapter 16

July–October 2003
The 'sexing up'
of the dossier

Britons were being held at the military prison in the US naval base in Guantanamo Bay, Cuba. Alistair Campbell, Blair's infamous spin doctor was accused by the BBC's defence correspondent of 'sexing up' a dossier. This led to further accusations that Blair had misled the House in order to declare war on Iraq. Weeks later, Campbell resigned.

⊰ 16 July 2003 ⊱
Dr Kelly is described as chaff under tough questioning
by the Foreign Affairs Committee

Dr Kelly, a senior civil servant and weapons inspector, was under the spotlight for leaking information to the BBC's defence correspondent, Andrew Gilligan. Later, he took his own life.

Bill Olner (Lab. Nuneaton), a member of the all-party Commons foreign affairs committee, yesterday asked a witness whether he had ever mentioned 'the C word'.

The witness replied: 'C word?'

Mr Olner: 'Yes, Alastair Campbell.'

That C word is of course not mentioned in polite society. The witness was a respectable Ministry of Defence civil servant who did not look the type to use such language. One could not imagine him telling anyone that they had behaved like a complete Campbell.

We were at the committee's renewed investigations into the BBC allegations concerning that C. The corporation's defence correspondent, it will be remembered, had reported that the Prime Minister's chief spin doctor had 'sexed up' some intelligence material about Iraq's weapons of mass destruction.

The Government demanded to know who had told Andrew Gilligan such a thing. Mr Gilligan and the BBC, as we journalists are apt to do, refused to disclose the source. Mr Blair and Mr Campbell have talked of little else since. This is not only because they are angry with the BBC. It is because it enables them not to have to talk so much about the actual weapons of mass destruction, or lack of them.

The committee had already held seemingly interminable hearings into the matter. In the middle of them, the above-mentioned respectable civil servant, Dr David Kelly, a weapons inspector with experience of inspecting weapons in Iraq, decided that he might himself be thought of as the source. Or at least, the Ministry of Defence announced that he might be the source. He confessed to having had lunch with Mr Gilligan.

Dr Kelly did not look like someone who would use the C word. But the committee members could not at first be sure. They suspected that he had. Otherwise, why had he volunteered to come before the committee? But as the questioning proceeded, it became clear that Dr Kelly was not the mole. He had not been the one who had revealed to Mr Gilligan that the material had been 'sexed up'.

The questions and answers seem to reveal that Dr Kelly did not know about the things that were in Mr Gilligan's story. 'I believe I am not the main source,' he said. 'From the conversation I had I don't see how he could make the statements he was making from the comments I made.'

It was then that Mr Olner uttered the C word. Dr Kelly conceded that it was Mr Gilligan, not he, who had used it. That could not have surprised the committee. Mr Gilligan is a journalist. That is the sort of language which we sometimes use.

Why, then, had Dr Kelly come forward? He explained that it was because 'other elements' of Mr Gilligan's report had matched what he had told him. As it dawned on the committee members that they had not found the mole, some of them became irritated. Especially pugnacious Andrew Mackinlay (Lab. Thurrock).

'You're chaff,' he told Dr Kelly – chaff, as far as one could recall from war documentaries, being material dispersed about the sky to deceive enemy air communications. Dr Kelly had been 'thrown up' by the Ministry of Defence so as to divert the committee from the real mole, Mr Mackinlay implied. Mr Mackinlay did not like being made a Campbell of.

There was not much that Dr Kelly could say in reply to Mr Mackinlay. He confined himself to a few words of polite dissent from the suggestion that he was chaff.

The committee departed with many answers unforthcoming. Who was the mole if it was not Dr Kelly? Had someone at the top of our intelligence services sent Dr Kelly to confuse the committee? Perhaps it was C himself. MPs nowadays think they are being tricked by a whole bunch of Cs.

Daily Telegraph

⊰ 18 September 2003 ⊱
The Hutton Inquiry: It is not exactly easy getting every detail right, is it Mr Scrumptious?

The Hutton Inquiry into Dr Kelly's death found the Government completely innocent of 'sexing up' any intelligence material or dossier. Frank attended one of the early stages of the investigation. After its results were published in January 2004, the Independent *had just one word on its front page: 'WHITEWASH'.*

Jonathon Sumption, the famously expensive QC appearing for the Government at the Hutton Inquiry, spent much of his cross-examination talking up the smallest mistakes of the BBC defence correspondent Andrew Gilligan. In due course, Mr Sumption mentioned a BBC official named Stephen Mitchell.

'Stephen Whittle,' Gilligan courteously corrected him. 'Stephen Whittle,' Mr Sumption replied, almost as if he were correcting Gilligan.

Later, cross-examining Richard Sambrook, the BBC head of news, Mr Sumption referred to a document written by a *Today* programme editor. 'The Miranda Holden document,' he said.

'Miranda Holt,' said Mr Sambrook. 'Miranda Holt,' Mr Sumption commented, in an authoritative sort of way.

So, then, it is not easy getting every detail right is it, Mr Scrumptious? 'Sumption, actually.' Sumption, exactly.

Now, if I may move on, Mr Assumption.

Yesterday's sitting was almost entirely about the Government, represented by this master of detail, trying to show that, because Gilligan had got a number of small things wrong, he had got a big thing wrong too. That is, a story the most essential aspect of which was that various figures connected with British intelligence thought that Mr Blair had exaggerated the threat which Saddam Hussein posed to Britain; in particular, Saddam's ability to deploy weapons of mass destruction in 45 minutes.

At one stage, Lord Hutton provoked laughter – concerning one of Gilligan's descriptions of Dr Kelly to the Commons foreign affairs committee – by intervening with the question: 'What do the words "Absolutely, Yes" mean, Mr Gilligan?' Gilligan replied: 'That is, I mean, I would characterise the source in the same way as I characterised him on the programme.'

I mention this because Lord Hutton may have put the finger on the central problem of his inquiry. 'Absolutely, Yes' is not really the appropriate phrase. More appropriate is the title of a play recently playing in the West End of London: *Absolutely, Perhaps.*

It was by the great pre-war Italian playwright, Pirandello. Though a genius, he was essentially a one-idea author. All his plays are more or less about the impossibility of knowing what is real. *Absolutely, Perhaps* concerns a woman who may or may not have married the same man twice. Did he have two different wives or just one? At the end, when asked who she is, she says she is his wife; thus leaving open both possibilities. The Hutton Inquiry has a similar plot. On the face of it, it is about whether the Government 'sexed up' some intelligence stuff in order to get a war past the Labour Party.

Dr Kelly's tragedy, though dreadful, is a subplot. The story could end with it being shown that the Government both sexed up the stuff, and did not believe that it did so. The public can then believe what it wants to believe. A less elevated comparison could be Agatha Christie's *Murder on the Orient Express*. They all did it.

Most of us have been Christie admirers at one time or another. But those of us who are not Pirandellians, content to leave it at that, we should still strive to discover which side – the Government or the BBC – has the most justification for its belief that it is in the right.

To that end, it appeared to this observer that Mr Sumption did not seriously undermine Gilligan's story. Gilligan proved a good witness. There will be much emphasis on his admitting, under Mr Sumption's cross-examination, various errors. For example, he had been wrong to describe Dr Kelly as being in the intelligence services. Mr Sumption seemed triumphant. But Gilligan also said that, in his successive BBC reports, he had merely said that Dr Kelly was involved in intelligence. That Dr Kelly undoubtedly was.

Gilligan also admitted that he had done wrong in revealing to MPs on the foreign affairs committee that Dr Kelly had been the source for a *Newsnight* report. He yesterday apologised. I am just trying to remember when, in this whole affair, Mr Blair has apologised. He may be the one who has the most to apologise for.

But we all make mistakes – as Mr Suction knows.

Daily Telegraph

⊰ 1 October 2003 ⊱
'More battered without and stronger within' –
Blair's fake heroics at the Labour conference

What happened was the opposite of what had been expected. Outside the hall, opponents of Tony Blair's Iraq policy demonstrated. But inside no one heckled or jeered him.

He had confronted an international bully and it would make no difference if the party agreed with his policy or not. Gordon Brown just had to be stopped. Mr Blair made it clear that, if necessary, he would do it again. He would go into that Islington restaurant and eat as much polenta as it took to beat Mr Brown.

Mr Blair's speech was just about as good a conference speech as we old hands had heard. It had everything needed for the occasion and for Mr Blair's predicament.

We are told that television has ensured that, at conferences, leaders must concentrate on addressing the whole country, not just their own parties. But the country was not Mr Blair's immediate problem.

He faced trouble from his party. Perhaps he will face trouble from the country too, but an election is two years away and he will worry about that when the time comes. At the moment he had to deal with the threat posed by what, for the party, he truly believed to be Mr Brown's weapons of mass self-destruction.

To confront that threat, he deployed jokes. He deployed incomprehensible, and presumably bogus, statistics. When he told of letters which parents of soldiers killed in Iraq had written to him, he wept – showing that, to overthrow this man Brown, he would stop at nothing.

The passage concerning the letters and the weeping were not in the section dealing with Iraq. They were in a generalised section towards the end about how hard his job was but, by implication, how suited he was to it. True, the sentence ending the passage did not quite make sense: 'After six years, more battered without but stronger within – it's the only kind of leadership I can offer.' Battered leadership, it seemed, was what the country needed.

The section solely about Iraq lasted only a few minutes. It began in a pleading manner: 'I ask just one thing: attack my decision but at least understand why I took it.' That was an anti-heckle device, as no one felt disposed to shout: ''Cos the Americans told you to, you poodle.'

Mr Blair was now free to remind his party that Saddam must have had weapons of mass destruction because he gassed lots of his people. Yes, but was there any danger that he might have gassed us here in Britain? There obviously was not, otherwise Mr Blair would have told us long ago.

Then he pointed out that Saddam's regime had been brutal. But he did not explain why he was not embarking on a series of wars against other brutal regimes. He was not, however, presiding over a course in logic. He was trying to stop troublemakers from heckling him in front of the cameras. In that, he was completely successful.

For suddenly, after a few paragraphs on Iraq, he changed the subject to the need to keep in with Europe as well as America, the mention of Europe resulting in applause, though not of course the mention of the US. The next thing we knew he was talking about fairness and equal opportunity. Suddenly, it was a case of: Briton Escapes Iraq Horror.

What of the other causes of Brownite unrest: foundation hospitals and university top-up fees? Mr Blair seemed to defend both with reference to Old Labour principles of educational opportunity and more money for health.

After the shock and awe of his attack on the Brownites, their situation became similar to that of the Iraqi Ba'ath Party.

Mr Brown had no alternative but to join in the applause. But his old spin doctor, Charlie Whelan, looked defiant. He is the Tariq Aziz of the Brown regime, without giving himself up to the Americans. Further unrest is inevitable.

Daily Telegraph

Chapter 17

October 2003–
December 2004

Yet another Tory leadership election, Cherie at the Vatican and other matters

Despite the fact that the Westminster Village was obsessed by the monumental events in Iraq, domestic affairs within the Tory Party were developing. Opinion polls showed the Tory vote plummeting. Twenty-five Tory MPs' signatures trigger a vote of no confidence in Iain Duncan Smith and a leadership election follows.

⊰ 29 October 2003 ⊱
A vote of no confidence in Iain Duncan Smith

Most Conservative MPs heard the news, appropriately, in accordance with the party's oldest tradition. That is, lunch. I was with one of them. The same scene was enacted at tables all over Westminster and the length and breadth of London's old Tory eating country.

It is the land where no polenta grows, where game and red meat lay down their lives for the party and where bread and butter pudding lives on. My companion – as the restaurant critics say – was an IDS loyalist, who would vote for him in a confidence vote, and then for David Davis. There we were, cheerfully parodying the article in the early edition of the *London Evening Standard* from the vastly experienced plotter, Francis Maude (Con. Horsham), announcing, now that it was safe to do so, that he had written his letter to Sir Michael Spicer, the 1922 Committee Chairman.

'I put my cards on the table,' I quoted from Mr Maude's article. 'Having spent months putting my knives in the back,' I added, doubtless with great unfairness to so transparent a soul as Mr Maude, but to my companion's amusement – or at least mine.

Suddenly, his mobile rang. He spoke to someone of whose identity I thought it prudent not to inquire. 'Really? Where did you hear this? Sky News. IDS making statement soon. That's it, then. Talk later. Byeeee.'

'That's what?' I asked. Silly question, really. Seconds later, the companion's bleeper – the sinister device with which modern Whips seek to control their parties – vibrated.

'Ah, um, yes, well,' he said, staring at the little screen.

'Can I see the message?' I pleaded.

'Oh, all right, then.'

The wording was unusually lucid for an important pronouncement in modern politics: Appropriate numbers of letters received for vote of no confidence in IDS tomorrow. Details on your e-mails and in the Whips' Lobby – Michael Spicer.

That was indeed it, then. In common with all those other tables, we fled the pudding; the first time that had happened, en masse, in Conservative history. Any night of the long knives would be preceded by the day of the short lunches. We made either for a television set in warm Westminster or for the chill outside Conservative Central Office.

Very soon, Mr Duncan Smith appeared, flanked by his wife, and the more ambiguous figure of Theresa May, the Party Chairman, who made a point of looking serious, something which her hostile critics deny that she truly is. The Deputy Leader, Michael Ancram, the Shadow Chancellor, Michael Howard, and Oliver Letwin, the Shadow Home Secretary, were there too. But no David Davis! As lawyers say, you will make of that what you will.

But a Davis supporter later assured me that the anti-Davis camp had 'deliberately' sought to keep him away from Central Office and make him look disloyal by not telling him that the 25 signatures had arrived.

'Right!' Mr Duncan Smith began, in a decisive voice. In his vow to contest the confidence motion he was, speaking without notes, more lucid and firmer-voiced than at other decisive moments of his time as Leader. But by one of the cruel laws of politics, as careers end, that is so often the way.

Then he was gone; back into Central Office, but gone from the leadership too, we were sure. We gave ourselves to such vulgar speculation as whether Mr Maude made known his letter only after safely ascertaining that the 25 were already in.

Darkness fell on Westminster. Lights burned in many a Tory office window long after the occupant, in these days of a huge Government majority and consequent poor attendance, would usually have gone home. The Chamber's Opposition back benches were deserted. The Conservatives gave themselves over to a night of intrigue around the Commons followed by weeks around the country.

Daily Telegraph

⊰ 31 October 2003 ⊱
Michael Howard, Shadow Chancellor, declares his candidacy for the Tory leadership

Declaring his candidacy, Michael Howard promised: 'I will lead this party from the centre.' Such was the mood of amazing optimism, some of us took that worrying news surprisingly well.

After the declaration, Andrew Marr, for the BBC, began his question by saying: 'A lot of people don't know you very well.'

Mr Howard looked relieved. Until then, his problem was that a lot of people thought they knew him very well indeed. Ann Widdecombe and the liberal media had seen to that.

Mr Marr added: 'Is there anything about you that you would want them to know?' To the relief of non-centrists everywhere, he failed to give the correct centrist answer, which is: 'Yes, I'm gay.'

Instead, Mr Howard replied that his most profound belief was that everyone was put on this earth to make the most of their abilities and he wanted to help them do so.

For yesterday was a demonstration of Conservative multiculturalism. The room was packed with Euro-sceptics, Euro-enthusiasts, right-wingers, left-wingers, no-hopers, hopers, a few brave souls who had fought in the last ditch for Iain Duncan Smith and plenty less brave ones who had fired anonymously from the ditches opposite.

Even though it was 3.30 in the afternoon, Nicholas Soames was present – presumably having interrupted his lunch. The attendance of Mr Soames at any gathering turns it into a festive occasion. But in any case there was a mood of jollity not experienced at a Tory event since election night 1992.

Such a mass of Tories usually needs Tory enemies to make the party go, or rather to make the party split. But here there seemed to be none. Then word went around that sour Eric Forth, the Shadow Leader of the House, who was not present, was angry about the crowning of Mr Howard without a vote from the grassroots. He would have to suffice as an enemy.

Mr Howard's was much the most impressive announcement any of us could remember of a Tory leadership candidacy – a genre of which we have had vast experience. He was both impassioned and charming. Charm is not something which the public has been conditioned to associate with him. But it is the one quality his friends emphasise most. Yesterday, for the first time, it might have been apparent more widely.

A Carlton TV reporter had a monster of an inquiry: what did he say to the suggestion that he was 'oily, smarmy, aloof' etc? A lesser politician would have sought to ingratiate himself, promising that people would think differently of him once they got to know him, or had heard his pensions policy. Mr Howard confined himself to replying: 'That was a very generous question.'

He knows that, sadly, there will be time enough for him to seek to refute the 'oily, smarmy, aloof' version of himself. It will be the Blair apparat's version for the next two years or so. But if Mr Howard maintains yesterday's form, he could defeat it, although it will be hard.

Six years ago certain newspapers put out this version of Mr Howard because they sought to ingratiate themselves with rising

Blairism. Now that the shine is off Blairism, it might not be in their interests to do it to him a second time. Mr Howard arrived to cheers. Non-IDS admirers pointed out to one another, amusedly, that one of IDS's smoother lieutenants had positioned himself near the door through which Mr Howard arrived, the better to demonstrate his acceptance of regime change.

Later, back at Westminster, the Liberal Democrats told us that they would shortly tell us more of their plan to eject Mr Howard from marginal Folkestone. Targeted assassination! Charles Kennedy was thus the Sharon to Mr Howard's Arafat.

Whatever might be thought of Mr Howard, after yesterday it cannot be denied that he has suddenly made our politics more exciting and dangerous to all concerned.

Daily Telegraph

Frank's description of the launch of my campaign for the leadership of the Conservative Party captures the mood of the occasion brilliantly. But then, of course it would. He was the master of the phrase which got to the essence of things.

I remember the event well. And it was just as Frank has described. I don't know, though, whether Charles Kennedy would welcome being likened to Sharon, anymore than I would welcome being cast as Arafat!

Michael Howard MP

◃ 7 November 2003 ▹
Michael Howard acclaimed new Leader

The clock's hands moved towards midday: the last moment for nominations for Conservative Leader. We tried to devote all our attention to trade and industry questions, but we kept watching that clock. All must have had the same thought.

Would word go around the Chamber that, against all authoritative prediction, a second candidate for the Tory leadership had just rushed up to Sir Michael Spicer, the Chairman of the 1922 Committee, with his or her nomination papers? With five minutes to go, Tim Yeo, the Shadow Trade and Industry Secretary, rose.

This provoked a certain hilarity on the Labour back benches. 'Leadership announcement,' someone cried. Mr Yeo was indeed talked about as a leadership contender. His hostile critics might say that the talk was mainly from himself.

Mr Yeo made a point about competition policy. Patricia Hewitt, the Secretary of State, prefaced her reply with: 'I am delighted that the Honourable Gentleman is in favour of the leadership of his own party.' This produced disproportionate hilarity on Labour back benches.

The Conservative benches began to empty. The 1922 Committee was to meet at noon in Committee Room 14, the usual scene of their private practices. At 12.20, Sir Michael would reveal to it definitely that Mr Howard was Leader. We would not, of course, be allowed in. The Tories believe that whatever they do, they should be allowed to do it in private, provided no one is hurt; except, at regular intervals, their leader.

But we of the written and televised word would be allowed to wait outside and hear Sir Michael's amplified, disembodied voice announcing the result. So we hovered in the committee corridor: London's longest corridor, it is said. Down its length trailed the Conservative Party in twos, threes and fours.

The mood was jolly. We laughed at them. They laughed back at us. The thought occurred: what was so laughable about us? They're the ones who keep having these laughter-making crises. How dare they laugh at us!

There were some odd couples. Mr Portillo arrived in genial conversation with the traditionalist John Hayes (Con. South Holland and the Deepings). Mr Portillo is a famed moderniser. Mr Hayes – faithful to Mr Duncan Smith to the end – is a less famous olden-iser.

What could they have found to talk about, as fate threw them together? Literature? Philosophy? David Davis? They share an interest in those subjects.

Then came Mr Howard, nodding a few greetings as he made his way past us. The door to Committee Room 14 closed. Within seconds, a deep rumble reached us in the corridor. I thought I told

Nicholas Soames to take something for that post-lunch stomach. But the sound was of Mr Howard being honoured with the traditional 1922 Committee salutation of desks being banged.

The door swung open to admit a latecomer long enough for us to note that many MPs were standing in front of their desks. That rumble, then, was the sound of a standing bang. And this with the next party conference a year away! Mr Howard was starting with the support of all the party's old bangers.

Either that, or it was the younger ones, constituting themselves into a West Indian steel band. The sound went on intermittently for 20 minutes, after which Sir Michael's voice reached us, saying that no other nominations had been received and Mr Howard was Leader of the Conservative Party and of Her Majesty's Opposition.

For reasons I hope will become relevant in a moment, I was reminded of the young woman who, irritated at having to queue in a North Wales post office, announced: 'Do you realise I am Lloyd George's daughter?' The clerk replied: 'There's lots round 'ere who could say that.'

Leader of the Conservative Party and of Her Majesty's Opposition! There's getting to be a lot around there who could say that. Let us hope Mr Howard stays that way longer.

Daily Telegraph

⊰ 22 November 2003 ⊱
President George Bush's state visit

Amid the tightest security ever known, London came to a standstill for the President's four-day state visit. A team of grammarians had ensured a massive security clampdown around his syntax.

The flaw in President Bush's visit has been its failure to produce a Bushism: those unwittingly imaginative uses of English on which his enemies seize, but that endear him even more to some. Usages such as his reassurance not long ago that 'border relations between Canada and Mexico have never been better'.

It was obvious what he meant, unless he believed that Mexico and

Canada shared a border, which assumption on his part would not worry me. Leaders have experts to explain these things when they need to know, which Mr Bush does not because, as he suggested, Canada and Mexico are good neighbours of America and, indeed, of one another.

On this trip, the team of grammarians who presumably now travel with him at all times have ensured a massive security clampdown for hundreds of yards around his syntax. No Bushisms for Britain, then; as I write, though, he is still with us. There is time for him, say, to assure the Duke of Edinburgh that Scotland was always one of his favourite parts of England; or to tell Michael Howard, on the assumption that he was the Australian Prime Minister John Howard, that he wished Australia well in today's big cricket game against France.

George V's official biographer, Harold Nicolson, wrote of the last state visit by an American president in 1918: 'Through decorated streets the King, with the President beside him, drove from the station to Buckingham Palace: the Queen and Mrs Wilson followed in the second carriage. The men and women who thronged the pavements and the windows welcomed the President with awe and hope: to them he seemed a theocratic figure, the prophet of a finer revelation. Mr Wilson responded to their respectful plaudits by raising his top hat and smiling a wide but arid smile.'

But George V's more recent biographer, Kenneth Rose, writing more than a generation later than Nicolson in 1983, could be more revealing. Nicolson merely says that on 11 December 'he [the King] returned to England [from France] to prepare for the reception of the President of the United States'.

But Mr Rose says that the King was 'surprised and hurt' at not being consulted about the arrangements because they curtailed what his Private Secretary told the Prime Minister was the King's 'much-needed and well-earned holiday at Sandringham' – and the shooting that entailed.

Mr Rose adds that Lloyd George 'brusquely' replied that the Imperial War Cabinet had 'overruled' the King's objections. 'So the sovereign dutifully remained at Buckingham Palace to hold a state banquet in his honour. Wilson made a deplorable impression. In reply to the toast to his health, he omitted any reference to the part played or the sacrifices endured by the British Empire in their joint struggle.'

The King told a friend: 'I could not bear him. A cold, academical professor – an odious man.' Mr Rose adds: 'Only the Sandringham pheasants rejoiced.' The Queen and the Duke would not have found Mr Bush cold, and certainly not academical. But we will have to await an unofficial biographer to discover whether there were any private Bushisms or whether our own John Prescott proposed a toast to Mr Brush.

Daily Telegraph

⊰ 27 December 2003 ⊱

The Blairs visit the Pope. Cherie expresses her disappointment at the lack of women in the Vatican Curia.

Searching in the end-of-the-year newspapers for any sign of what the new year would be like, a *Daily Telegraph* headline struck the eye: 'Get rid of sexism, Cherie tells the Pope'. So 2004 'like most years in these past three decades or so' will be a year for diversity.

Mrs Blair was delivering the Tablet lecture. She had visited the Vatican privately during the year with her husband and children. She had not liked what she saw. Most of us, when we visit Rome, see various wonders of antiquity and Renaissance. But Mrs Blair keeps an eye out for gender inequality, and similar cruelties. 'After the trip,' said the *Telegraph*, by way of background to her lecture, 'she expressed her disappointment at the lack of women working in the Vatican Curia, the Church's equivalent of the Civil Service.' We were not told the Pope's opinion of her. 'That Signora Blair,' he could well have confided to a senior member of the Curia, 'she was the guest from hell.'

'You mean, literally from hell, Holy Father? A representative of the Devil? We must exorcise her at once.'

'No, worse, a representative of Signora Greer. She complained to me that all the apostles were men, and that not one of the gospels put in the Bible was by a woman, even though she knew that women wrote plenty of gospels in those days but the Church burnt them. Burnt the books, she meant, but also the women. She said women in the Bible get all the unskilled jobs, like washing Our Lord's feet with their hair. But, I told her, a woman was chosen to bring Our Lord into the world. Being Our Lord, he could have done it himself. She said that was all very well, but the Bible makes it pretty clear that she didn't have the chance to go to university, and be a barrister just like her.'

'And what was her husband doing while she was going on like this, Holy Father?'

'He rolled his eyes upwards, and winked at me. He was very nice. Later we had a quick word together, when she went off to check how many women there were in my Swiss Guard. He was very devoted to her. He said, "You know what it's like when you've lived with a woman for many years. You get used to their little ways." I told him, "Of course, I don't. I'm the Pope." But I knew what he meant.'

Mrs Blair is in a noble tradition among British women. She knows what is good for us. Florence Nightingale knew that better field hospitals were good for our troops. Lilian Baylis, founder of the Old Vic and later Sadler's Wells, thought that serious drama, opera and ballet would be good for the London working class. But, it may be objected, an opinionated barrister 'whose opinions never surprise us' is hardly the same as Miss Nightingale or Miss Baylis, especially since, unlike those two, she also seems to have a taste for the material joys of life when offered free.

But most people must make do with the predominant values of the age in which they live. Miss Nightingale and Miss Baylis, though separated by several decades, were born into ages of earnestness. Mrs Blair is a child of the self-indulgent 1960s and 1970s. It is as well that she did not found Sadler's Wells, since it would resound to heavy metal and Bob Dylan if she had. Mrs Blair's age does not think that the workers should be led, in the arts, to the tastes of the elevated. It believes that nearly all tastes are equally 'valid'. So Mrs Blair's generation must espouse what the age most values. This seems to be two, on the face of it, incompatible things: diversity and equality. But they are not incompatible in Mrs Blair's mind. For her, people of diverse background should have an equal opportunity to be the same as one another. That is liberal and feminist. For many of us, this would be a dreary spectacle. But the 'many' in the 'many of us' is important. Mrs Blair would get her way in Scandinavia and Holland, and probably has already. But in an eccentric country such as Britain, there are enough of us not to conform to her orthodoxy.

Spectator

⊰ **5 February 2004** ⊱
Seven demonstrators are evicted from the Gallery.
The Hutton report is a 'whitewash'.

*The House debated the Government's claims that British bases in
Cyprus could be attacked by Saddam Hussein 'within 45 minutes'.*

There was the Prime Minister, making a persuasive case, to his own satisfaction, as to how Lord Hutton had produced a most objective report. A shrill voice interrupted from the Public Gallery: 'No more whitewash!'

At first he must inwardly have assumed that Clare Short had reverted to her demonstrating adolescence. But then he would have remembered: that was when she was in the Cabinet. Her behaviour had been relatively restrained since then.

The gallery attendants rushed to remove the offender, dragging him across the laps of the two people sitting next to him, a young woman and a young man. Mr Blair resumed his speech. A couple of minutes later, the young woman rose: 'No more whitewash.' She too was dragged out. In 20 years' time, she could well be the token left-winger in a New Labour Cabinet. One has to start somewhere.

All in all this exhilarating process was repeated five more times, bringing the total of those ejected to seven: five male, two female. Miss Short, gazing up from the Labour back benches, perhaps thought that deplorable. The number of males and females hauled off should have been equal. In future, organisers of Commons gallery demonstrations must follow equal opportunities guidelines.

As each demonstrator was dragged out, another rose in a completely different part of the Gallery. Many of us eventually assumed that the entire Gallery consisted of demonstrators. So far they had been young, and dressed as for a well-behaved evening of police-tolerated cannabis consumption in Camden.

But we suspected that what looked like several *Saga* readers, in their golden years, up for the day from Godalming, would soon join in. Anti-war fervour affects all classes.

After the seventh young shouter was dispatched, however, the Speaker, Michael Martin, interrupted Mr Blair to suspend the sitting and order the Gallery cleared. All further shouting came solely from MPs.

For most of his speech, Mr Blair was the impressive master of his brief, or Lord Hutton's, which amounts to the same thing. But in the middle of a passage denying political influence on the famous published dossier about the Iraqi threat, a Tory backbencher intervened to point out that the inquiry transcript showed his own chief of staff, Jonathan Powell, asking what would make a *London Evening Standard* headline. The paper came up with the 45-minute weapon threat – a threat which the Government later had to disavow.

Mr Blair replied that if he could correct every wrong *Standard* headline, he would be a happy man. But that was sleight of hand. This was one *Standard* headline which served the Government's interests. That, perhaps, was why Mr Blair did not try to correct it.

Mr Howard was restricted by his acceptance of the Hutton report, to which he committed himself before its publication. But he cleverly showed that Mr Blair was now admitting something which he had constantly denied when Mr Howard asked: that the Government leaked Dr Kelly's name. Mr Blair only now admitted it because Hutton found nothing wrong with it.

The Scots and Welsh Nationalists questioned whether Ann Taylor, the former Labour Chief Whip now appointed to the Butler Inquiry, would lend objectivity to her task. As chairman of the all-party intelligence committee, she had received an advance copy of the Hutton report. 'She's part of the process,' Adam Price, a Welsh

Nationalist, several times called out. The Welsh and Scots suspected her of being an English agent.

Boris Johnson (Con. Henley) was brilliant. This was because he alone understood that the notorious dossier was a bit of sensationalist journalism. Alastair Campbell, an ex-sensationalist journalist, was really its editor. Those grand spies were just like a staff trying to give their editor the sort of stories he liked.

Mr Campbell wanted Iraqi terror-weapons stories. The spies gave him them. 'Andrew Gilligan was right.' If an editor likes stories about pheasants, he gets stories about pheasants, Mr Johnson explained. Mr Johnson, a journalist, has worked for both Sir Max Hastings and Charles Moore, though never for an editor who did not want pheasant.

Daily Telegraph

After Iraq had been conquered, the Blair Government commissioned a report by a top judge, called Hutton, into all the lies they had told in making the case for war. The report was expected to be a whitewash. It was. Here Frank watches Blair escape yet again, slipping through Tory fingers like a greased piglet. But in the course of an otherwise useless debate, he observes two key facts: that it was the Government that leaked the name of the poor weapons inspector, David Kelly, who had blown the whistle on their exaggerations; and there was certainly political pressure, from Number 10, to make the absurd claim that British bases in Cyprus could be attacked by Saddam Hussein 'within 45 minutes'.

Boris Johnson

⊰ 7 February 2004 ⊱
Charles Moore and the BBC

Mr Charles Moore, the former *Daily Telegraph* editor, denouncing the BBC in that paper last week in the light of the Hutton report, observed: 'It seems to me that the BBC today is the enemy of conservative culture in Britain.' The 'It seems to me' is the sort of phrase which suggests that a writer has but tentatively arrived at a conclusion, and even then only after weighing the alternatives. But some of us remember it 'seeming' to Mr Moore for some time. In the months before he left the *Daily Telegraph* editorship last summer, he ran an entertaining series, 'Beebwatch'. Its purpose was to monitor what the *Daily Telegraph* saw as the Corporation's delinquencies. So rather than 'It seems to me', 'As I've been saying for years' might have been more apt.

Mr Moore's piece of last week continued: 'How does the BBC approach subjects such as American power, organised religion, marriage, the EU, the actions of the armed forces, the rights of householders to defend their property against burglars, choice of schools or any perceived inequality? . . . If someone appears on a programme described as a "property developer" with someone described as a "green activist", who will get the rougher ride? If a detective drama features a feisty lesbian and a chilly aristocrat, which is more likely to be the murderer?'

No one could disagree with Mr Moore on any of that. The issue, for those of us whose disposition is conservative, with either sized 'c', is whether we would wish it otherwise. For us, the broad lib-left-wingery of BBC current affairs and drama adds savour to life. It is something by which we measure our Conservatism or conservatism. We positively enjoy pointing out the sublimely ignorant one-sidedness of the BBC's employees and contributors about almost anything political, either when they talk of the present or of the past.

We listened rapt to a recent radio series about the 1945 Labour Government, which was actually called, apparently without irony, something like *The New Jerusalem*. Hardly any room was given to the possibility that that Government's lumbering NHS, vast housing estates, nationalisations and taxation might have stored up trouble for decades to come. We did not hear, for example, that the Attlee Government's hospital building compared unfavourably with that before the war. Nor did the programme dwell on Aneurin Bevan's forecast that, because of his health service and because people would be healthier in general under successive Labour Governments, the cost of the NHS would fall. It was bliss for us. We contentedly mocked or fumed for days, until it was replaced by a discussion of the Spanish Civil War by experts, none of whom mentioned any Republican wickedness – only Franco's.

As a fellow employee of the Telegraph group, I have been Mr Moore's comrade-in-arms in many a war against many a feisty lesbian in support of many a chilly aristocrat. But three-quarters of the thrill of battle was the knowledge that the BBC had the heroes and villains the other way around. We had some sort of media establishment against us. It would not be so exhilarating if we in fact were part of the media establishment.

But what would the dramas and current affairs be like from this BBC which would be sympathetic to Mr Moore's world view?

8pm. BBC1: First in a new series of the award-winning *Green Murders*. Genial Master of Foxhounds Lord Grenville Hot-Toddy, the most popular figure in the village, is found dead with a hunt saboteur's placard buried in his skull. But the issue is: which environmentalist did it?

9pm. BBC2: *Canadian Dreyfus: How Tweedy Browne framed Conrad Black*. A disturbing documentary.

11pm. BBC1: *A People's History of Eton* (repeat). This is the episode in which presenter Charles Moore ignores the scholarship winners and puts in a good word for the boys who got there by dint of sheer, hard lineage.

Midnight. BBC2: *Couples*. Sexually inexplicit scenes, in context of stable marriage. Warning: no nudity.

There would be nothing to fulminate against. I like the BBC just as it is.

Spectator

I think the BBC had just committed one of its many outrages of bias about the Iraq War, over which it was determined to destroy Tony Blair, and I know that I was getting pompous about it. Frank's resulting column is a classic of his comic world-view – his realisation that, for columnists, it is essential to love thine enemy, if only because he provides you with so much material.

Charles Moore

⊰ 26 February 2004 ⊱
The Tory party in flagrant breach of the Nasty Party guidelines

Kevin Barron (Lab. Rother Valley), questioning the Prime Minister yesterday about fertility treatment, commended the 'nice guidelines'. A colleague later explained that the guidelines in question were those of the National Institute for Clinical Excellence (NICE).

But I only found that out afterwards. I was able to spend the rest of Prime Minister's Questions assuming that the Government's Nice Guidelines were about enforcing niceness, if necessary with prison sentences or a heavy fine for a first offence.

Two Conservative conferences ago, Theresa May, then Chairman, announced that the reason the Tories had lost by two successive landslides was that they had been thought of as the Nasty Party. She did not explain why the Tories won three elections in a row under Lady Thatcher; Lady Nice, as she has somehow not gone down in history.

Mrs May is no longer Chairman. But, since that speech, the Tories have become nicer and nicer: to gays, ethnic minorities, the NHS, single-parent families, two-gay-parent families, Labour public spending plans. The Tories are now nice to everyone, except of course to one another. Only yesterday it became known that Mr Howard was going to hold a 'pink summit' at which that minority could look to the Conservative Party for redress.

Thus, whether under Iain Duncan Smith or Mr Howard, they have been in flagrant breach of the Nasty Guidelines. Lord Tebbit, previously in charge of enforcing observance of the Nasty Guidelines, must be distressed.

Yet Mr Blair, and the Labour Party, continue to insist that, especially under Mr Howard, the Nasty Guidelines are still in force. Mr Howard is still greeted by hissing from certain Labour women when he rises in the Commons, not so noisily as when he rose on the day of the Hutton report, but still faintly.

Mr Blair constantly reminds the country that Mr Howard had much to do with the poll tax, which is seen as flagship Nasty legislation of many years ago.

Mr Howard yesterday raised the subject of council tax. Labour had broken a 'manifesto pledge' to bring local government bills down. They had risen by 60 per cent since Labour came to power in 1997.

Mr Blair replied: 'We have kept our promise to fund councils. Central grant has gone up 30 per cent in real terms, compared to a seven per cent cut under the Tory Government, with all councils getting an above-inflation boost this year.'

Massive numbers of Labour backbenchers, having the advantage of not understanding a word the Prime Minister was talking about, cheered hugely.

Mr Howard rose a second time and blamed the council tax increases on the burdens that the Government had imposed on councils, increased national insurance contributions, red tape and so on.

Mr Blair (of course): 'I'll take no lessons in waste in local government from the person who introduced the poll tax.'

Mr Blair, Mr Howard and lesser politicians now constantly 'take no lessons' from one another about all manner of things. Perhaps it began with Mr Howard, at one of his first Question Time contests with Mr Blair, being the grammar schoolboy who would 'take no lessons' in equality of opportunity from that public schoolboy. The phrase nearly always secures time on the evening television news.

Later, Mr Howard mocked Mr Blair for announcing random drugs tests in schools without apparently realising that the relevant department had already announced them. Mr Blair attacked Mr Howard for opposing the tests. Mr Howard indicated that he was for them, and was just pointing out Mr Blair's incompetence.

Mr Blair retorted that, in saying something hostile about the policy, but not really being against it, Mr Howard was 'opportunistic'. Mr Howard: 'I'll take no lessons in opportunism from the Prime Minister.'

Perhaps a generation of schoolchildren will arise who assume that lessons are things that they should not take. Eleven-year-olds will shout out in the classroom: 'Mr Speaker, I'll take no lessons in maths from that maths teacher.'

As so often, the politicians are unwittingly storing up unrest in our schools.

Daily Telegraph

Here, as usual, Frank illuminates the sterile nature of parliamentary exchanges. Of course we, the politicians, don't see them like that at the time. They form an essential part of the trial by combat that is at the heart of our model of democracy. Gaining an advantage at Prime Minister's Question Time is treated like an advance of a mile on the Somme.

It is doubtful whether the electorate see it quite that way. And Frank was the master at deflating our pretensions. He did it gently and always achieved one great objective. He got us to laugh at ourselves.

Michael Howard MP

⊰ 23 October 2004 ⊱
Boris apologises to Liverpool

Boris Johnson, MP for Henley and editor of the Spectator, *allowed an editorial to go into the magazine accusing Liverpudlians of wallowing in their victim status over the murder of Ken Bigley, held hostage in Iraq. Michael Howard sent Boris to Liverpool to apologise.*

For reasons beyond our control, this column was unable to be present in Liverpool to witness The Great Apology. As the years pass, so vast was the event, it will be embarrassing to admit that we missed it.

We will convince ourselves that we were there in person. Books will be written about it. Artists will paint 'Boris Before the Scousers'. Poets will capture the moment when Johnson was forced by his cruel leader Howard to eat humble butty.

But the hardest task will be that of the historians. Painters and poets are not expected to be accurate. Mere accuracy is not for artists. Historians, however, are supposed to provide the facts.

They will have to discover whose idea The Great Apology was. Most of the newspapers said it was Howard's. But Boris says that it was his own.

Howard: 'Boris, you've got the party into a lot of trouble. I order you to Liverpool to make it clear to the Scousers that you've been an idiot.'

Boris: 'I've had exactly the same idea myself, Mike, I mean, Leader.'

We do not need posterity to confirm, however, that the Conservative Central Office press and public relations experts brilliantly mismanaged the visit. Among other absurdities, they tried to hide Johnson from the national media descending on the city. They were thus trying to hide from the national media a figure who spends much of his life trying to appear in the national media. Yet the inconsistency, and resultant scope for ribaldry, seemed not to occur to Central Office's media experts.

In the face of this provocation, my colleagues who went up from London acquitted themselves magnificently. Johnson – in lamenting early in the day that he had not yet met any 'real people', only media – may have balked at their presence. But, as they sing on the Kop, 'You Never Balk Alone'. Those ornaments of my profession continued to intrude into his privacy.

I have already convinced myself that I was among them – hounding and doorstepping him.

Me: 'Have you found any mawkish cultures of sentimentality and grief so far, sir, except from Central Office, I mean?'

Johnson: 'Who do you write for?'

Me: 'The *Spectator*.'

Johnson: 'I never read it.'

Daily Telegraph

⊰ 4 December 2004 ⊱
Looking back on the Granita pact

After John Smith, leader of the labour party for just under two years died, Blair and Brown met at an Islington restaurant, Granita, and allegedly came to an agreement that Blair would run for the leadership and in due course hand the torch over to Brown. Here Frank looks back at the details, such as they were.

Concerning the unedifying Blair-Brown scandal with which the newspapers have sought to titillate their readers all week, a few observations.

It is hard, perhaps impossible, to arrive at the facts, since they all seem to be disputed. But friends of Gordon Brown, who subsequently turned out to be Mr Brown himself, claimed that, when their relationship was more intimate than now, Tony Blair, over dinner *à deux* in a fashionable Islington restaurant, promised to 'fast-track' Mr Brown as his successor at Number 10. Later, Mr Blair allegedly reneged on this promise. He is now said to be seeing a youthful, burly Northerner named Alan Milburn, presumably with a view to fast-tracking him.

Mr Brown is said to be 'devastated'. There is certainly no doubt that he is in love with Number 10. All he wants is access. The idea that his future happiness has been snatched away from him, before he can enjoy it, is unbearable to him.

Relations between the two have now completely broken down. They communicate only through the tabloids.

Mr Brown's friends say that they could never understand what he saw in Mr Blair. They say that Mr Blair is just a coquette, or as the less well-bred of them put it, a slapper.

To them, he is a shallow, social-climbing networker. That explains his choice of that modish restaurant in modish Islington, where he then lived. He simply used Mr Brown for reasons of personal advancement – to enable him to reach Number 10. He cast Mr Brown aside when he was no further use to him.

Neither side comes well out of it all. Mr Brown is clearly driven by one of the deepest and most personal of emotions to penetrate the human heart (ambition). Mr Blair is determined to keep his family together in Number 10.

The British people will surely conclude that there is much right and wrong on both sides. There must be a full inquiry with a wide remit. For example, who paid for the Islington dinner? Did Mr Brown subsidise Mr Blair's polenta and sun-dried tomatoes, or vice versa?

But a resignation would be a disproportionate outcome. It is politicians' own business, what they do to one another in private. Without sin . . . cast first stone . . . judge not . . . importance of family . . . intrusion . . . Boris . . . tabloids . . . Those are my final thoughts.

Daily Telegraph

⊰ **24 September 2005** ⊱
Cherie puts the Queen at ease

A new book, *Tony and Cherie: A Special Relationship*, by Paul Scott, perhaps unwittingly offers useful tips for anyone intending to have Mrs Blair to stay. At Balmoral 'Cherie Blair had lain awake in terror of a large and ugly statue at the foot of her bed, which . . . had taken on a ghoulish menace.' When Mrs Blair comes to stay, then, do not put a statue at the bottom of her bed. I never do. If she requests a statue, we always offer her something liberal and progressive, rather than ugly and ghoulish; something resembling that pregnant disabled woman now on a plinth in Trafalgar Square. 'Mrs Blair is said to despise the Balmoral rituals of a 6am reveille by a bagpiper.' One should therefore give one's bagpiper the weekend off. Or perhaps the passage is ambiguous, and it is not the bagpiper to whom Mrs Blair objects, but his presence as early as 6am, in which case he should not start blowing until, say, 10am by which time Mrs Blair would have digested her muesli and completed her yoga and indeed her yogurt.

The Queen's corgis also set off an allergy from which Mrs Blair suffers. 'Every time she walks into the place her eyes bulge, go red and begin to water,' said one insider. 'She comes out in red blotches and her nose runs constantly.' It is hard to see what the Queen and the Duke can do to help her here. They could charge extra Kleenex to the Civil List for the duration of Mrs Blair's visits. But that might not be enough, since 'the corgis pose a particular problem', the book says. 'Cherie absolutely despises the creatures.'

Let us hope that this passage is not misunderstood. Mrs Blair is presumably a sound animal-welfarist. She cannot despise the creatures because they are corgis, there being nothing they can do about that. As a good progressive with republican tendencies, she presumably despises them only because they are royal corgis. She sees them as having sold out to the system, rather as her husband has had to. If they occasionally bit the Queen, or defecated on the Duke, she would have a higher opinion of them. As it is, they are just another example of this country's all too prevalent deference.

Nor did Mrs Blair enjoy having to attend an afternoon tea party for the late Queen Mother's 'elderly women friends during a Balmoral holiday'. According to the book 'it was not just tea but a steady supply of sherry that was on offer to the titled OAPs. The party began in a genteel enough manner, but as the afternoon progressed it steadily descended into a raucous sing-along with the Queen Mother leading from the front and insisting that a mortified Cherie join in every tune.'

To those of us of the 'God bless y'ma'am' generation, such an occasion sounds like heaven. We would enjoy nothing more than a raucous sing-along with the Queen Mother and various titled OAPs on a Balmoral afternoon. But Mrs Blair is a child of the 1960s. She would not have known the words to 'A little of what y'fancy does y'good', or 'Don't 'ave any more, Mrs Moore'. Still, I cannot believe that any occasion over which the Queen Mother presided would have been anything other than enjoyable in the end, even to the Prime Minister's wife.

'Know any Joan Baez numbers, ma'am?' Mrs Blair would have demanded.

'I don't think one does, Mrs Blair. But please sing us one.'

Mrs Blair (singing): '. . . babies dying in the ghetto . . . corporate profits . . . egregation . . . woe, woe, woe.'

The Queen Mother: 'How lovely!'

Sherry-sodden titled OAP (changing the melody): 'That's enough of that, y'miserable cow. Now, all together: My ole man said follow the van . . .'

The Queen Mother: 'Would you like a smoke, Mrs Blair?'

Mrs Blair: 'Now y'talkin'. Just a little joint will do.'

As always, the Queen Mother's tact would have saved the situation. But, as we have seen from Mrs Blair's point of view, the Queen herself can be a tiresome and demanding hostess, although eventually Mrs Blair, with her breeding, would have put her at her ease.

Spectator

Chapter 18

September 2005– December 2006
The rise of Compassionate Conservatism and other matters

David Cameron, MP for Witney since 2001, became Leader of the Tory Party in the autumn of 2005. His liberal Conservatism resuscitated the party and he established a lead in the opinion polls. Leading 'Cameroons' are his Shadow Chancellor George Osborne, MP for Tatton since 2001, and Michael Gove, MP for Surrey Heath since 2005.

⊰ **22 September 2005** ⊱

Was this a gay wedding? No, it was democracy in the Tory Party.

I always loved reading Frank's sketches. He combined an instinctive understanding of the Conservative Party and all its machinations with a unique ability to poke fun at it.

This article, on the voting process for the 2005 leadership election, is a classic example.

In a thousand words, he cuts a swathe through all of us – Clarke, Widdecombe, Fox, Bercow, Davis, with the best of all reserved for George Osborne and me.

Frank liked to prick the pomposity and self-importance of Members of Parliament. In this article I love his account of Conservative MPs walking past him and claiming their views on the leadership were 'well-known', and his response that, in fact, he didn't know their views or, indeed, who they were. I am sure that wasn't true – as he knew the party better than most – but it is a wonderful remark.

If Frank had merely been trying to record this event for history, I am not sure what historians would make of it. But I know that if I were to read his account in 30 years' time, it is likely to bring back clearer memories than any more formal report of what leadership election day was actually like.

David Cameron MP

What would, say, the Iraqis make of all this? Not an unreasonable speculation as we of the press hovered in the Commons committee corridor for the first vote in the Conservative leadership election. It was an exotic country. All around us were Barry and Pugin's mock Middle Ages. The party holding the election was the direct descendant of that which had opposed the First Reform Bill that extended the franchise and at first opposed the Second. Not until 1965 had its MPs the vote in leadership elections which they were about to exercise. Elections had not always been devices of which its leaders had approved.

Yet, one o'clock in the afternoon having struck, down the corridor began a steady stream of simple Tories, determined to vote. For weeks the old regime – that which brought the country to its knees in 1979 and of which Michael (now Lord) Heseltine was the last candidate – had sought to intimidate them into voting for its last hope, Kenneth Clarke. He was 'a big beast'. He was the only one who could win a general election. He had a paunch. He was a bloke. Odd this last, since the regime has little time for blokes on such subjects as immigration and capital punishment.

Yet by the end of the afternoon the Tory back-bench masses had voted Mr Clarke out. The regime's candidate was gone. The regime, that is, of Foreign Office officials, merchant bankers, 'One Nation' Conservative MPs, BBC producers, liberal newspapers, Oxbridge heads of college, Chatham House lecturers and corporate magnificoes; all who tend or aspire to govern Britain, no matter which party is in power. Who needs a Ba'ath when a nation has such a shower?

For months it had urged Tory MPs to vote for its last Conservative embodiment: 'Ken'. But they voted against him. It was hard not to admire the way in which these humble Tories stood in line, for minutes on end, to vote. What courage. Who says that the West cannot bring democracy to the Tory Party? What an inspiration to other countries this was. If Mr Clarke and the regime had had its way, the party would now have to wear the Bercow. Instead, by Tuesday, Mr Clarke's noisiest backer, John Bercow, the MP for Buckingham, was standing at the edge of the television screen, as Mr Clarke had no choice but to accept defeat. Never mind the discomfiture of Mr Davis, the elimination of Mr Clarke was the glory of this entire leadership election. It did not matter who led the party compared with the importance of ensuring that it was not Mr Clarke. There is no evidence that he could win a general election – there is no evidence that any Conservative could win a general election – but there was every evidence that his Europeanism would have caused the Government to raise Europe at every opportunity, and split the Tories. It is becoming clear yet again that split parties tend not to win elections. 'Who do you want?' a colleague asked a Labour MP strolling down the corridor as we waited. 'Well, Clarke,' he replied. That man understood politics. Yet the regime insisted that Clarke was 'the one Tory Labour feared'.

Back to just before one o'clock that fateful Tuesday. Miss Widdecombe was already at the committee room door. She was for Mr Clarke; for the regime. The voting hour struck. Miss Widdecombe, an MP whom we did not recognise, and Desmond Swayne – the Member for New Forest West but, more to the point, unlike most neo-conservatives, a soldier who had taken time off from Parliament to do his duty and serve in Iraq – seemed to be in competition to be the first to vote. They hurried towards the door. It remained shut. It was the wrong door. They hurried down the corridor and rushed to the next door. It opened. In the ensuing carnage to be the first to vote, one's money was of course on Miss Widdecombe to crush the soldier. But he later claimed that he was indeed the first. Perhaps he briefly detained her in a nearby personnel carrier. Anyway, he was for Dr Fox.

The afternoon wore on. We asked each arrival how he or she

would vote. 'My view is well known,' several said, or words to that effect. Some tended to be more obscure. Not only did we often not know how they would vote; we often did not know who they were.

As they came down the corridor, the leadership candidates made a point of being relaxed. That only made them and us the more tense. Mr Cameron and his accomplice, Mr Osborne, came down the corridor side by side. Tremendous affection flowed between the two young men. It was like one imagines a gay wedding. But both abandoned themselves to heterosexuality in adolescence and have apparently stayed that way inclined. What a loss to Tory modernisation.

In due course, for no logical reason, Ken Livingstone appeared in the corridor. He was about to enter another committee room when he inquired of us: 'Is that where we buy the Charlie?' I inquired of a more worldly colleague as to what he was talking about. 'Charlie's what they call cocaine,' the colleague explained.

The corridor filled. Labour Members came to mock and to be jolly. So too did Mrs Edwina Currie, in her capacity as a television representative. Tory MPs were admitted to the committee room to listen to the result. Mrs Currie, though no longer an MP, slipped in. We protested to the two policemen at the door. They did nothing to drag her back. This confirmed that our politically correct police are reluctant to deal with people who flout middle-class standards. Fortunately, a Tory spotted her and she had to leave. Presumably she then climbed in through one of Barry's fanlights.

The result came. Then the candidates appeared in front of the cameras on the pavement outside. It was interesting to note which MPs got into the picture. Close behind Mr Cameron was a prominent latecomer to his campaign, Bernard Jenkin. Very near Mr Cameron was Alan Duncan who, not long ago, when Mr Davis looked the winner, had declared Mr Cameron's candidacy 'impudent'. Despite, or perhaps because of all this, I love the Conservative Party.

Spectator

◄ 7 January 2006 ►
Is Gandhi's relaxed dress code
the precursor of Cameron's ?

First, Mr Letwin became the first prominent politician since Mr Benn publicly to advocate redistribution of wealth. Then it was announced that Bob Geldof would advise the Conservatives about world poverty. Then Mr Cameron, in his New Year message to his country, invoked, with approval, Gandhi.

Mr Cameron pronounced: 'As Gandhi said, "We must become the change we want to see in the world."'

This is threatening to get out of hand. Plenty of us understand the game that Mr Cameron is playing, and think he has no choice but to play it. He disagrees with those on the right who say that many of the voters who stayed out of the polling booths on the last two general election days were true Conservatives who abstained because the party was not right-wing enough. None of the three books about the 2005 election which I have so far read – there have been at least two others – confirms this.

People stayed at home for other reasons. Either they thought that the results were not in doubt and that there was no point in voting. Or there was a more 'sociological' explanation: the old blue-collar base of the mass electorate no longer exists, its last service to the country being to move at successive elections from Labour to Margaret Thatcher. Voting has since become a mainly middle-class activity. The middle class – secure in the knowledge that union abuse of power and excessive inflation have, thanks to Mrs Thatcher, been beaten – can afford to go through a liberal phase. They do not realise that the only possible definition of the redistribution of wealth is to tax the better-off and give the proceeds in one form or another to those defined as the poor. When pressed, Mr Letwin will deny it. He will say that the money will come from 'growth' or 'cutting waste' in which case it is not redistribution but simple distribution. Mr Letwin's explanation will reinforce the middle-class assumption that his redistribution just means making the poor the beneficiaries of some unspecified source of money. Concerning Sir Bob, the middle class assumes that his heart is in the right place. They are rather hazy about Gandhi. But there was a film about him a while ago. Disguised as Sir Ben Kingsley, he looked poor, so his heart was probably in the right place too. Looking at this incurious, unquestioning electorate, Mr Cameron assumes that for the time being anything that looks Conservative has no chance of being popular, and he is probably right. The Conservatives have had similar periods in their history, and were returned to office.

Still, wealth redistribution, Sir Bob and Gandhi are probably unnecessary to the Cameron grand strategy. The middle class will continue to like Mr Cameron without them. And this unlikely trio could cause the Conservatives trouble eventually. There could be an embarrassing coming-together of Sir Bob and Mr Letwin. Some rock concert could be addressed along the lines of: 'Ollie Letwin and me – we wanna redistribute focking wealth, y' smug middle-class bastards.'

Sir Bob's choice of language puts one in mind of a story about the late Queen Mother when she was Queen, during the war. She was visiting a wounded airman in hospital. 'I got shot up over the Channel by a Fokker,' he told her. 'Had to bale out into the drink. I was lucky. I looked up and saw the sky was full of other Fokkers.'

'Yes, yes,' the Queen replied. 'I and my husband the King entirely share your view of the Germans. But what kind of plane shot you down. A Messerschmitt, or what?'

Today's middle class could in the end prove less tolerant than that Queen. But whatever happens, Conservative columnists will be found to write that Mr Cameron's latest gesture towards centrist or indeed left-wing opinion is consistent with Conservative policy. Great Conservatives of the past will be invoked. Some journalists are doing so already. 'Bob Geldof is very much in the tradition of Disraeli or Bolingbroke. Something of a troublemaker. Never an Establishment man.'

And Gandhi? What was it Churchill, campaigning from the Conservative back benches against the India Act, said about him? Something like: 'A half-naked fakir' who presumed 'to treat with the King–Emperor'. Gandhi was not in favour of India becoming a modern economy. He wanted the people to practise simple crafts in their villages. This seems to be taking Mr Cameron's environ-mentalism rather far. Certainly, Gandhi would disapprove of the India of today.

How, then, did he get into Mr Cameron's New Year message? We can imagine the Cameroon inner circle discussing his suitability.

George Osborne: 'Brilliant. The Gandhi is the best tandoori in the whole Notting Hill area. It would be a great way of showing that we want more immigration.'

Mr Gove: 'I meant Gandhi the politician.'

Mr Cameron: 'Yeah, the one who went around in public in a loincloth, naked from the waist up.'

Mr Osborne: 'I didn't know Mrs Gandhi was like that. Are there any pictures?'

Mr Letwin: 'The one Michael has in mind was a man.'

Mr Osborne: 'Well, we can't have everything. Let's shove him in. Then one of those hacks will say that he was just like Disraeli or Bowling-alley.'

Mr Letwin: 'You mean Bolingbroke, George.'

Mr Osborne: 'Do I? He sounds useful too. We could explain, or one of our columnists could, that this Gandhi was the precursor of Dave's relaxed dress code. Gandhi too would not always have worn a tie. So Dave's in a Tory tradition, and so is Gandhi.'

Mr Cameron: 'Gandhi wore hardly anything. How far do you want me to go, George?'

Spectator

⊰ 24 May 2006 ⊱
How did an immigrant get into the Home Secretary's office?

News that various Nigerian cleaners, working on Home Office premises dealing with immigration, were themselves illegal immigrants was amusing enough. But people are always wandering around Home Office premises whom staff cannot be expected immediately to identify, no matter how hard staff might try.

First Nigerian cleaner: 'Excuse me, sir. Do you work here?'

John Reid: 'Aye.'

'For how long?'

'About a week. Just gettin' t'noo the place.'

Second Nigerian cleaner: 'What language is he speaking?'

First Nigerian: 'English, but with a foreign accent. He obviously wasn't born here. Do you have any means of identification, sir?'

Mr Reid: 'Ah doo nay need it.'

Second Nigerian: 'We've all got to have our passes, mister. But I won't call security yet. You're obviously one of us. We illegals must stick together. Then, in the end, they'll let us stay. But we'll not help a terrorist. You're not one, are you? You say you've been here a week. Where did you work before that?'

Mr Reid: 'At the Ministry of Defence.'

First Nigerian: 'That means he's been involved in bombing. He could be dangerous. How long were you there?'

Mr Reid: 'About a year.'

Second Nigerian: 'And before that?'

Mr Reid: 'Department of Health.'

First Nigerian: 'And for how long were you there?'

Mr Reid: 'About a year.'

Second Nigerian: 'Bit of a drifter, eh? How come you've been sacked so often? You can't be a competent cleaner.'

Mr Reid: 'Listen, Jimmy. I've had to clean up after one Cabinet Minister after another – the latest being that Charles Clarke. Heard of him?'

First Nigerian: 'Never heard of him. Is he an illegal too?'

Second Nigerian: 'Clarke? I remember him. The fat guy with the ears. Kept on losing foreign criminals. Useless cleaner too. Blair had to deport him. No wonder this new guy's frightened.'

First Nigerian (addressing Mr Reid authoritatively): 'If you are deported too, do you have a well-founded fear of persecution in your country of origin?'

Mr Reid: 'Absolutely. I'd have to live there. That bastard Brown would see to that if he gets Tony's job. But I aim to stop him.'

First Nigerian: 'That sounds like a threat to the Chancellor of the Exchequer. You're a crazy. What's your religion?'

Mr Reid: 'Blairite. In my country, there's a Macfatwa against us. I'm not threatening anyone. Brown's threatening me. Please don't send me back.'

Second Nigerian: 'Relax, man. We don't like Brown either. He keeps on going to Africa to be photographed with our children. That's not healthy. Also, by handing total control over interest rates and monetary policy to the Bank of England, he's a crypto-Friedmanite, whereas I'm an unreconstructed Keynesian. Just you slip away, and good luck.'

Later a Home Office official, asked by the all-party Commons Home Affairs Committee how many former Home Secretaries were still in the country, replied, 'I haven't the faintest idea.'

Spectator

⊰ 28 October 2006 ⊱
Prescott dropped on Japanese. Tory polls go up.

It was announced this week that John Prescott, our Deputy Prime Minister, was to visit several Far Eastern countries as the representative of the British Government. Historians and moral philosophers will probably debate until the end of time whether, in the autumn of 2006, Britain was right to drop John Prescott on Japan.

Liberals, but not only liberals, will argue that, quite apart from all the moral issues involved, Japan was by then clearly beaten. Others will argue that, at the time Prescott was used against Japan, it was only 61 years since Japan had surrendered. Japan could have been kidding in 1945. In 2006, there was still a lot of fight left in the country. For decades, she had been hitting us with her television sets, cars and laptops.

We had to do something. Deploying Prescott was the only answer. No Japanese female civil servant would be safe. No Japanese interpreter would be able to decipher his English. He would express the wish to get stuck into some Sunni when he meant sushi. This, by itself, would sour Japanese relations with the Sunnis: that is, most of the Arab world. Japan is dependent on the Arab world for much of her oil. Panic would spread among the Japanese population.

I confess to being torn on the subject. On balance, however, I would argue that no country, however aggressive its export of television sets, cars and laptops, deserves to be hit by a Prescott.

Last week I argued here that David Cameron's embracing of Lib Dem-ery was laughable, but successful. Whereupon he and the Conservatives declined in the polls. My thesis looked wrong.

Now they are back up again. But, even if they were not, he would still be successful. The Conservatives were only a little behind Labour. The vital point was that their percentage was still in the high 30s, which is more than the Tories managed under their three previous leaders.

Daily Telegraph

⊰ 6 December 2006 ⊱
New Conservatism: Is this some sort of hoax?

It must be odd, joining the Conservative Party today. What do newcomers favour? The worldly-wise have long explained that Conservatism does not stand for much. It is what Tory politicians have to say to the voters in order to win office. Some Marxists say so, which is inconsistent with the Marxist belief that Conservatism is one of the means by which we are forced to live under capitalism. If that were so, there must be limits to how liberal or progressive the Conservative Party can be. Otherwise the cost of Ms Toynbee's welfare state would intrude on the profits of the fat capitalists. To circumnavigate this problem, Marxists invented 'false consciousness'. To distract them from overthrowing capitalism, the workers are lulled into believing in childish institutions and causes: the monarchy, patriotism, religion, wars. Having thus distracted the workers from the masses' true interests, the capitalists are free to make their profits.

There are signs that this system, if it ever existed, is breaking down. The capitalists have nothing left with which to distract the workers. The Iraq War, for example, has not inspired mass patriotism.

Mr Cameron is the first important post-Thatcherite politician. Mrs Thatcher's causes were so popular among those falsely conscious workers – though she herself was not – that John Major and Tony Blair had to say that they would not undo them. But voters have short memories. They take it for granted that the unions no longer cause winters of discontent. It is safe for politicians to confront ills about which nearly everyone agrees: greenery, the ozone layer, Africa.

Hard causes remain. Healthcare cannot be reformed unless more private money is spent on it. But that is now considered too dangerous a cause for a Conservative to espouse. Private healthcare is thought to favour only the rich. So, everywhere the First Post-Thatcherite turns, he is faced, to an extent endured by no previous Tory Leader, with his party being thought solely the party of the rich. The Iraq War's unpopularity shows that he cannot appeal to patriotism. Denunciations of immigration and illegal asylum-seeking are thought to upset the Liberal Democrat vote on which Mr Cameron relies for victory; the traditional Tory vote being thought not big enough. He has only one course: he must disown his party.

Yet there will always be those of us who think of ourselves as Conservatives. Today is hard on us. Still harder on the young, coming new to Conservatism.

Conservatism, contrary to popular belief, has often attracted the young. The 1960s, lazily thought of as the decade of left-wing youth, was also the decade of right-wing and libertarian youth: that of Hayek's revival, Friedman's arrival. Perhaps these idealists could telephone Conservative Central Office and offer to serve the cause even though the only people who are welcome these days seem to be donors.

'Conservative Central Office speaking. If you want to destroy the Conservative Party as it has existed for 150 years, press one. If you loathe Lord Tebbit, press two. If you are a careerist who wants Nicholas Winterton's seat, press three. If you are Nicholas Winterton, resign your seat and make way for someone who's not barking. For all other inquiries, please hold.' Music: Bob Dylan medley: arr. Toynbee.

Further recorded message: 'All of our agents are busy at the moment. But your call is going up in the queue.'

Eventually, a live human voice: 'Hello, Francis speaking. How can I help?'

'I want to join the Conservative Party.'

Mr Maude: 'Is this some kind of a hoax?'

'No, not at all. I feel I can make a real contribution.'

Mr Maude: 'How much?'

Spectator

PART TWO

CHAPTER 19

Our life in France

In 2003 Frank and I bought a house high up a mountain surrounded by vineyards in Languedoc Rousillon. France was always an obsession with Frank. He was fascinated by its cathedrals, its cuisine, and most of all its history. Many a lunch was had surrounded by the most beautiful scenery, with Frank not looking up once but concentrating on his cassoulet or escargots and debating with the historian Andrew Roberts and others where the Allies should have landed on the south coast of France.

These three pieces, all written for the Spectator, *describe expeditions we embarked on in 'la France profonde'.*

⊰ **16 August 2003** ⊱
Hitler and Pétain meet, only once, at Montoire-sur-le-Loir

The British who reach here – the Midi – from the Pas de Calais through la France profonde at this time of the year think of the history through which they drive as cathedrals, abbeys and chateaux. There are plenty of those.

The great events of 20th-century France are associated with the north; say, the battlefields of the Somme. But, if they pass near it, or see it signposted, they should consider stopping for half an hour at Montoire-sur-le-Loir in the Vendôme, where Ronsard was born, deep in the countryside of the chateaux de la Loire – not, though, for any chateau.

'Montoire says one of those white signs on one of those silent, narrow, deserted country roads that crisscross all central France – a sign spotted perhaps on the way to or from a restaurant recommended off the autoroute. At first nothing is thought of it. But wasn't Montoire a place visited by, of all people, Hitler? Isn't that where he had his only meeting with Marshal Pétain just after he conquered France? No. Can't be the same one. There must be many Montoires. The one where those two met must be on the Franco-German border, hundreds of miles away. Why should Hitler have come here? Hitler in la France profonde? No.

But, of course, it is indeed the right Montoire. They met in its modest railway station waiting-room. 'Of Montoire, one will quickly forget the sadly famous railway station,' says the green Michelin guide to the region, 'in order to remember instead its beautiful old houses, its ravishing bridge, and its adorable chapel painted with frescoes in beautiful colours.' One does not have to be a sensationalist to think that Hitler's having once been in town is even more interesting to the passing Anglo-Saxon, or indeed German.

Not that they much advertise it locally. There is no mention of it in the window of the tourist office in the square. When we parked there for lunch, we had not consulted the entry in the green guide, and were still under the assumption that this could not be the right Montoire. But it seemed reasonable to call in on the tourist office and ask.

The place was deserted of customers, and dusty. The world did not seem to beat a path to Montoire-sur-le-Loir. For that reason, it seemed a blessed spot. An elderly woman looked up from the counter. The inquiry called for some diplomacy in case, as we had assumed, it was the wrong Montoire. 'Excusez-moi, probablement non, Madame, mais est-ce-que votre ville – er, votre ville charmante – le lieu du rencontre entre . . .'

'Hitler et Pétain,' she replied. We had the right Montoire, she reassured us. Was any written information available about it? Certainly, she said, cheerily. Now, where had she put it? She opened an old cupboard. She knew there was something on it somewhere. Eventually, she produced a pamphlet published in 1997 by the tourist office 'of the land of the poet Ronsard'. It was entitled 'The "handshake" of Montoire'. The one photograph issued after the meeting showed the two principals shaking hands.

The woman behind the counter seemed the right age. 'You are too young, but do you at all remember the meeting?' Of course. That morning, in October 1940, she had set out for school as usual. But the town was full of German soldiers and gendarmes. Someone said that there was to be no school that day. Everyone was to stay at home – adults too. The next morning they read in the newspaper and heard on the radio that Hitler had been in their town.

The pamphlet was strikingly good, offering all the basic information. The French motive for the meeting, it explained, was to try to improve the harsh conditions of the armistice signed at the fall of France five months earlier. The German motive was that Hitler, having drawn a lesson from his failure to invade Britain, had decided to break British lines of communication with the Mediterranean. For that, he needed the benevolent neutrality of, or an alliance with, Franco's Spain and a collaboration with France which still held North Africa.

It also had a paragraph headed 'Pourquoi Montoire?' The answer was that Hitler was travelling by train from Berlin to Hendaye near the Pyrenees for his one meeting with Franco. For the related meeting with Pétain, he needed a small town on the way which was peaceful, far from a city and had a railway station with a tunnel in which he could take refuge if there was a British air raid, which the leaflet noted was 'assez improbable dans cette époque de l'occupation'.

And so Montoire became one of those blameless places whose names, by history's chances and accidents, become symbols – often for the bad – like Vichy itself. On returning from Montoire, Pétain delivered a radio address at Vichy containing words which, for much of the world, were to undo his reputation once Germany had lost: 'It is in honour and to maintain French unity, a unity of 10 centuries, in the setting of constructive activity in the new European order, that I enter today down the road of collaboration.'

That was to destroy the reputation of Philippe Pétain as assuredly as, a generation before, his victory at Verdun had created it. If only for the sake of a quiet life, most people, including perhaps most French, now assume that that is true. Few care to be blackguarded by today's liberal classes as apologists for right-wing authoritarians who collaborate with even more right-wing authoritarians. Pétain and Montoire are consigned to history's dark side. Much for that reason, Pétain, and Montoire, have few defenders now.

But for at least a decade after the war, both did. In a second-hand bookshop, near here in the Midi, was to be found Montoire: *Verdun Diplomatique*, published in 1948 while Pétain was still in prison for treason, by Louis-Dominique Gerard, a civil servant whom Pétain had asked to be his chef de cabinet. Here was a different story: the marshal had defeated the Germans diplomatically at Montoire just as he had militarily at Verdun. For example, he had refused to enter the war in North Africa against the British. Thus Britain kept Gibraltar, and Germany lost the Mediterranean.

Today, such reasoning is scoffed at rather than refuted – refuting it being a harder task. Whatever the truth, vast events, then, from a little town on the way down from the Channel ports.

Spectator

⊰ 4 June 2005 ⊱
Wine-growers vote '*non*' in the timeless hamlets of the Languedoc

Our TGV, slipping through la France profonde from Lille to Montpellier three days before the referendum, would now end its journey earlier, at Nîmes, the intercom told us: unspecified faults on the line. *Midi Libre*'s headline had it the next day: 'Vineyard-owners' discontent, travellers in trouble.' Militant winegrowers had damaged the line. It was to do with the referendum. The wine-growers were for '*non*'. But since they looked like winning, why damage the railways? It confirmed the traditional English view that, in a nation with a revolutionary tradition, important politics must if possible include token revolutionary acts.

We reached the village – a hamlet, really, the nearest shop six miles away – where we have a small house. There is a vast view across vineyards. Wine was the only issue down here. Probably the constitution mentioned nothing much about wine. But the French were not voting about the document as such; the exit polls had unemployment as the first discontent. The second – felt by 40 per cent – was the untranslatable *ras le bol*, which the French-English dictionaries have as 'fed up'. 'Fed up' – is that not what much of French history has been about people being? We were in the midst of continuity down here in Languedoc.

We called on neighbours at the local winegrower's solid stone house. All would vote '*non*'. Cheap Spanish wine was everywhere. The foreigners were allowed to put more chemicals in, which helped make it cheap to produce. Also, the labour that produced it was cheaper than in France. With EU enlargement, Bulgarian wine threatened. But wouldn't the French prefer to drink the better French wine? I phrased it that way, even though Britons who seem to know about wine are less sure that the average French wine is that much better now. But price was vital.

Then there was cheap foreign labour. Too many cheap Polish builders. Good workers; old ally of France; brave in the war; but this is economics. The Albanians were a different matter again. They were Musulmans, apart from other things. France had nothing against Islam, but France was not an Islamic country. I pressed them on the fear of Islam, but they did not dwell on it. No Le Peniste sentiment emerged.

Did they not still believe in the European ideal? A pause. It was good once, in prosperity and full employment. Then there was Turkey. They're not Europeans. But did France not see Europe as a balance to a too powerful United States? No. Did they fear United States power in the world? Perhaps surprisingly, no. They were against the Iraq invasion. 'Only good thing Chirac's done, keeping us out of that,' one said, but none of them was anti-American.

Russia? No fear of them? Not a great power any more, they thought. Germany? One replied by asking me, did I feel *méfiance des Allemands* [distrust of the Germans]? I am not sure I do, but for discussion purposes I said I did. No one else did. Localism, it seems, was not the same as 'paranoia'.

The winegrower's wife is the mayor's secretary. Would we like to come to our little village's *mairie* and sit in on *le dépouillement* [the count] with the mayor and councillors? I wonder if a similar invitation would be extended to a French couple in rural England.

Come Sunday, and there was a certain hum even in these timeless hamlets. It was agreed that the referendum had aroused more interest and debate than any presidential or parliamentary election since the early Fifth Republic. At the *mairie*, we joined eight councillors, mainly middle-aged, a couple elderly and one a man in his twenties. They laughingly greeted us with cries that everyone had voted '*non*'. They fell silent and looked at their watches as close of polling approached. A golden early evening sun slanted in. The mayor rose, a M. Elie Kubica, whose parents were born in Poland. They cannot be that bigoted. To an English eye, he is rural France incarnate: round, jolly, appalled by Beziers rugby team's new relegation to Ligue 2, nothing having gone right for them since they built that expensive new stadium that will be used for the World Cup in three years' time. '*C'est le temps*,' the mayor announced. '*Oui*' ballots to his right, '*non*' to his left. The vineyard owner, M. Taillefer, took the first from the brown envelope. '*C'est oui*,' the mayor announced, rhetorically and loudly, putting it to his right. Silence around the room. A sensational upset in our village? The mayor took the second paper. '*Non*'. The next. '*Non*'. Then: '*Non*', '*non*', '*non*'. Fifty-six ballots were cast out of an electorate of 59 in six hamlets. A landslide for the '*non*' deep in the Midi. We accompanied the votes to the canton headquarters 10 miles away, where the results from the surrounding villages were being written on a board. '*Non*' from everywhere. There was no jumping up and down. There would have been no one to jump up and down at: no Parisian or Strasbourg pro-*oui* haute bourgeoisie. Ours is not a place of rootless *fonctionnaires*.

Spectator

⊰ **10 September 2005** ⊱
The accused rose in the High Court and replied,
'Pétain, Philippe, Maréchal de France'

Leafing through *Massif Central* magazine in France this August, I spotted that the tourist office at Vichy had a new guided tour: the main sites from when it was capital of the French state (1940–1944). It is now 60 years – to the summer – since the president of the High Court in Paris began proceedings with: 'The accused will rise, and state his surname, first name and rank,' and the accused rose and replied: 'Pétain, Philippe, Marshal of France.' Sixty summers later, that man is a tourist attraction. I and a friend drove up from the south to join the tour.

The Germans having occupied Paris, and having allowed the French a non-occupied zone mainly comprising central France and the south, Vichy became the capital partly because, being a spa, it had plenty of hotel rooms for civil servants. So gentility became, to the British and the Gaullists, notoriety. It is as if Britain had been occupied, a comparable capital had quickly to be found, and all these years later we still asked the question of famous British public figures, 'Yes, but what did he really do under Cheltenham (or Bath, or Tunbridge Wells)?'

There were about 20 of us on the tour – mainly middle-aged, but including two females who looked the French equivalents of chavs: mother and daughter, perhaps, or sister and older sister. The older looked uncomprehendingly bored, but wore a strained look as if she was irritated at herself at not understanding what the guide was talking about. The younger made no pretence at wanting to know, and kicked the earth and pebbles in her boredom. Some of the older ones looked old enough to remember. When the guide began to utter the regime's three-word slogan, replacing *Liberté, Egalité* and *Fraternité*, a couple of elderly women joined in: *Patrie, Famille, Travail*.

In a fine rich voice, the male guide told the story plain and well – referring formally to the main characters of the summer of 1940: le Président de la République, M. Albert Lebrun; le Président du Conseil, M. Paul Reynaud; and above all Le Maréchal. He led us up and down a strip of green, bordered by plane trees, and enclosed by an elegant wrought-iron canopy from the Second Empire when the town's potential was established. Around it were the biggest hotels; above all the Hotel du Parc. Now a block of flats; then the Foreign Office, and the Marshal's bureau – the latter now empty, not open to visitors, but maintained, as *Massif Central* wrote, by 'a rather obscure association of the extreme Right'.

Around us, Vichy the place, rather than Vichy the idea, lived on.

Elderly couples waltzed to a band, playing old Trenet and Brel tunes, at a tea dance in a Second Empire pavilion by the green. Pétain was found guilty of treason in 1945, dying in prison aged 94 in 1951. He would have said that he saved those dancing old people from what would have been a far worse German occupation had he not risked the opprobrium of collaboration. Most Britons jeer at him for saying that. A few of us – certainly I – have never been so sure. Whatever the truth, it should not be denied that a man who was once his country's most admired soldier, but who died in prison a convicted traitor, is the stuff of tragedy. But that is what so many people, most Britons, and now perhaps most French, do deny, which makes him more tragic still.

Spectator

Chapter 20

Frank's passion for opera and ballet

Frank became interested in opera when, as he describes in the first piece of this chapter, his sink school in the East End of London was chosen to provide the children for the Royal Opera House stage at Covent Garden. This led to his lifelong passion for opera and later ballet, of which he often wrote. As an adult he rarely missed a production at The Royal Opera House or at the English National Opera. He would very often see the same ballet several times in a week to see how each different cast interpreted the roles.

Opera

⊣ 1982 ⊢

**Embraced by Maria Callas on stage
at the Royal Opera House**

Experience has taught me that one interesting thing has happened to everyone, but only one. Politicians, most columnists and nearly everyone who goes on television are under the impression that everything that has happened to them is interesting. Such people are no exceptions to this remorseless law. Only one thing is likely to have happened to them too, if as many as that.

All of which is by way of being an overture to the announcement that the interesting thing that happened to me took place amid the fog-Clean Air Act London 25 years ago this very night when I appeared with Maria Callas in the first two performances at Covent Garden of Bellini's *Norma*.

The secondary school in Shoreditch of which I was an inmate happened to supply the human material for the children's parts at the Royal Opera House. The qualification for getting into this academy was stiff: one had to fail the 11-Plus. In my day one had to be almost feral to fail the 11-Plus. I shall always be grateful to my early teachers that I managed the feat.

Having won a place in the school, the privileged pupils discovered that, because the rehearsals took place during the day, if you volunteered for the opera, you got out of maths. On the strength of a few mid-1950s television programmes, I disliked opera. On the strength of a few lessons, I feared maths. I volunteered for the opera.

My Covent Garden debut was in 1955 as one of the Nibelheim dwarfs in *Das Rheingold*. We were required to scream when the late Otakar Kraus, the greatest of Covent Garden Alberichs, cursed the ring. Over the next three years, we were the urchins in Act One of *Carmen*, the urchins in Act Two of *Bohème*, the urchins in Act One of Janacek's *Jenufa*, the urchins in Acts One and Two of *Otello*, and both Trojan and Carthaginian urchins at various stages of Berlioz's immense *The Trojans*, wearing, in both Troy and Carthage, I seem to recall, the same costume.

We were also the aristocratic officer cadets marching around the garden in St Petersburg in which is set Act One of Tchaikovsky's *Queen of Spades*. In this latter role, we were less convincing, the Shoreditch school being long on urchins and screaming dwarfs, but short on aristocrats.

It was extraordinarily casual. In some of the works we were required to sing. *Carmen*, after all, contains urchins' chorus of some complexity. But of the vocal arts we were entirely deficient. We simply shouted with the utmost vigour, usually in English, such was Covent Garden's linguistic policy at that time, but in *Otello* in phonetic, cockney Italian. Happily, this dark era in Covent Garden's history has ended, and the school which provides the lads today achieves higher standards.

Early in 1957, we learned that there was an opera coming which would require only two of us: *Norma*. Apparently, the heroine of that name had two children, whom she decides to stab to death, changing her mind at the last minute and opting instead for a duet with a mezzo-soprano. I and a boy called Arthur were chosen. The choice was dictated by our height rather than innate musicality, which was just as well since no singing was required. Furthermore, Arthur and I had no history of artistic collaboration. Being even smaller than me, he was the one by whom I was always courageously refusing to be bullied.

I embarked on this memoir resolved to be honest, to tell only that which I could remember. So now the sad truth must be faced: of this, the one moment of my life which makes me immortal, I can recall very little. Just a few images in my memory. For it was 25 years ago, and I was just turned 14. So today, I never trust the childhood reminiscences of autobiographies.

I remember that there seemed to be something exciting and tense about the atmosphere in the weeks before the performance. Arthur and I were constantly enjoined to be on our best behaviour, especially at the first rehearsal. At some point, we must have learned that someone exceptional was involved, which meant someone with a foreign name. Hitherto, under the Covent Garden regime, the singers tended to have such names as Elsie Morrison and James Johnston, the latter a ringing Irish tenor who used to tell Carmen: 'Carmen, oil never leaf your soid.' We had been the choirboys whom Mr Tito Gobbi had terrified in Act One of *Tosca* and he seemed jolly enough, for he had fed us Italian gobstoppers during a rehearsal and asked us about football.

Then, probably in the *Daily Mirror*, Arthur and I learned with some consternation that a woman was coming to Covent Garden who was known as 'Opera's Tigress'. Furthermore, she had been in a 'storm' in New York. She had got the sack for a baritone who had held a final note longer than she had in a duet.

The latter was untrue, as the books now make clear, but that was no good to Arthur and me at the time.

As a result of the *Mirror*, household and neighbours were alerted. There was some doubt as to whether Norma was the name of the opera or the name of the great singer. 'My boy's appearing with that Norma,' my father would sometimes explain. By word of mouth down the street, this was occasionally transmuted into the Johnson boy appearing with Yana, a popular television artiste of the period.

Came the rehearsal. The late Christopher West, the producer, seemed nervous. An efficient-looking woman came in wearing sculpted horn-rimmed glasses, a tight black sweater, a green two-piece suit and stockings with black seams down the back to which were affixed stiletto heels in accordance with the fashion of the day. (Pubescent boys take note of such details.)

'That's her,' Arthur said. 'Don't be bloody daft,' I distinctly remember telling him. 'That's West's secretary.' But Arthur was right.

'These are the children,' West said to the great soprano of the age. 'They're a little big,' she replied, speaking I recall with a sort of American accent. At this, West, a somewhat epicene figure, began to flap his wrists with some consternation. He gabbled something about younger ones not being allowed on stage under British law. Callas stared at us. Arthur and I cowed. If this bitch gets the boot for baritones, what would she do to us, we no doubt pondered, I regret, in our rough way.

'I understand,' Callas told West, who breathed again. But there was still trouble. It came, however, not from Callas but from the mezzo-soprano, the late Ebe Stignani.

She was singing Norma's rival in love, the 'young temple virgin Adalgisa'. Stignani was 52 at the time. I now know that she was a singer of much distinction. 'Her acting was all in the voice,' says my edition of the *Oxford Dictionary of Opera*, which was just as well, because she was a short, round woman with a terrifying face. 'Not understand to him, not understand to him, Maria,' she told Callas. 'They're too bigga.' Though I cannot claw the precise words back from memory, Callas replied with something about even the great Stignani having to abide by the law. West giggled.

I forget the actual rehearsal. Indeed, the policy of honesty compels the admission that I remember little of the two performances themselves. But I do recall that when we emerged from Covent Garden underground station, people were already at the barriers offering clusters of £5 notes for return tickets.

And I could not forget that when Callas bore down on us with the knife, her nostrils flared; that when, dropping the knife, she repentantly clasped us to her bosom, her perfume smelt like that of an aunt who was always kissing me; and that at the first performance on 2 February there penetrated, into my left eye, the top of the diva's right breast, which partnership remained throughout the subsequent duet with Stignani.

In that eye I felt the most distinct pain as that voice of myth and legend rose and fell. In the other eye, all I could see was the exit sign at the far corner of the gallery. At the second performance, I ducked and secured a safer refuge in a more central portion of the diva's bosom.

And that is all. Still, there are few men who can truthfully say that their eye made contact with the right nipple of Maria Callas. So it is not necessarily true that someone who has passed much of his adult life in the Press Gallery of the House of Commons has never glimpsed greatness.

Opera

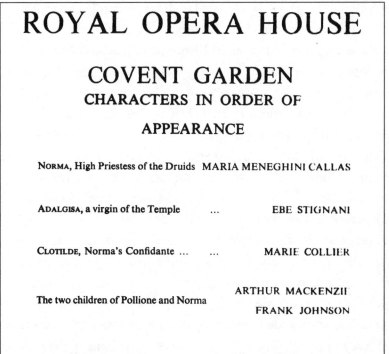

ROYAL OPERA HOUSE

COVENT GARDEN

CHARACTERS IN ORDER OF

APPEARANCE

NORMA, High Priestess of the Druids   MARIA MENEGHINI CALLAS

ADALGISA, a virgin of the Temple   ...   EBE STIGNANI

CLOTILDE, Norma's Confidante ...   ...   MARIE COLLIER

The two children of Pollione and Norma   ARTHUR MACKENZIE
FRANK JOHNSON

Druids, Bards, Priestesses, Warriors and Gallic Soldiers.

Programme for the opera *Norma* in which Frank appeared alongside Maria Callas.

◄ 5 March 1989 ►
Benjamin Britten's whimsicalities are profound and beautiful

As an impressionable youth in the 1950s and early 1960s, I endured the unceasing propaganda of the nation's arbiters of taste about Benjamin Britten being a great operatic composer. True, much of this agitation was the work of what might be termed the homosexual school of music criticism: certain post-war critics who were gay before their time. What was Britten's swooning *Billy Budd* if not the all-male *Madam Butterfly* – though without the same melodic inspiration? But articles in the influential magazine *Opera*, which was under broadly heterosexual control, would routinely throw Britten into the succession of acknowledged greats: '. . . Mozart, Wagner, Verdi, Puccini, Strauss, Janacek, Berg and Britten'.

In his autobiography, Lord Harewood, founder of *Opera* (magazine) and later the English National Opera Company's managing director, is unrelenting on the subject of Britten's tenor companion, the late Sir Peter Pears – he of the strangulated high tones, curdled lower ones, and general whooping. Pears, says Lord Harewood, was 'the peer of Callas . . . the inspiration of Benjamin Britten . . . He would have been King Lear if Britten had written it.' Nowadays, one unashamedly regards the loss of Britten's *Lear*, starring Sir Peter, as a lucky near-miss. But, at the height of the Britten-Pears Terror, it was not so easy. I began to believe in Britten's greatness myself.

The rest of the world, however, decided differently. Britten's operas are not much performed abroad. There will still be people for whom Britten's whimsicalities and maunderings will be profound and beautiful. But they will mainly be British.

The two activities in which historically Britain has done best are literature and parliamentary government. We should be content with that. When our influential classes were more self-confident, we were indeed content with that. Very few cared when a pre-1914 German wrote a rude book about us called *Das Land ohne Musik*. It did not matter to our rulers if we were 'the land without music', even if it were true, which it wasn't. They were happy to be the land with Shakespeare and the rule of law.

This lauding of Britten then, is to do with our loss of self-confidence. That, and our liking for the brave trier who does well against Germans and Italians in the opera house. But for the recovery of that self-confidence, it is essential that in our hearts we should not believe a word of it – nor care.

Sunday Telegraph

⇥ 11 June 1989 ⇤
Domingo 'has improved,' Pavarotti announces

Next Sunday, Luciano Pavarotti will give a concert in the new London Arena. The following night Placido Domingo will complete five performances of *Il Trovatore* at Covent Garden. People who know nothing about opera know one thing. Those are the world's two greatest tenors. But if they are, why?

Domingo and Pavarotti, in strictly alphabetical order, are 'great tenors' as the term is popularly understood (not that this detracts from their greatness). They are associated with the sound which most people, whether they like it or not, seem to recognise as the sound a great tenor is supposed to make. That this sound became the world's idea of the tenor was not inevitable. It was because of Caruso (1873–1921). He began a line which continued through Gigli (1890–1957) to the present.

Caruso was perfect for the new *verismo* (realism) operas which emerged early in his career, such as Mascagni's *Cavalleria Rusticana*; Leoncavallo's *I Pagliacci*; and the works of Puccini. At first, audiences in the lower part of the house found Caruso's style uncouth. But he appealed literally over their heads to the gallery. This was particularly good for his career in the new country, and the new country of the common man.

New York in the early 1900s was flooded by Italian immigration. Caruso was made by New York as much as by Milan. So there is a case for arguing that the 20th century heart-bursting tenor is almost as much an American creation.

Domingo was born in Madrid, in 1941, and Pavarotti at Modena, in 1935 – though there is a school of thought which claims that

Domingo is just as old as Pavarotti. Domingo was the son of singers of *zarzuelas*: Spanish light operas. Pavarotti's father was a baker, who had been in the local opera house chorus. Pavarotti – aged 26, six feet tall, weighing just under 15 stone compared with his present 25 stone or so – made his debut as the wan poet Rodolfo in *La Bohème* in 1961.

He was engaged by Covent Garden in 1963 for the final performances of a run of *Bohème*s begun by di Stefano, a star of the period. According to a diary of performances which I then kept, di Stefano was at times inaudible, and ducked the highest note in his great aria.

It cost more for a seat to hear di Stefano than to hear this new man, Pavarotti, who had no trouble with any note. At only 42, di Stefano – much admired by the young Pavarotti – was finished. He had paid the price for the reckless demands which he had for years made on a glowing, though faultily produced voice.

Pavarotti 'gives' as much of himself as did di Stefano. But there is nothing faulty about his technique. It is generally equal to the demands he makes on it. For that reason, at 54, he does not sing so often in the roles and arias which enabled the record company to call one of his early albums *King of the High Cs*.

Domingo started in the National Opera in the early '60s in Mexico, where his parents had emigrated. His rise was very quick. At his Covent Garden debut – *Tosca*, 1971 – he was far more famous than Pavarotti had been at his. No cheaper prices for him.

The big difference between the two is that Domingo began his career in the lower category of voice: baritone. Domingo's voice is darker. Pavarotti avoids the heaviest Italian part, Verdi's *Otello*, and Domingo avoids high Cs; though that leaves plenty of other parts and notes which they have in common.

Domingo's variety of parts is far greater. He learns them very quickly. He is the better – certainly, the slimmer – actor. Domingo is the tenor for opera-goers who take the 'serious' stage seriously – who go to the National Theatre, and the Barbican, and regard the director as being at least as important to performance of Italian opera as the singers.

The world has never before been reduced to just two 'great tenors'. (There is a case for another Spaniard, José Carreras, as a third. But even before his recent struggle with leukaemia he was punishing his beautiful voice by singing parts too big for it.)

When asked about one another, Domingo and Pavarotti adopt the courtesies which people use when they do not approve of each other. Ever since he was first conscious in the late '60s that Domingo would be his lifelong rival, Pavarotti has used the same formula: 'Placido has improved.' Pavarotti is conscious that – being the Italian – he has the advantage. His sound is simply more authentic.

A great authority on singing once wrote that when Everyman sang in his bath, it was Caruso whom he fancied he heard. As we have seen, some fine social distinctions exist between the supporters of today's great two. Whether it rings with Domingo or Pavarotti can tell us a lot about a man's bathroom, and the man.

Sunday Telegraph

⇥ 24 June 1998 ⇤
Since Puccini's 'Nessun Dorma', great melody continues to sleep

A man at the Music Discount Centre in the Strand reports that people who have never before bought a 'classical' record have been flocking to his shop asking for 'Nessie Dorma' or just 'the World Cup Song'.

It may be surprising that the BBC should have chosen 'Nessun Dorma', an Italian operatic aria, to advertise the World Cup. But the public's response does not surprise me. I would make big claims for 'Nessun Dorma'. I believe it to be the last great tune ever written.

Its emergence into the world in 1926 ended a phase of musical history which had lasted for more than 200 years, and started another – although no one realised it at the time.

Claiming 'Nessun Dorma' as the last great tune is not to deny quality to some of what came later: the 'Villjalied' from Lehar's *Merry Widow*, say, or 'Lili Marlene' or Cole Porter's 'Night and Day', or Edith Piaf's 'La Vie en Rose'. They, and plenty more, are good tunes – beautiful, even. But they are not great. They do not move and stir in the way that 'Nessun Dorma' does. They would not propel the masses towards record shops in which they had not previously set foot.

To achieve that, a great operatic composer is needed. More specifically, an operatic composer from the line that stretches from Handel through Mozart, Rossini, Bellini, Donizetti, Verdi and Puccini. Some of those composers were far greater than others. No one suggests that Puccini was the equal of Mozart. But they all had one thing in common. They could write tunes which appealed to a vast number of people in the way that 'Nessun Dorma' does.

It is sometimes claimed that in those days opera audiences in Italy were mainly working class, that the same people went to the opera as would today go to a football match. But Italian opera houses, even in their great age, still had to be subsidised from the public purse, which suggests that opera was not mass entertainment.

A majority of the audience was probably from the urban lower-middle class. But a good proportion was from the peasantry and the proletariat. Such audiences required tunes. Without tunes, composers and operas, as happened all the time, were forgotten.

Puccini was the last composer to give them tunes of the requisite quality, and 'Nessun Dorma' ('No one shall sleep') is the last one he gave them. It comes at the start of *Turandot*'s last act. The cruel Chinese princess Turandot issues an order to all the city: because the hitherto unknown name of a certain prince must be discovered by daybreak, no one shall sleep. In a moonlit garden, the prince hears the offstage populace's repeated cry of 'Nessun Dorma!' He takes up the phrase, and spins the melody with which Pavarotti seems to have entranced the British football-watching public.

The aria ends with a top B – which is not in Puccini's own score, but which tenors rightly think is expected of them – on the word 'Vincerò!' The prince is confident that at daybreak his name will remain unknown, and he will be victorious.

After that aria, Puccini completed about half-an-hour's more music for *Turandot*. Then, at Brussels, on 29 November 1924, he dies of cancer, aged 66, the opera unfinished.

It was completed, with the help of Puccini's drafts, by his pupil

Alfano. But at the première in La Scala, Milan, on 25 April 1926, the performance ended on the note Puccini had reached. The conductor, Toscanini, then turned and addressed the audience. Accounts differ as to his exact words. According to one report, they were: 'Here, at this point, Giacomo Puccini broke off his work. Death on this occasion was stronger than art.'

But no one in the audience knew the full significance of that moment. It was more than the end of Puccini. It was the end of popular opera. *Turandot* is the only opera written in the last 65 years with so much as a single phrase which any BBC executive would risk as the signature tune for the World Cup.

Puccini's contemporary Richard Strauss (1864–1949) had entered the popular repertory with *Der Rosenkavalier*. But that was in 1911. Straussians would offer his *Arabella* (1933), or a couple of duets within it. But even they would not expect anything in *Arabella* to compete for the crowds with 'Nessun Dorma'.

Britten's *Peter Grimes* (1949) has a foothold – which I suspect is slipping – in the popular repertory, but I cannot think of any passages in that work which its admirers would put in for the World Cup.

Is this because operatic composers cannot write great tunes any more? Before 1926 they had written them for centuries, and there is no reason to suppose that they had suddenly lost the talent. Rather, their talent gradually became unwanted.

Sometime in the 1920s opera houses, like other cultural institutions, began to fall to modernism. To stay alive, opera houses still needed the old operas. But modernism dictated that there should be no more like them. Admittedly, a work like *Peter Grimes* is not modernist, or would not be regarded as such by modernists. But it shares modernism's unwillingness to indulge in the long-breathed, formal melody for voice.

History suggests that such melodies, to be great, can only be written by operatic composers – or songwriters of the standing of Schubert. Composers of musicals, ballads and pop songs, however good, can never quite do it.

Some optimists say that, with the rout of modernism in most of the arts, and the rise of 'post-modernism', opera composers will work the spell once more. Meanwhile, since 'Nessun Dorma', great melody continues to sleep.

Sunday Telegraph

⚔ 28 January 2001 ⚔

'What's the world coming to? A prince of the Royal House at the funeral of a bandleader!'

A review of John Rosselli's The Life of Verdi.

One hundred years ago this weekend, Giuseppe Verdi died in a Milan hotel at 88. The crowd lining the city's streets for the funeral procession was vast. Vast too are the centenary commemorations now going on all over the world. Yesterday, Radio 3 devoted its entire day's programmes to him.

Many people, including people not much interested in opera, will probably not find it odd that he should command this attention 100 years on. They know that, with Puccini, he is the world's most popular opera composer.

But for at least 50 years after his death, people would have found it very odd indeed. Over those 50 years, his operas' survival was not at all certain. It seemed impossible that we would ever arrive at today's position: more than 20 of his 27 operas performed regularly; all recorded, most more than once.

John Rosselli does not quote it in this book – so I hope it is true – but the aged nobleman, Count dal Verme, who was in the honour guard at Verdi's funeral, heard an old officer exclaim, on noting a King's relative among the mourners: 'What's the world coming to? A prince of the Royal House at the funeral of a bandleader!'

By general consent, *Don Carlos* is one of his greatest. Last weekend I saw it on successive evenings in Munich and Stuttgart. It is such a standard part of the repertory that, as with Shakespeare, producers feel free to make of it what they like. Taking place in the Spain of the Armada king, Phillip II, it contains an auto-da-fé : a ceremonial burning of heretics, watched by court, clergy and people.

Both productions illustrated this book's thesis, that Verdi was, as well as being a composer, a man of the theatre. In Munich, the production was what nowadays passes for traditional (a large wooden box doing service as forest, palace, and everything).

In Stuttgart, the producer set this scene somewhere resembling George W. Bush's Texas. The court women were dressed in Houston and Dallas finery. They air-kissed, and complimented one another on their frocks, while being bitchy about them later. The court men were in black tie. The clergy were fundamentalists. Television interviewers with microphones roamed the crowd for celebrities. A satellite dish stood ready to televise the burning. The producer, believing – probably rightly – that a 16th-century auto-da-fé is too remote to horrify the kind of educated bourgeois who go to the opera in modern Germany, was using modern imagery that would. It was tremendous theatre.

But producers can only play around with a classic if classic is what the audience recognises a work to be. Otherwise the piece is not well known enough for the reworking to have any effect. Yet in 1933, not a long time ago in musical history, the English-speaking world's leading critic, Ernest Newman, in effect agreed with that old officer at the funeral. He wrote of one of *Don Carlos*'s then rare performances that Verdi knew neither how bad the opera's libretto was, nor how bad the music was. Even at Verdi's death, most of his operas had fallen from the repertory. It was as a nationalist icon, not a composer, that he was mourned.

Mr Rosselli writes that in its dip and rise Verdi's reputation matches that of his contemporary Charles Dickens. Both were called crude, noisy and melodramatic. 'Only in the last 50 years or so have *Bleak House, Little Dorrit* and *Our Mutual Friend* been studied as great works of art, intricately wrought out of a wide and deep vision of society. Not by accident, that period has also brought a mighty growth of serious critical interest in Verdi.'

That Mr Rosselli – one of the three or four best interpreters of 19th-century Italian opera, who died last week at 73 – could write this beautiful little book proves the point.

Sunday Telegraph

Ballet

⊰ 25 March 2000 ⊱
Frederick Ashton's *Marguerite and Armand*
and history's fallen women

A rt's most famous fallen woman is yet again before the London public. At Covent Garden, the Royal Ballet's great French ballerina, Sylvie Guillem, is dancing Marguerite in Ashton's *Marguerite and Armand*. That is, ballet's version of the *Lady of the Camellias* tale.

That tale began as a novel in 1848 by Alexandre Dumas *fils*; became a play, also by Dumas, in Paris in 1852; an opera, *La Traviata*, by Verdi in Venice in 1853; a film, *Camille*, in Hollywood with Garbo in 1937; and this ballet by Ashton in London with Fonteyn in 1963. Via Fonteyn, Garbo and now Guillem, the fallen woman in question has been embodied by three of the relatively few great performing artists among the women of the 20th century, and now early 21st. To them must be added Callas, the 20th century's most famous Traviata.

The tale, it may be remembered, is the one about the expensive Parisian courtesan during the July Monarchy (1830–1848) who to her surprise falls in love with a not especially rich young man of good family from Provence, abandons her way of life to live with him idyllically in the countryside, and is then visited by his father. That forbidding gentleman tells her to leave his son because the scandal is ruining the chances of his daughter making a certain rich and socially prominent marriage. She of course refuses. He then assures her that his son will leave her once her beauty goes. On hearing that she agrees to leave the young man. She returns to Paris and to a former wealthy protector – without telling the young man of the reluctance with which she is doing so. The young man follows her and publicly insults her at a big party. The rich protector challenges the young man to a duel in which the young man gets the better of the rich man. The fallen woman starts to die of consumption. Both the young man and his father arrive separately at her death-bed. The father is full of remorse. She and the young man are reconciled. She dies.

My purpose in raising the subject here, however, is not for reasons of interdisciplinary comparison. My purpose is altogether less elevated. What exactly was – or is – a courtesan? How did she – or does she – differ from what the mass press calls a 'vice girl'? Not that I disapprove of the mass press in these matters. An owner of the *Washington Post* once said that journalism was 'the rough draft of history'. Not if history relies on broadsheets such as the *Washington Post* it isn't. Dumas' Marguerite is based on a real person: Marie Duplessis. We would know all about her, and her trade, if the July Monarchy had had a halfway efficient *News of the World*. ('Exclusive: Why Love Has Made Me Quit The Game – by Marie.')

The importance of the mass press is even greater in our present age. Unlike the France of Marie's time, ours is not an age of political, ideological or philosophical conflict. We are post-Thatcher. Whatever our party allegiance, most of us tend to agree on basics. Politics and public controversy is now about what the pious disparagingly refer to as 'personalities'. People either crave celebrity or crave knowledge of, or acquaintance with, celebrities, or 'celebs'. Some of us may deplore this, but it is useless to deny it. We tend not to find out enough about celebrities in the broadsheets, though their 'decline in standards' has improved our knowledge a bit. Future historians, writing about the present Age of Celebrity, will be wise to rely on the tabloids and the glossies, and I hope, for the more elevated discussion of the celebrities concerned, the *Spectator*. So trying to find out what a courtesan did was not easy.

The London Library is good on 19th-century France, as it is on most subjects, but had no separate section on Fallen Women, and I did not like to reveal to the librarian that this was my specialist subject. But dedicated research revealed that Marie Duplessis played in a Premier Division of about a dozen fallen women who dominated the sport in its heyday: roughly from the 1830 July Monarchy until a little after the 1871 defeat by Prussia which rather depressed things. I discovered that, apart from Marie, I had heard of one of the other famous players: Cora Pearl. Her scoring rate was second only to that of Marie. But I had not known what I now discovered: she was British. One felt a surge of pride comparable with what was felt in front of the television when the English XV overwhelmed France last month. We had thrashed them at something at which they considered themselves the best in the northern hemisphere.

Cora was born Eliza Emma Crouch in Plymouth in about 1835. Rupert Christiansen, in his lively book on the years 1869–1876, *The Tales of the New Babylon*, says her real surname might have been Emma Crutch. That suggests that she was even wiser to change it; Cora Crutch being likely to arouse ribaldry, given her choice of profession. The writer Alphonse Daudet mocked her 'comic English accent' but that could have been her unique selling point.

It emerged from my researchers that a courtesan differed from a 'vice girl' in that she chose her own customers. There was also a pretence that they were not customers at all, but a series of lovers who just happened to be rich, famous in the arts, or well connected. Some authorities referred to some courtesans keeping several such clients on the go at the same time, but did not explain how this worked in practice. Was it a time share? Past 40, Cora, who once charged 10,000 francs a night, had to cut her price to only 100 francs – a fantastic bargain offer.

Marie Duplessis did not have to go downmarket, since consumption claimed her at 23. One of the books described her average day: rise at 11; *petit dejeuner*, read newspapers; 15 minutes' piano practice; dress; drive in the Bois; receive visitors; dinner; theatre or opera; supper at the Café de Paris; dancing and gambling; work. A modern courtesan's day would presumably consist of: rise at six; jog; half a grapefruit; receive personal trainer; visit analyst; lunch on Caesar salad; visit plastic surgeon; Condé Nast drinks party; home at ten; minimum of work to avoid stress.

Paris's Fallen Women, then, were more fun than today's. For France remained fascinated by them. Covent Garden's *Marguerite and Armand* evening includes Ashton's *pas de deux* to music from Massenet's opera *Thaïs* (1894). A courtesan in Hellenistic Alexandria falls for a monk. He rejects her. She converts to Christianity. He loses his faith. He catches up with her in the desert where she has sought refuge. He now desires her. She rejects him and dies, inspiring from the first-night gallery the immortal cry of, 'Quick, now! While she's still warm.'

Spectator

⊰ 4 December 2004 ⊱
A kinswoman from Stoke Newington, the great British ballerina Alicia Markova passes away

My ballet-going started just too late for me to have seen, in any of her great roles, Alicia Markova, who has died at 94. But I almost believe that I saw her in her greatest, Giselle, because of a brilliant phrase of the American critic Edwin Denby; that she danced it with 'a chaste abandon'.

She was born Lilian Alice Marks in Stoke Newington. Likewise, Margot Fonteyn was really Peggy Hookham. It was assumed that the pre war public would be more likely to turn up for someone who sounded like that era's notion of a great ballerina, as well as looked it.

Since then, such was the astounding progress of British dancing in the second half of the 20th century that British ballerinas became happy to dance under such down-to-earth surnames as Collier, Penny, Wells, Sibley and Bussell.

Who would have thought that the prosaic British would become so good at the – on the face of it – unBritish activity of classical ballet? Not just at dancing it, but at creating it, as was the case with Frederick Ashton, to whose centenary the present Covent Garden season is dedicated.

That should be seen by all patriotic Britons, and any passing Russians.

Daily Telegraph

⊰ 21 May 2006 ⊱
Fireworks backstage with Sylvie Guillem

Shortly, on Channel 4, a lithe woman of 41 will curl her body around two fit younger men for 20 minutes. The programme will also include her curling her body, for roughly the same length of time, around herself. Not unusual for Channel 4. But for thousands of viewers, normally of other channels, it will be enough to know that the woman doing the curling is Sylvie Guillem, for 15 years as great a ballerina as any in the world. For Guillem is one of the few performers – like Placido Domingo – who have reached such a level of fame that whatever they do is watched or listened to.

But there is something about the dancer that differentiates her. Domingo's repertoire, though vast, stays within established tradition. Guillem, who has spent much of her life as the tragic woman-into-swan, the jilted Giselle, or the awakened Sleeping Beauty, has been crossing over into modernity. The Channel 4 programme consists of three dance films of work by the contemporary choreographer Russell Maliphant. Sylvie Guillem has travelled far from ballet's lakes and castles. But she was still in that kind of country when I met her in her Covent Garden dressing room – appearing in the Royal Ballet's *Romeo and Juliet*. She is one of the tallest of great ballerinas, so I surprised myself with my own first words: 'You're shorter than I expected.' By which I meant that she was shorter than my own 5ft 10in. She smiled and rose on *pointe*, bringing herself to my own modest height – but tall for a ballerina. The taller ones look tall only on stage.

We talked about the first things about ballet and herself that came into my head. Except for one thing that was in my head, but which – being an old balletomane and therefore deferential in the presence of a great ballerina – I left unraised: her reputation. So, I was relieved when she did so herself. 'My reputation precedes me all the time, but I'm not the monster people think I am,' she announced suddenly.

'How disappointing,' I replied.

'It is disappointing,' she responded.

How did she acquire this reputation? 'Because, most of the time, people speak without knowing. But I can't say I'm easy, because I'm not . . . I just don't like authority.' She corrected that to: 'I do like authority when I respect it.'

Which brought us to her attitude to authority in the form of the Royal Ballet choreographer, the late Kenneth MacMillan. Established gossip has it that they did not get on. He is said to have sat groaning in the stalls as she danced one of his ballets, protesting that she was not dancing the steps he wrote, but her own. When he rebuked her, she is alleged to have told him that people came to see her, not him.

She arrived at the Royal Ballet from the Paris Opera Ballet in 1989, three years before MacMillan's death. 'Your relations with MacMillan were sometimes tense,' I suggested.

'Really?' she replied, and laughed. 'I think I arrived from Paris too late. He wasn't able to cope with someone like me. It was not an easy time in that everything was new for me.'

What was the final state of her relations with him? She was pretty definite: 'We were not talking to each other.'

'So you would dance his Manon or Juliet and he would be in the audience, but afterwards you wouldn't talk to him?'

'I really don't know if he was in the audience. I never saw him after a show.' I sensed that I had exhausted, not the subject, but all that she would say about it – though she had been candid by Royal Ballet standards. So what did she think the rest of her life was going to be like? Given that, like all performing artists, she had had to make sacrifices. Most performing artists like hearing that sort of thing about themselves, but this one replied: 'What sacrifices?'

'Well,' I floundered, 'you have not had any children.'

'That's not a sacrifice. That's a choice. I've never said, "Oh God, I have to go on doing what I have to do, and I cannot have a child." I think it's a very complex feeling that I have about this. As a physical experience, it must be something incredible.'

Me: 'Not as difficult as 32 *fouettés* [a reference to a challenging series of turns in *Swan Lake*].'

Her: 'No, be serious. Then, afterwards, you have the responsibility for someone in the world that we are living in.' I suggested that the world we lived in was a lot better than the world that, say, her parents grew up in. But, turning a French adage into English, she replied: 'We are all sawing at the branch we are sitting on . . . With this planet, very crazy. People will find that they will turn the taps on, and there'll be no water. They start to think about it too late.'

I suggested that these were small problems compared with those of her parents' generation. 'Terrorism is not a small problem,' she said. But she agreed that plenty of people still lived well. 'There's an abundance. Come on, it's fantastic. I'm just thinking that in 25 years, you know, you will have Le Mad Cow, then you have the chicken that now you can't eat. What are they going to do, the poor kids? So it's not a sacrifice, no.'

'But you've had a pleasurable life.'

'Yes, but it was not always easy. It doesn't mean that I didn't have bad moments. I made it the best I could.'

'But none of the bad moments were to do with ballet?'

'It can be that also . . . You know, you think: everyone's picking on me.'

To which all I could say was: 'Surely it's a very long time since anyone picked on you?'

Daily Telegraph

Chapter 21

Great men remembered

⊰ 30 April 1981 ⊱

**Harold Macmillan, aged 87, addresses an
audience at Caxton Hall**

Eighty-seven years old, very frail and alarmingly lucid, Mr Harold
Macmillan spoke at a meeting in Caxton Hall, London,
yesterday. He addressed the Primrose League on the subject of
Benjamin Disraeli, the centenary of whose death falls this year.

The aged voice swung to and fro in that grand, singsong, pendu-
lum-like delivery that, one imagines, was the standard intonation of
Grand Old Men in Mr Macmillan's youth and of which he is the
final master. Probably he sounded a bit like that already when he
was 45 or even younger. For one can never escape the suspicion with
Mr Macmillan that all his life was a preparation for elder statesmanship, his only regret being the necessity to clock in with the
actual long and arduous political career before taking up televised
reminiscence and elegiac appearances such as yesterday's.

Certainly, he knows the tricks like no other today. 'There were
great men in those years, great men,' he quavered, as he told us about
Disraeli's own long, slow haul before being able to take to the
reminiscence circuit.

'Russell . . . Palmerston . . . Gladstone.' Mr Macmillan gazed
around us, as if pondering whether to chance his arm with a sudden
flourish of: 'As a young man, I knew them all.'

He is also a master of the strategic mumble ending with a word
spoken with sudden clarity, so as to emphasise its importance. All
this box of tricks was on show yesterday.

If Disraeli came back today, would he be surprised by the world? Mr Macmillan did not really think so. All sorts of things had developed which had started in his day. For example, religion was already under assault from someone Mr Macmillan called 'Mr Darwin'.

Instead of an age of faith, we lived in an age of credulity. 'There isn't a society which cannot collect money for its obscure and nefarious activities.' Moreover, people believed in something called 'the expression of the individual'. Mr Macmillan was against that. So was Dizzy. Yet it would not surprise him today.

Whiggism, liberalism, even Marxism, had their points: he and Disraeli granted that. But 'they are like the classical buildings that followed the Renaissance. Beautiful in their way, but incapable of growth.'

All this was achieved with many a marvellous mumble and bulging of the cheek. We sat transfixed. Under their richly decorated lampshades and embroidered coal-scuttles, the women of the Primrose League, the last of the Tory hat people, were in a state of collective trance.

He several times said that the Tories must be the One Nation Party; a wet code phrase, that. But he also said Mrs Thatcher was courageous, and that drew much applause. Disraeli was well-served. But so, once more, was Mr Macmillan.

The Times

⊰ 8 July 1992 ⊱
**What is high culture? Malcolm Muggeridge
(1903–1990) reveals all.**

L ast Sunday, I tried in the *Sunday Telegraph* to say what high culture was. Various friends have gently mocked the attempt.

I should explain that trying to define high culture is not something I go around doing all the time, like other people who go around trying to cut down on drink, or to slim. There was a wider purpose: to justify taxpayers' subsidies for opera, Shakespeare – high culture in general.

My attempt was, of course, a failure. If it was any comfort, attempts at a definition of high culture have been going on continuously since the days of the ancient Greeks, and they have all failed too. That there have been so many attempts suggests that, however impossible it is to define, it exists, and that it is always in the news.

For example, the present Secretary of State for Education, John Patten, says that great literature must be taught in all state secondary schools.

Whereupon, various smartie boots retort that it is impossible to define what great literature is.

They are right, but the impossibility is the beginning of the problem, not the excuse to abandon it. When on Sunday morning I rang Alan Watkins – the *Observer*'s political columnist – his first words were: 'I'm in the middle of reading you on high culture, ha, ha, ha. Well, y'know, I've always denied that opera is high culture.'

I reminded him that, in addition, he had always denied that Shakespeare was high culture either. He agreed that that was so. Over the years, Mr Watkins has assured me that Shakespeare was an example of the vulgarity of the English. (Mr Watkins is Welsh.) The plays, he says, mainly consist of assorted thugs greeting each other with such cries as: 'How now, Northumberland?'

Normally, this would be intolerable, coming from the average journalist-oik. But, as any reader of his work can see, Mr Watkins is highly literate. So another problem is raised: it is not just what is said about high culture, but who says it.

Before the early 19th-century romantics, Shakespeare was widely believed, particularly in France, to be uncouth. But that was not offensive because one of the Frenchmen who held that view was Voltaire.

Likewise, it is hard to imagine any people more couth than the Bloomsbury Group. One of them, the art critic Clive Bell, in his book, *Civilisation*, which seems to have been to its day (the 1930s) what Lord Clark's television series of the same name is to ours, wrote: 'We do feel that some artists are highly civilised, Phidias, Sophocles, Aristophanes, Raphael, Racine, Molière, Poussin, Milton,

Wren, Jane Austen, and Mozart; we do feel that others are not, the builders of the Gothic cathedrals, Villon, Shakespeare, Rembrandt, Blake, Wordsworth, Emily Brontë, Whitman, Turner, Wagner, and the Congolese fetish-makers.'

Some of us are rather weak on our Congolese fetish-makers. But we can see what Bell meant. Transferred to our contemporary situation, it is that Shakespeare, were he alive today, might not be civilised enough to pass one of the Secretary of State's new tests on great literature.

But at least Bell did not deny Shakespeare's greatness, and he was trying to be helpful. Generally, however, those intellectuals who raise difficulties about definitions are trying to be the opposite.

The late Malcolm Muggeridge was a master at it. Alan Watkins and I used to go on pilgrimages to him at his cottage at Robertsbridge in Sussex. 'Ah, yes, culture [Kul-chaw],' he once exclaimed. 'Dear boys, it is the sort of thing that Australians come over here to look for – you know, those Aawh-stralians who write about the arts, and go on television.'

He had them asking passers-by at Heathrow or Earl's Court: '"Excuse me. Could you tell me the way to culture?" Eventually, they are directed to various literary parties in central London.'

Malcolm reached out, and several times made the gesture of some-one lifting something up, to see if there was anything underneath it. 'They search the room, picking up potted plants, and trays of wine glasses, to see if there's any culture underneath. But to no avail. The culture has always gone – completely GHAWN.'

I suspect that Malcolm had in mind, among others, Mr Clive James. I do not care about the weight of numbers of envious Britons who say the contrary: even though he makes jokes on television, Mr James is cultured by any definition. But what is the definition?

Daily Telegraph

Frank and I paid several visits to Malcolm Muggeridge and his wife Kitty at their house near Battle in Sussex (it was a bit bigger than a cottage). He had two favourite impersonations. One was of Sir William Haley, the former editor of The Times, *the other was of Clive James, the author and performer. Malcolm would depict James searching in vain for Culture, behind the curtains or on the mantelpiece. For Haley, he would climb precariously – 'like a little monkey', Malcolm would say – in his quest for Wisdom. Alas, no Wisdom was ever to be found.*

Alan Watkins

⊰ 1 April 2000 ⊱
Harold Pinter (1930–2008): The Chekhov of the working class

I have never been able to think of Pinter plays, as so many of both his admirers and detractors do, as unrealistic. We read that Chekhov caught to perfection the speech of the minor Russian country gentry. Pinter is the Chekhov of the London proletariat. To me, as a Londoner from roughly the same part of the city as Pinter, the non sequiturs of the following passage from *The Caretaker* were what I heard all the time from relatives and neighbours:

'You remind me of my uncle's brother . . . Very much your build. Bit of an athlete. Long-jump specialist. He had a habit of demonstrating different run-ups in the drawing room round about Christmas time . . .'

Why round about Christmas time? the logical middle-class mind might ask. But Londoners scorn such literalism. The character does not elaborate on why that particular season, but continues:

'Had a penchant for nuts. That's what it was. Nothing else but a penchant. Couldn't eat enough of them. Peanuts, walnuts, Brazil nuts, monkey nuts, wouldn't touch a piece of fruitcake. Had a marvellous stopwatch. Picked it up in Hong Kong. The day after they chucked him out of the Salvation Army. Used to go in number four for Beckenham reserves . . . Had a funny habit of carrying his fiddle on his back.'

The same character has another immutable passage:

'You've got a funny resemblance to a bloke I once knew in Shoreditch. Actually he lived in Aldgate . . . When I got to know him I found out he was brought up in Putney. That didn't make any difference to me.'

Persons of an unimaginative, bourgeois cast of mind might object:

why on earth would it make a difference to him? But the character presses on:

'I know quite a few people who were born in Putney. The only trouble was, he wasn't born in Putney, he was only brought up in Putney. It turns out he was born on the Caledonian Road just before you get to the Nag's Head. His old mum was still living at the Angel. All the buses passed right by the door. She could get a 38, 581, 30 or a 38A, take her down the Essex Road to Dalston Junction in next to no time. Well, of course, if she got the 30 he'd take her up Upper Street way, round by Highbury Corner and down to St Paul's Church, but she'd get to Dalston Junction just the same in the end.'

Passages like this can still be overheard on tubes and buses from a certain generation. Pinter wrote *The Caretaker* at 30. At nearly 70, he has lost none of his gift for creating real Londoners. His new play, *Celebration*, captures the speech of those who have moved out to Essex and become rich: the self-made Thatcherite wealthy whom Mr Blair won over in 1997 by promising no higher taxes. It is to be doubted whether Pinter has met any of them, but he knows them. He is a genius of language as well as a genius in general. Would that there was a Pinter of the distinctly non-cockney world in which Pinter now moves. Perhaps, in his next play, it will be Pinter.

Spectator

⊰ 8 August 2000 ⊱

Robin Day: That tremendous heart which at last has given out

I spent last Christmas with Robin Day. How jolly, you may think. Like most curmudgeons, he is bound to be good with children; sentimental; perfect material for the Santa Claus kit. All of which is true, but this particular Christmas was not for all that.

I was spending it in hospital. Suddenly, he arrived in the room next to mine.

His heart – that tremendous heart which at last has given out – was giving him renewed trouble.

Since it started to play up a decade or so ago, he had had much experience of hospitals. I, however, had not.

Barely out of the operating theatre, I was confronted with a new potential terror: this eruption of the life force – of jollity and joshing. That's all I needed. But like so many political journalists who had been his companion – and butt – of an evening at party conferences, or in the Commons press gallery canteen, I had been jollied and joshed by Robin for years.

His presence in hospital, over Christmas at that, was a link with one's world, and it is one's world which seems too distant at a time like this – especially since the suspicion must be that it is getting by perfectly well in one's absence.

'Just in for checks, old boy,' he roared. 'I hear your situation is more serious.' In a way, his arrival was a reassuring link with my previous life until now. He left his door open. He made endless telephone calls, announcing to his friends where he was spending Christmas.

Since he was under the impression that everyone else was, like him, a bit deaf, he bellowed down the telephone, and I lost count of the times I heard the same patter.

'Guess who's in the next room to me?' he would roar, if he was talking to anyone who had remotely heard of me, and plenty who had not.

He would announce my name, accompanied by a lengthy routine as to which of the many journalistic Johnsons it was. 'He's had a tuma,' he would eventually proceed, '. . . well, I know he seems perfectly fit, but that's an irrelevance, darling [or dear boy] . . . I keep on calling it a tuba . . . He gets annoyed . . . He says if it was only a bloody tuba inside him, it would have been less trouble ejecting it.'

As night fell, he would put his head round my door. 'How's your tuba. I think it's time for some more champagne, don't you? Is it the turn of one of your bottles, or one of mine? Shall we get a couple of nurses smashed? I like that Aussie one, don't you?'

I explained to the nurses who he was. They were too young. They thought him tremendous, but they had no idea that he was for a long time as famous as anyone in the country. For it had been about a decade now since he had ceased to appear on the screen all the time, and we are beginning to learn that almost no fame fades so quickly as the fame which is dependent on that screen. Other images soon occupy the retina of the young.

In his heyday as a national figure – and it was a long heyday, lasting from the late '50s to about 10 years ago – you could walk along the promenade with him at a party conference, and every head would turn; something which did not happen when one was alongside all but two or three Cabinet Ministers.

At the time of his death, he was of course still much recognised, but not by the young. I wonder if that hurt him, for he loved the young and when they got to know him the young loved him.

But, then, those of us who knew him a bit tended to wonder a lot of things about him.

He seemed proud of his achievements. He cared passionately about the quality of politics, and perhaps even more, about the quality of the reporting of politics.

Yet did he also consider himself a failure? He was always saying he did.

He was always saying that he would rather have been a lawyer or a politician; ideally both, like the politicians of old, such as F.E. Smith and Hartley Shawcross.

For the Robin Day paradox was that the man who had so much to do with the biggest influence of his time – television – was not really a man of his time.

Unlike the age in which he flourished, he was not cynical about Parliament, monarchy, and country.

To him they were the same as they were in the olden time of his orator heroes, of whom naturally the greatest to him was Churchill.

To make the paradox still more complete, this man – who won fame for his brusque way with them – considered most politicians to be serious people engaged in a serious enterprise.

It was because they – and it – were serious that they should be able to withstand his way with them. He was no failure.

Daily Telegraph

The brilliant Hugh Trevor-Roper,
Lord Dacre (1914–2003)

Lord Dacre – Hugh Trevor-Roper, the historian who has died just turned 89 – was not what he seemed. He would have liked that. For people, and things, which were not what they seemed fascinated him all his long life.

He wrote about the Soviet agent Philby – who when the British considered appointing him head of our espionage early in the Cold War was certainly not what he seemed – and about Backhouse, the master forger.

Trevor-Roper was recruited into the world of deception when young, becoming at the start of the Second World War what we now call an 'intelligence analyst'. Soon he formed the opinion, based on the study of intercepted German cipher traffic, that the head of the German secret service, Canaris, was an anti-Nazi: another figure who was not what he seemed.

Perhaps his early experience of the secret world was what attracted him to the study and observation of things which were not what they at first appeared. Perhaps it was in his nature.

This suspicion, that there was something which lay beyond appearances, helped make him a brilliant historian. It extended to his view of other historians.

In the early 1950s, Arnold Toynbee, mainly as a result of the Americans taking him up and putting him on the cover of *Time* magazine, was the most famous historian in the world. His many-volumed *Study of History* sold in its millions, though those millions would not have got through it. Trevor-Roper, in a single devastating article, exposed it as a vast exercise in mystification.

Trevor-Roper's origins were certainly not what they seemed. As early as his Oxford undergraduate days he was assumed to be upper class, probably of the intellectual upper class like Toynbee. In fact, in the GP's home into which he was born in rural Northumberland there were no books except manuals of racing form. The tenor of his home, he said, was remorselessly anti-intellectual. He was discouraged from asking too many questions. 'Curiosity killed the cat,' his mother told the boy who was to grow up into, in both senses of the word, one of the most curious of English historians.

Trevor-Roper's father was a racing man. So was Hugh in his youth. That meant gambling. On the young Hugh's first visit to Germany, just before the war, the future historian of the last days of its worst son was drawn to the casino at Baden Baden. He devised a system for roulette and kept on winning.

He changed his winnings and at Cologne – it being illegal to take German money out of Germany – changed it into sterling and posted it to himself in Oxford, where it kept him in claret and luxuries for some time. Or so, late in life, he liked to tell his friends, one of whom – to my pride and pleasure – I became.

Nor was he what he at first seemed to the Fellows of Peterhouse, Cambridge, whose Master this essentially Oxford figure became. They thought they had appointed a malleable figure, a reactionary like themselves.

They discovered that he had beliefs of his own – rather liberal ones – which he intended to put into practice. Or, again, so he liked to tell it. Those Fellows have a different version. But, then, Hugh was as enthusiastic about academic politics as he was about international politics. And as witty. 'The Fellows of Peterhouse have been brought to order if not to life,' he told a friend.

His fascination for the previously unknown was to lead him into the calamity of his life: the incident by which, cruelly, the multitude will remember him. In 1982 he authenticated, for Times newspapers, the forged Hitler diaries. He soon changed his mind but the damage to him was done for ever.

The case against him, in the matter, was again not what it seemed. In a tape-recorded conversation with me many years later he made a good defence of himself, suggesting that he was as much deceived as anyone else.

Lovers of brilliant historical writing will prefer to remember him as the finest historical essayist since Macaulay, one of his heroes, and a dazzling man.

Daily Telegraph

⊰ 12 June 2004 ⊱

There was nothing slow about Ronald Reagan.
He spotted me for an Englishman right away.

Ronald Reagan (1911–2004) fascinated me from the moment he became governor of California in 1966. He was a right-winger who had won office. In those days right-wingers never won anything. Every office-holder or potential office-holder in every democracy – Labour, Tory, Democrat, Republican – seemed to be a liberal or a centrist. All the authorities said that that was the only way democracies could be governed.

I had only just become interested in politics, and was bored by the subject already. If no one could do anything differently from anyone else, when would I witness any of the great clashes that I had just started reading about in books?

Then came Reagan. He was apparently a fading actor, and a former Democrat who had for some years been making a living out of pro-capitalist and anti-communist speeches for various institutions which were that way inclined. He then made a stirring television speech in support of the hopeless Goldwater candidacy in 1964. Immediately afterwards, some southern Californian multimillionaires paid for him to run for governor. The Democrat incumbent, Pat Brown, patronised him. Reagan won overwhelmingly. This was interesting.

Pieces began appearing in the broadsheet British press warning against this dangerous man. That made him even more interesting. Neither I, nor the British broadsheet press, was to know that in truth, as governor, he had not done anything particularly right-wing. He had staged a quarrel with the Californian universities for letting New Left students run riot about Vietnam. But the welfare budget was just as big as ever. He talked right-wing. He did not do right-wing. This was to be the pattern of his career and the explanation for his success. He was good at stringing right-wingers along. In 1969, he came to London to address the Institute of Directors in the Albert Hall. I hurried there in my capacity as a London reporter for a northern English daily. He had come to elective office late, and must already have been nearly 60. He looked 40. Magnificently, he assured the assembled directors that they were entrepreneurs yearning to breathe free if only government would throw off their shackles of regulation and punitive taxation. Most of them were doing perfectly well out of the Wilsonian, soon to be Heathian, corporate state, in league with the unions. But Reagan seemed somehow to make them wish that a more heroic destiny was possible for them.

I next set eyes on him about 10 years later when he came to Europe in an effort to establish 'foreign policy credentials', having decided to contest the presidential election against President Carter. I was one of a group of Tory journalists invited to have breakfast with him at his hotel. He was late. Mr Bill (now Lord) Deedes complained in my ear that he could well go off this governor fellow because he (Lord Deedes) was not a man who liked being kept waiting for his brekker; my own sentiments entirely.

The governor arrived after about an hour. More importantly, so did the brekker. A young man from the Institute of Economic Affairs (IEA) – the first and greatest of the London free-market think tanks – asked the first question. Could the governor explain how he had privatised garbage collection in California? A Reagan aide took it upon himself to answer: 'The governor began with a pilot scheme in Santa Barbara.'

Reagan intervened: 'No, it was Santa Monica.' The aide corrected himself: 'Excuse me, Governor, you're right. We had some problem with the bigger trash bins we needed, and we got on top of that at our next pilot in Laguna Beach.'

The governor: 'No, we only got on top of the bigger trash bins once we tried them out in Palo Alto. Then we went statewide with the whole programme. That was the year we changed those road signs from steel to rubber, figuring that we'd rather have the signs crushed than the motorists hitting them get killed. It sure cut down on fatals.'

Who said this man had no grasp of detail? The IEA stalwart pressed for further and better particulars on that garbage. As a result, we touched only briefly on the Soviet threat.

My next sighting of him in the flesh was when reporting the New Hampshire Republican primary for the first time, in 1980. He had just lost the Iowa caucus to George Bush Sr. Most of us thought that he was too old now (69) and that Bush would win the nomination. But I and a couple of other British reporters still thought that it would be more fun first to follow Reagan. We asked one of his staff where the governor was campaigning that day. The reply was 'Berlin'. This worried my compatriots. No wonder his campaign had gone wrong. But I remembered Theodore H. White, the first journalist to evoke the New Hampshire primary, in his book on the 1960 Kennedy campaign. I knew that in the south of the state, where it was, the towns have names like, speaking from memory, Bedford and Plymouth; but in the north, Hanover and Berlin. We drove north through beautiful snow. 'Could you tell us the way to Berlin?' we frequently stopped to ask. No one knew where it was. Eventually, a policeman asked us to write it down. 'You mean, Buuurln,' he said. Soon we saw the sign: 'Berlin'. We just had not known how to pronounce it.

We found the governor walking down the main street. It was all but deserted. He heard us talking behind him. In lieu of anyone else to talk to, he turned around: 'Am I right in thinking that you guys are from England?'

'Yes, Governor Reagan,' I replied. (Though no longer a governor, American political etiquette dictates that he still be thus addressed.)

He put his hand on my shoulder, and sighed, 'My films were never really big in England. Something about that innate English good taste.'

Me: 'No, no, Governor. I saw one only last evening on late-night New Hampshire television.'

He sighed again, and in that husky voice confided, 'I know. I know. My opponents will stop at nothing.' Then he nudged me with his elbow and inquired, 'D'you think I should demand from the television company the right to reply?'

As he himself said of the soldiers who stormed Omaha beach, 'Where do we find such men?'

Spectator

⋈ 16 July 2005 ⋈
And a monster, Chairman Mao

The Guardian's *reaction to Mao's death and* Mao: The Unknown
Story *by Jung Chang and Jon Halliday.*

It is good to see, at the top of the non-fiction bestsellers, as proof that not all is dumbed-down, the first great political biography of the 21st century: *Mao,* by Jung Chang and her husband Jon Halliday. One of the book's many qualities is that it confirms what many of us have always believed about the 20th century's ideological mass murderers: that their crimes were not simply committed in order to further their ideology or their beliefs but were, like all mass murder, the product of character. Ages before our own had no difficulty in deciding what it was about their characters that caused their crimes: they were evil.

But the 20th century did not believe in the existence of evil. It believed in 'psychology' as an explanation for, say, a Hitler. That, and 'economic structures'. Hitler came to power and did what he did because he was a tool of monopoly capitalism. When Stalin died, the Left accepted that Stalin was a mass murderer, though it had not done so in his lifetime, but ascribed it to 'state capitalism'. Mao, in his lifetime, got off lightly from the Left because he continued to make radical noises to the end.

Jung Chang and Jon Halliday, however, show that, as he rose in the Communist Party in the 1920s, Mao 'discovered in himself a love of bloodthirsty thuggery. This gut enjoyment, which verged on sadism, meshed with, but preceded, his affinity for Leninist violence. Mao did not come to violence via theory. The propensity sprang from his character . . . this propensity caught Moscow's eye, as it fitted into the Soviet model of a social revolution.'

How different from what was widely written when Mao died in 1976. 'The death of Mao Tse-tung removes one of the most remarkable characters in history,' said the *Guardian* then. 'By his ideas and actions the most populous country in the world was translated from near-feudalism into a modern centralised state. His career is assessed by Jerome Chen, professor of Chinese history at York University, Ontario, and John Gittings [the *Guardian*'s then China expert].'

The rest of the article contained no mention of the numbers killed in this translation from feudalism into a modern centralised state. The murderous 'Cultural Revolution' had happened only a few years before. Yet here it was depicted as a mere 'struggle of ideas', with Mao and his followers among 'China's youth' seeking 'to create new socialist values'. The article reassured the readers of 1976: 'Even the disorders which Mao deliberately stirred up may turn out to be beneficial.' Jung Chang and Jon Halliday have ensured that no one would dare write that kind of thing about Mao again, though they no doubt will about the next left-wing mass murderer.

Spectator

That Mao's crimes were not simply committed in order to further his ideology, communism, is a key observation in our book, and something that only gradually dawned on me during our decade-long research. I became convinced that certain ideologies just suit mass murderers, who use these ideologies as tools to serve their personal goals. Frank highlights a point that is central to the understanding of evil in our troubled world.

Jung Chang

Chapter 22

A few last thoughts

⊰ 12 February 1986 ⊱
Anatoly Shcharansky comes in from the cold
at the Glienicke Bridge

Frank wrote this piece from Germany.

Mr Anatoly Shcharansky got out of a yellow minibus at the East German end of the Glienicke bridge.

The appropriate ingredients for an East–West prisoner exchange were all around him. There was the gaunt iron bridge, spanning a frozen lake and linking East Germany with West Berlin. The sun was pale, the temperature below freezing. All around were woods.

On the first occasion that this remote place was used for this purpose in 1962 – the U2 pilot Gary Powers and the Soviet 'master spy' Rudolph Abel walking towards each other from opposite ends of the bridge, did not look at each other when they passed in the middle, got into cars, and were driven away to obscurity – the scene was watched by a few reporters from a West Berlin newspaper.

This time, the powerfully symbolic proceedings were watched by several hundred television crews, herded behind steel barriers on either side of the road leading from the bridge.

The US Ambassador to East Germany ushered him into his car and drove him to the middle of the bridge. There he got into the car of the US Ambassador to West Germany. It was then that Mr Shcharansky came fully into view: a short man in a fur hat and dark overcoat talking vigorously. The ambassador guided him by the shoulder and held open the car door. East German and Soviet officials remained a blur in the background.

The ambassador's Mercedes, accompanied by West Berlin police cars and American military vehicles, swept past us down the wooded road towards Tempelhof Airport, the flight to the American airfield at Frankfurt, Mr Shcharansky's first embrace of his wife since 1974.

Thirty minutes after Mr Shcharansky, we were passed by the bus containing the freed Western spies – five anonymous figures, of varying ages, looking like a representative group of the West German middle class.

The Times

⊰ 11 December 1987 ⊱
Gorbachev asks whether US immigration stand on the Mexican border with machine guns

M r Gorbachev prepared to fly home last night after – according to yesterday's *New York Times* front page – 'borrowing one of Mr Reagan's patented political tactics and taking his case directly to the American people'. The paper added: 'The strategy seems to have paid off.'

What was more likely was that Mr Gorbachev had taken his case directly to the American politicians – a very different, more impressionable lot. That certainly seemed to have paid off.

When he met members of Congress on Wednesday, one of the legislators was sufficiently emboldened to complain to him about how few people were allowed to leave the Soviet Union.

Mr Gorbachev raised a mock rifle in his hands. 'You stand on the Mexican border,' he said – implying that the United States shot Mexicans trying to leave Mexico.

Officers of the US Immigration and Naturalization Service do not, as a rule, stand on the border and shoot Mexicans trying to get in. If they did, there would be many more premature deaths among Mexicans.

But Senator Robert Byrd, the Democratic majority leader, commented of Mr Gorbachev's debating thrust: 'There was not a hell of a lot we could say in response.'

Why not? The Soviet Union's problem with potential immigrants is to do with people trying to get out. That of the US is to do with people trying to get in. This would seem to tell us something about the relative popularity of the two countries as places in which to live.

Mr Gorbachev should be the one without a hell of a lot to say in response. Instead, Mr Robert Michel, the Republican minority leader in the House of Representatives, gushed: 'He's a very smart individual, very attuned to our system, how it operates.' Mr Tony Coelho, a Californian Democrat representative, added: 'He's one of us – a political animal.'

To those of us who are neither Soviet nor US citizens, it does not seem as if Mr Gorbachev is one of them – an American political animal just like Mr Coelho. Mr Coelho underestimates his own craft. Mr Gorbachev is good at impressing American political animals. But that is easier than being one of them himself. For that, he would have to be electable.

We have yet to see whether he is electable in the Soviet Union, and we probably never will. It is even more problematic whether someone like him could be elected at the end of one of those long US campaigns.

By that time, Americans would have got to know him much better than they have at the end of a three-day visit. They would notice that his way with hostile questions – such as the one he was asked about Soviet emigration – suggests that he is someone who is not used to being asked them.

Also, he does tend to lecture. 'The Soviet Union has its own interests, and the United States has its own interests,' went one typical passage. Every nation has its own specific interests.

The Times

⊰ 20 February 1991 ⊱
Columbo, the greatest TV detective of all

If Holmes is the greatest detective created for print, Columbo is the greatest detective created for television. He returns on Saturday to ITV.

Columbo is Holmes's equal in ratiocination. But, in a typical

Columbo story, we know at the start who committed the crime. It is not a who-dun-it? It is a how-will-he-find-out-who-dun-it?

This convention is rarely departed from. The opening scenes show the crime being committed. Usually, it is the 'perfect' murder. The police are called, sometimes by the murderer himself, so confident is he, or occasionally she. Forensic experts dab around the corpse.

Enter Columbo of the LAPD (Los Angeles Police Department). Peter Falk has been playing him for 20 years now. The actor, and presumably the character, are now 62. Fortunately, although Falk is youthful and rather handsome, the part does not depend on glamour.

The detective arrives in a battered and unreliable car. He wears an old light brown raincoat of the kind immemorially associated with dirty book shops. He smokes a wilting cigar. Sometimes his dog is in the car – a tedious animal who never jumps either out or in when Columbo wants him to. Columbo potters about the murder scene. Either there, or later, he meets the murderer.

Here we arrive at a second convention: the murderers are nearly always rich or powerful, and sometimes famous, and they patronise Columbo. Surely this shambling wreck can be no threat to the perpetrator of the perfect crime?

Columbo is deferential. If famous, the murderer will be subject to much gush from the detective. 'Gee, Mrs Columbo – ah, that is, my wife – is one of your greatest fans, sir. She never misses your programme. Wait 'til I get home and tell her I met you.'

This woman, always referred to by her husband as 'Mrs Columbo', is a constant presence, but we never see her. We know nothing of their marriage. It is unclear whether they have any children. She probably nags him a little, but not so much as to make him change his car, overcoat or smoking habits.

For a long time, the murderer is satisfied that Columbo suspects nothing. But the detective has a habit of returning for the one last apparently irrelevant question – sometimes arriving, without prior notice, at the murderer's home. So, after a while, the murderer's patience is exhausted.

'Now look here, Loo-tenant. I've told you all I know. If you persist in bothering me, I'm afraid I'll have no alternative but to complain to my friend, the Police Commissioner. Anyone would think that I committed the murder.' But wealth or power avails these criminals naught in the end. Columbo always spots something that does not quite add up.

The belief that wealth or fame confer power is very American. But American, too, are the institutions which alone can curb that power – police departments, the rule of law, courts. Only in a country where shabby men in dirty raincoats, if enough of them vote the same way, can defeat presidents and senators, can they also defeat those whose superior position makes them think that they can get away with murder.

Before democracy, when inexpert militias dealt with crime, which criminals went to the gallows was a matter of luck or ill-luck. Few of Columbo's murderers would have met such an end. Instead, they would have used their position to make sure that the suspicious Columbo did.

Professional detection, and therefore detective fiction, rose with democracy. This April sees the 150th anniversary of what is generally accepted as the first detective story: *The Murders in the Rue Morgue*, by the American writer Edgar Allan Poe. Except for his uncommon powers of reasoning, Columbo is the common man – a bit of a slob, even. That he is a citizen of the country of the common man means that those powers of his can be used against the murderous rich and powerful who scorn the common man.

Daily Telegraph

⇥ 9 September 1992 ⇤
De Gaulle and Khrushchev at Stalingrad

Alan Clark, former Tory MP, former Minister of State for Defence, and author of a book on the Second World War's Eastern Front, has just reminded us in a newspaper that this summer was the 50th anniversary of the outbreak of the Battle of Stalingrad. This reminded me, not of that awesome engagement, but of a tale told to me by a French diplomat who specialised in de Gaulle stories.

He admitted that most of them were made up. But he insisted that this one was true.

As French President, during a state visit to the Soviet Union many years after the battle, de Gaulle was taken to Stalingrad. Khrushchev, or Brezhnev, or whoever it was, announced: 'This was where the Soviet people hurled back the Fascist hordes.'

'*Un grand peuple*,' de Gaulle replied. '*Un grand peuple.*' Khrushchev, or whoever, swelled with pride. The embodiment of one great people had recognised the greatness of another.

'*Un grand peuple*', de Gaulle continued to muse. '*Un grand peuple – les Allemands.*'

Daily Telegraph

◄ 1 November 1993 ►
Joan Collins/the Albert Memorial

I regard Miss Joan Collins in the way that other Londoners regard the Albert Memorial. I realise that, as a construct, she is rather over-done. But the style in which she was designed reflects the taste of the age in which she was built.

The nation is about to celebrate the 60th anniversary of her creation.

According to *Who's Who* – which, deplorably, she only got into this year – she was born on 23 May 1933. Celebratory articles are already beginning to appear. But it is important that she is not taken over by intellectuals and men of letters. That happened to the Albert Memorial. Until Lord Clark and John Betjeman started celebrating mock-Gothic, Londoners thought of the memorial as hideous, ridiculous but lovable. Then, aesthetes started saying that it was a work of art.

It is not, and neither is Miss Collins. But she is ripe for Betjemanisation.

We can be sure that some fogey, young or old, is about to pronounce that custom has not staled her infinite variety, and that she doesn't look at all 60. Of course custom has bashed her infinite variety a bit. And 60 looks about right. These days hardly any women of 60 look 60. Or rather, they do – but not in the way they did until about 20 years ago. In this, Miss Collins has been a pioneer.

The envious, or less kindly disposed, hinted that she must have had a facelift. If she has, I would have been against it. It is to me a Heritage issue. Any of the materials used to carry out the work would have been inauthentic. Plastic and foam rubber were not used on women during the time when she was built.

If there is to be renovation work on Miss Collins, it should be supervised by a Fine Arts Committee. But similar misguided attempts have been made to give the Albert Memorial a facelift. I do not like the idea of Miss Collins being boarded up and closed to the public for years, especially since I am only 10 years younger than her and therefore expect her to outlive me.

Daily Telegraph

⊰ 30 October 1994 ⊱
The corridors and catwalks of power: Frank
reports on fashion in Milan and Paris

At first, the basic principle of the autumn fashion shows did not seem to be much different from the autumn party conferences. In Milan, as so often in Blackpool, there was soon a split.

True, a split skirt rather than a split party; but, for those of us trained to politics, any split will do. An outsider could begin to feel at home. As Milan continued, and on in to Paris, there were splits of many kinds: down the front, up the back, round the side, between the top and the bottom. The only difference was that, at Blackpool, the designers had a vested interest in covering the splits up.

There were other similarities. There was, for example, Nadja Auermann. She was referred to simply as 'Nadja', placing her in that category of woman, like Colette or Mistinguette, referred to by a first name only. Nadja was the new supermodel, a very tall blonde who seemed to be everywhere – a German consisting almost entirely of legs and hair. She was the Heseltine. Not as much of a show-off, certainly; but quite enough of one to do her job properly. Except that, on reflection, if she was new, she could hardly be the Heseltine. He has been on the conference catwalk for decades.

Perhaps Nadja was a sort of nordic Portillo but twice as tall; giving the audience and the photographers very much what they wanted, shorn of nuance. She was in nearly all the big shows. She would stalk to the end of the catwalk – where the photographers are banked – and make her leadership bid. Naomi Campbell, Linda Evangelista, Claudia Schiffer and Carla Bruni seemed to be, in comparison, the moderates. (Before we can understand any situation, we politicos have to sort out who are the moderates and who are the extremists.) They could not match the extremism of Nadja's legs. Wisely, they usually countered with a bosom or bottom policy.

And with smiles. Claudia's smile was especially radiant. Nadja was not much given to smiling. One gained the impression that a smile from her would be no laughing matter.

The first show I went to, within an hour or so of reaching Milan, was small, with a short catwalk, and only one model – Nadja. Presumably, it was a sort of fringe meeting. This was for a label called Oliver, designed by Valentino. Oliver, it was explained to me, was the name of Valentino's dog. As the Milan shows proceeded, I was to discover that one or two of the other labels – and a few of the models – were also dogs. But that was not true of anything that Valentino had a hand in. I may have been a pagan in the temple of beauty, but like most of us, I recognise genius when I see it, even if it is not my subject. Valentino did not seem to me to be the supreme genius of the art form – I shall say at the end who I thought that was – but he seemed to me to be a derivative genius; one of those artists capable of executing brilliantly the forms pioneered by an even greater artist who has gone before.

Oliver, however, seemed to be minor work in the Valentino canon. It being a small show, we were able to stand close to the proceedings. Nadja's legs swung out from behind a curtain, and began to advance into the room. Her torso followed some time later. Once the whole of her was in view, the procedure had about it the air of Paul Raymond's Soho. Except that Nadja, seated on a stool, started to put things on rather than take them off; garters and bangles and baubles.

She brandished a long cigarette holder. Fishnet stockings sheathed her endless legs: an operation seemingly requiring as much wide-mesh material as once protected Normandy's Westwall. Her golden hair was sculpted into waves. Her face was an eerie white. The show seemed to have been inspired by Marlene Dietrich, or possibly Marlene Dietrich's corpse. I was becoming worried. I had read that whole seasons could be inspired by a single idea. Perhaps I had got the dead Marlene season. Depressing. I would rather be with Labour in Blackpool, for the dead socialism season . . .

As we all milled our way out, I found myself next to Valentino himself. As we shook hands, he inquired as to whether there was anything I wanted to know from him. Er, er, er, what was his favourite Italian football team? I asked. Well, I could hardly ask him anything intelligent about his work, could I? The whole point of my being here was to cast an ignorant eye over it all.

He smiled a worldly smile. 'Whoever's winning,' he replied. Thus, he seemed to be a true son of Italy. But I returned to the hotel full of foreboding. I found Dietrich something of a bore when she was alive, let alone when she was embalmed.

Next morning, however, everything became livelier. The show was by Dolce e Gabbana – two Sicilian gentlemen, it seems. I soon became acquainted with the system. The mob of fashion editors and buyers seethes around the door. Then part of the crowd thunders in and secures the best seats. They are the ones without the right tickets. The owners of the tickets arrive later. Thus is achieved a basis for negotiation. The essential rule seems to be that if someone is caught in a seat to which they have no right, they regard it as fair cop, and vacate the place to the rightful owner . . . Loudspeakers emitted a few bars of the intermezzo from *Cavalleria Rusticana* which, because it is set in the designers' native Sicily, precedes all Dolce e Gabbana presentations. But this quickly changed to the pulverising rock which accompanied every show, be it Milan or Paris. A procession of models entered who were wearing smart, pin-striped business jackets and carrying briefcases, but who had omitted to bring their skirts, and possibly their knickers. This was the first sign that skirts were to be either extra short or extra long this year.

The procession was led by Isabella Rossellini, puffing on a cigarette-holder. Memory recalled that she had been sacked from Lancôme's advertisements, reportedly for being too old. She seemed to be the Mother of the House – the Edward Heath figure. But much jollier; when she reached the end of the catwalk, she camped it up ruthlessly for the massed photographers.

Once the shows start, nothing goes wrong but what goes especially right? Which outfits were a success and which a failure? This, to the layman, was hard to discern. At all shows, male American fashion writers, in particular, would shriek their approval personally to Armani, Valentino and Versace, only to commiserate with one another in the street outside.

'Well, face it, it was a one-frock show.'

'Y'mean the trouser suit with the tie?'

'Yeah, the trouser suit with the tie.'

The one house which I was sure had got it wrong was Byblos, whose two designers were apparently Britons. One of their big ideas was to put bits of underwear outside the frocks rather than under them. Perhaps they had been inspired by the Pompidou Centre in Paris or the Lloyd's building in London, structures which reverse the normal order of things, and put the plumbing outwards. The effect, when applied to women, was powerfully un-erotic.

On to Paris. It was the same, only more so. Here was where Valentino, as opposed to Valentino's dog, put on his main show. We milled and waited amid high excitement. A wavy brown wig entered under which walked our own Joan Collins. The rock music thumped yet again. All the supermodels took to the catwalk. Nadja managed a smile, making her even more terrifying. The authorities pronounced Valentino to be in brilliant form, especially with a final burst of sequins and chiffon.

It was towards the end, in Paris, that I was encouraged to doubt the authenticity of one or two breasts. That is, one or two pairs of breasts. At the catwalk, in conversation with a fashion doyenne beside whom I found myself seated, I expressed admiration at the altitude achieved by two particular breasts which passed by at eye-level.

The doyenne gently explained that nature alone could not achieve such lift-off. In politics, especially if you are the Opposition, there can never be too much spending on infrastructure. But on learning that it went on in modelling, I felt cheated. Nadja's legs were now all I could cling to for certain.

Finally, to Yves St Laurent. Here, it seemed to me, was the supreme genius: the artist from whom all else has flowed ever since. St Laurent could make Nadja look normal – though I suppose that is not the point of her. His work was unstrained and authentic, even if that was not true, so to speak, of all his breasts. Some of the American males assured one another that he was out of date. But all that meant was that, in St Laurent, I had seen work which, unlike in politics, was not a slave to fashion.

Sunday Telegraph

24 July 2004
The Stauffenberg plot to kill Hitler
failed – and a good thing too

If only the assassination attempted 60 years ago last Tuesday had succeeded, we have heard all this week. But what was the conspirators' idea of success? In particular, what did the awesome man whose sonorous name we have heard this week really believe? Colonel Claus Graf Schenk von Stauffenberg was of his time and his class, we are told. What then was his attitude to, say, Slavs and Jews?

But first, to recount what happened 60 years ago last Tuesday. It is untrue that Stauffenberg and the other leading conspirators resolved to kill Hitler only once they knew that Germany was going to lose the war. They had long been anti-Hitler. By 1944, Stauffenberg, aged 37, was Chief of Staff to Colonel-General Fromm, head of the reserve army. Stauffenberg had been called from Berlin – to brief Hitler – on 20 July at Hitler's eastern headquarters, the luridly named Wolf's Lair in East Prussia, now Poland. Stauffenberg rose early that day at his Berlin home. A staff car took him to a Berlin airstrip. A bomb was in his briefcase.

On arrival in East Prussia, he was driven the 10 miles to the Wolf's Lair. He had breakfast, and set out with the Chief of Defence Staff, Keitel, for Hitler's conference. Stauffenberg asked Keitel to excuse him for a moment, since he wanted to 'freshen up'. In fact, he went to prepare the bomb for detonation and put it back into the briefcase. Nothing could now prevent it exploding 10 minutes later.

Hitler returned their salute as they entered the room. Stauffenberg placed the briefcase under the table. He had told Keitel that, while awaiting Hitler's order to speak, he might have to leave the room to take a call from Berlin connected with the briefing. He left the room and stood several yards away, smoking.

At the table a general was ending a briefing on the deteriorating situation on the Eastern Front. Keitel, who liked these meetings to go smoothly, whispered irritably to a junior officer, 'Where's Stauffenberg? It's his turn now.' The officer went to look, but reported that he could not find him. This was later to set up a suspicion in Keitel's mind. Another junior officer then made perhaps history's most famous or fateful shift of an inanimate object. Finding that Stauffenberg's briefcase prevented him standing comfortably at the table, the officer pushed it to the side of a heavy wooden support, thus protecting Hitler from the full blast.

The gist of the briefing officer's remarks were eerily prophetic. 'The Russians are pressing in towards the north with strong forces west of the Duna . . . If our forces are not finally withdrawn from Peipussee [near the Russians] then we face a catastrophe.' The bomb exploded. Keitel shouted through the smoke, 'Where is the Führer?' Hitler was still there, alive. Stauffenberg, looking in from outside, was convinced that no one could have survived. Soon he was on an aeroplane back to Berlin and the War Office in the Bendlerstrasse – now Stauffenbergstrasse – where the rest of the conspirators waited. At this point, we come to another of the day's mysteries. Fellgiebel, a signals officer in the plot, did not carry out his mission to destroy communications between the Wolf's Lair and the rest of Germany.

The English historian Wheeler-Bennett is hard on Fellgiebel, who was later executed. But the Irish-American writer Constantine FitzGibbon says that cutting the communications was not that easy.

They were complex. But why did not Fellgiebel telephone the Berlin conspirators to reassure them that Hitler was dead, and that they could put into operation their full plan? Was it because he soon realised that Hitler was alive? One man who 'knew' when he reached the Bendlerstrasse that Hitler was dead was Stauffenberg. But Keitel managed to secure a call to Stauffenberg's chief, Fromm, and assure him that Hitler had survived. Fromm had earlier been part of the plot. Nearly all of us, in our workplaces and in our observation of politicians and others, know Fromms. They go with the winner. 'You must shoot yourself immediately,' he told Stauffenberg. Stauffenberg and other officers instead arrested Fromm after a scuffle.

The conspirators sent a Major Remer – jailed for neo-Nazism post war – to arrest Goebbels. Goebbels asked him whether Hitler had personally decorated him with the medal he wore. He had. So Remer would recognise that voice if he heard it on the telephone? Goebbels put Remer through to Hitler, who ordered him to lead a detachment to arrest the conspirators. Remer somehow reached Fromm who finally succeeded in arresting Stauffenberg and others. It was now past midnight. Fromm had Stauffenberg and three others shot under car headlights in a dark courtyard, Stauffenberg dying with a cry of 'Long live holy Germany'. That did not save Fromm. The Gestapo discovered his earlier involvement and he was hanged.

We must remain in awe of Stauffenberg. Nonetheless, he belonged to a group of officers from some of Germany's oldest military families who could not explode a bomb correctly. They could not cut those communications. They could not spot a Fromm. Instead of shooting Goebbels, they sent a suspect officer, not part of the plot, to arrest him. Even if they had killed Hitler, they seemed disunited as to what should happen next. Some, perhaps most, wanted to make peace in the West and fight on in the East. The Western Allies would never have accepted that. On 20 July there were no enemy troops on German soil, just as there had not been at the 1918 armistice. There would have been another 'stab in the back' legend: Germany had not been defeated in the field but had been stabbed in the back by treacherous politicians and defeatist officers. We can imagine the Nazis, and the crowds, greeting the returning troops in 1944 as betrayed heroes. It is reasonable to speculate that there would have been something like civil war, with perhaps the Russians moving in to support the Communists. The Nazis would have argued that at the moment of betrayal, Hitler was perfecting the secret weapons, such as the V-rockets, which would have turned the war, and was probably about to build a nuclear bomb too. There could have been strife in Germany for years.

Spectator

The trip that Frank, Virginia, the historian Simon Sebag Montefiore and I made in June 2004 to Hitler's East Prussian headquarters, the Wolfsschanze (Wolf's Lair), was always going to be something of a pilgrimage. We went in part to pay homage to Colonel Stauffenberg's heroism, and to visit the memorial where the bomb went off (the hut was not rebuilt after the explosion). The flight in a flimsy ancient Soviet-era aircraft from Warsaw had left almost everyone airsick – except the pilot who rather heroically chain-smoked throughout the flight. Once there, we walked through the dark pine forest, seeing Hitler's private bunker and other parts of the vast Fuhrer-HQ that nature was slowly reclaiming. Frank's fascination for the issues and personalities of the war sparked endless conversational sallies, discussions, speculations and jokes. Only at the small but dignified memorial itself did we all fall silent, in awed contemplation of that momentous day in world history: Thursday, 20 July 1944.

Andrew Roberts

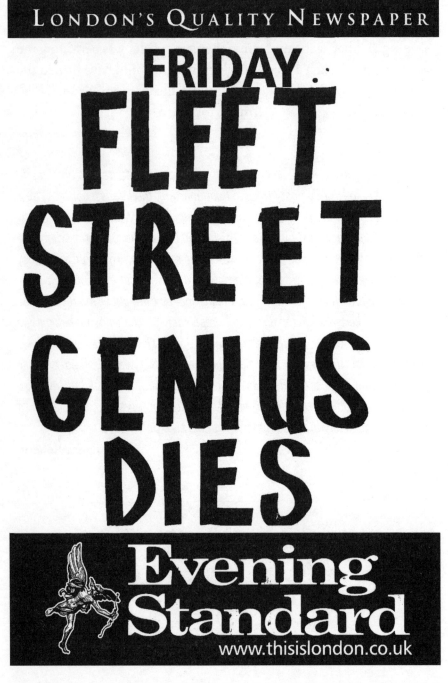

The *Evening Standard* poster on the day of Frank's death.

Index